THE BHARAT VARSHA

THE BHARAT VARSHA

HOW THE EVOLUTION OF CIVILIZATION TAKE PLACE

Title: The Bharat Varsha: How the Evolution of civilization take place
Author:Umang kartikey
CoverDesign&Maps:Umang kartikey
Illustrations & Diagrams: Generated and compiled with assistance from AI tools, archaeological sources, and open-access archives
Editor:Umang kartikey
Publisher:Self-Published
ISBN:978-93-343-7472-8
FirstEdition
Indore,India
2025

For permissions or inquiries ,pleasecontact
umangkartikey6@gmail.com
Printed in India

For my family and friends who have supported me

CONTENTS

Introduction

India's ancient civilization stands as one of the most remarkable in human history—deeply layered, continuously evolving, and richly diverse. Long before the rise of empires or written histories, the subcontinent was home to sophisticated cultures, advanced urban settlements, and profound spiritual inquiry. This book explores the story of Indian civilization from its earliest roots in the prehistoric rock art of Bhimbetka and the agricultural communities of Mehrgarh, through the grandeur of the Indus-Sarasvati cities, and into the transformative era of Vedic thought. The journey spans not just centuries, but modes of knowledge—oral and written, material and metaphysical. More than a linear history, this is a civilizational mosaic one shaped by continuity and change, debate and devotion, trade and tradition. The Vedas, Upanishads, and other early texts are not just relics of a distant past but living voices that continue to shape Indian identity. Likewise, the ruins of Harappan cities are not dead stones but silent testimonies to an intelligent and organized people.

To guide readers, the book includes special features—excerpts from original texts, insights from archaeological discoveries, comparative views with other civilizations, and contemporary debates in scholarship. These are designed to make the ancient world come alive and to invite critical reflection. This work does not claim to answer all questions—indeed, many remain unanswered. But it aims to present the best of what we know, and the best of what we are still learning, about a civilization that continues to inspire wonder and inquiry. Whether you are a student, researcher, or a curious mind, may this book serve as both a foundation and a starting point on your Journey into the heart of India's ancient past.

1
Head Start

The story of human civilization starts with the quiet revolution that occurred in Africa tens of thousands of years ago. Here, in the cradle of humanity, our ancestors first developed the fundamental capacities that would distinguish our species and lay the groundwork for all subsequent civilizational achievements. This African foundational layer represents humanity's first great leap forward—the development of fire control, toolmaking, language, social cooperation, and early astronomical observations that would become the bedrock upon which all later civilizations would build.

Yet while Africa provided the essential foundation, it was in the Indian subcontinent that this foundational knowledge found its most fertile ground for continuous development and expansion. India's unique geographical position, climatic advantages, and cultural continuity created conditions that allowed for an unbroken chain of civilizational development spanning over 60,000 years. This extraordinary head start would enable Indian civilization to develop sophisticated systems of mathematics, philosophy, medicine, and social organization that would eventually influence the entire world.

The African foundation layer represents humanity's first great cognitive revolution, occurring approximately 70,000 to 100,000 years ago. This was not merely a technological advancement but a fundamental transformation in human consciousness the emergence of abstract thinking, symbolic representation, and the capacity to manipulate the environment in increasingly sophisticated ways.

The mastery of fire stands as perhaps the most significant achievement of this foundational period. Fire was not simply discovered but conquered, controlled, and integrated into human society in ways that would transform every aspect of human existence. The ability to create and maintain fire provided immediate practical benefits: warmth in cold climates, protection from predators, and the capacity to cook food. However, the implications extended far beyond these immediate advantages.

Cooking food fundamentally altered human evolution. Cooked food is easier to digest and provides more available nutrients, which supported the development of larger brains while reducing the energy required for digestion. This freed up biological resources that could be devoted to cognitive development, creating a positive feedback loop between technological achievement and intellectual capacity. More importantly, fire became the focal point around which human communities gathered. The controlled flame created the first truly human spaces—areas of warmth and light where people could gather safely after dark, share food, and engage in the complex social interactions that would become the foundation of culture itself. Around these fires, the first stories were told, the first songs were sung, and the first systematic knowledge was passed from generation to generation.

The mastery of fire also represented a crucial conceptual breakthrough. It demonstrated humanity's capacity to harness natural forces for human purposes, to transform the environment rather than merely adapt to it. This represented a fundamental shift in the relationship between humans and nature—from passive recipients of environmental pressures to active agents capable of reshaping their world. The development of sophisticated tool-making techniques represented another crucial component of the African foundation layer. Early humans developed increasingly complex methods for shaping stone, bone, and wood into implements that extended human capabilities far beyond their biological limitations.

Tool-making required not only manual dexterity but also sophisticated cognitive abilities. The creation of a stone tool involves visualizing the desired end product, understanding the properties of different materials, and executing a complex sequence of precisely controlled actions. This process demands forward planning, spatial reasoning, and the ability to maintain focus on long-term goals—cognitive capacities that would prove essential for all subsequent human achievements.The tools themselves evolved in sophistication over time, from simple choppers and scrapers to complex composite implements that combined multiple materials and required elaborate manufacturing processes. Each advance in tool technology represented not merely a practical improvement but a leap in cognitive capacity and cultural sophistication.

Perhaps most significantly, tool-making became a cultural activity passed down through generations via demonstration and practice. This created the first technological traditions—accumulated bodies of knowledge about materials, techniques, and applications that could be preserved and improved upon over time. These traditions established the pattern of cumulative technological development that would characterize human civilization. The development of language represents perhaps the most revolutionary achievement of the African foundation layer. Language did not emerge suddenly but evolved gradually from earlier forms of communication, developing increasing complexity and sophistication over thousands of years.

Language transformed human society in fundamental ways. It enabled precise coordination of group activities, allowing for more sophisticated hunting strategies, collaborative construction projects, and complex social arrangements. Language made possible the sharing of knowledge about tool-making techniques, environmental conditions, and survival strategies, dramatically accelerating the pace of cultural development. More profoundly, language enabled abstract thought and symbolic representation. With language, humans could discuss concepts that were not immediately present, plan for future events, and contemplate abstract relationships. Language created the possibility of mythology, philosophy, and scientific thinking—the capacity to construct mental models of reality and manipulate them symbolically.

Language also enabled the preservation of knowledge across generations with unprecedented accuracy. While other animals can pass on some information through demonstration and imitation, language allowed for the precise transmission of complex information, detailed instructions, and abstract concepts. This created the possibility for cumulative cultural evolution—each generation could build upon the accumulated knowledge of their predecessors rather than starting from scratch. The development of different languages as human populations spread and diversified also created the first recognition of cultural diversity. Different groups developed different ways of organizing and expressing knowledge, leading to the emergence of distinct cultural traditions while maintaining the underlying human capacity for symbolic communication.

Social Cooperation and Cultural Emergence

The African foundation layer also witnessed the development of sophisticated forms of social cooperation that went far beyond the simple group coordination found in other species. Early human societies developed complex systems of reciprocity, shared responsibility, and collective decision-making that enabled groups to function as coherent units while respecting individual autonomy. These social innovations were not merely practical arrangements but reflected deeper developments in human psychology and morality. The capacity for empathy, fairness, and reciprocal altruism created the psychological foundation for complex societies. The development of social norms, shared values, and collective rituals established the cultural frameworks that would enable larger and more sophisticated forms of human organization.

The emergence of leadership roles, specialization of tasks, and systems for resolving conflicts demonstrated sophisticated understanding of group dynamics and social psychology. These early social innovations established patterns that would be elaborated and refined in all subsequent civilizations. Among the most significant achievements of the African foundation layer was the beginning of systematic astronomical observation. Early humans were keen observers of celestial patterns, noting the regular cycles of the moon, the seasonal changes in star positions, and the relationship between celestial events and earthly phenomena.

These observations were not merely casual but represented humanity's first systematic attempts to understand the cosmos and their place within it. The recognition of regular patterns in the sky led to the development of the first calendars, enabling precise timing of seasonal activities and the coordination of group activities over extended periods. Early astronomical observations also represented the beginning of humanity's quest to understand the underlying order of the universe. The recognition that celestial events followed predictable patterns suggested that the cosmos was not chaotic but governed by underlying principles that could be discovered and understood through careful observation.

The development of astronomical knowledge required sophisticated cognitive abilities: pattern recognition, numerical thinking, spatial reasoning, and the capacity to maintain accurate observations over extended periods. These cognitive skills would prove essential for all subsequent scientific and mathematical development. As human populations expanded beyond Africa, they carried with them not only their genetic heritage but also their accumulated cultural knowledge and technological capabilities. The migration out of Africa, beginning approximately 70,000 years ago, represented one of the most significant knowledge transfer events in human history. However, understanding how these early humans reached the Indian subcontinent requires examining both the routes they took and the compelling genetic evidence that traces their journey.

The Coastal Route: Following the Arabian Sea

The primary route that early humans used to reach India was likely the coastal pathway along the Arabian Peninsula and the shores of the Arabian Sea. This route offered several crucial advantages for migrating populations. Climate change during the late Pleistocene period (around 70,000-60,000 years ago) had lowered sea levels significantly, exposing larger coastal plains and creating land bridges that made coastal migration more feasible. The coastline provided reliable sources of fresh water from rivers and streams, abundant marine resources for food, and familiar environments for populations already adapted to coastal living in Africa.

Archaeological evidence supports this coastal migration theory. Shell middens and early human artifacts have been found along the Arabian Peninsula coast and in southern India, suggesting continuous coastal occupation. The presence of similar tool technologies along this entire coastal route indicates that migrating populations maintained their cultural traditions while adapting to new environments.

A secondary route likely took early human populations through the Fertile Crescent region of the Middle East before turning eastward toward the Indian subcontinent. This route would have followed river valleys and oasis systems that provided water and resources necessary for long-distance travel.This northern route may have been used during different climatic periods when the Arabian Peninsula was more arid and coastal resources were less accessible. Populations using this route would have encountered different environmental challenges and opportunities, potentially leading to the development of different adaptive strategies and cultural innovations.

Genetic Evidence: The DNA Trail

Modern genetic analysis provides compelling evidence for these migration patterns and helps us understand both the timing and the routes of early human movement to India. Several key genetic markers support the migration theories:

Mitochondrial DNA Evidence: Studies of mitochondrial DNA (inherited maternally) show that most Indian populations carry genetic markers that trace back to African origins around 60,000 70,000 years ago. The specific genetic lineages found in Indian populations (particularly the M and N haplogroups) suggest that the founding populations of India were among the first to leave Africa, indicating that India was one of the earliest destinations for human migration outside of Africa.

Y-Chromosome Analysis: Paternal genetic lineages (traced through Y-chromosome DNA) also support early migration to India. The presence of specific Y-chromosome haplogroups in Indian populations that are closely related to African lineages but show unique mutations suggests that these populations have been in India for tens of thousands of years, long enough to develop distinctive genetic signatures while maintaining clear connections to their African origins.

Autosomal DNA Studies: Analysis of nuclear DNA (inherited from both parents) reveals that Indian populations show a complex pattern of ancestry that includes both the original African-derived populations and later genetic contributions from various sources. However, the foundational African component remains clearly detectable, supporting the theory of very early settlement.

Ancient DNA from Archaeological Sites: Recent advances in ancient DNA extraction have provided direct genetic evidence from archaeological sites in India and along the proposed migration routes. These studies confirm that the genetic signatures found in modern Indian populations were already present in ancient populations, supporting the continuity of settlement over tens of thousands of years.

Genetic Diversity Patterns: The pattern of genetic diversity in Indian populations also supports early settlement. Populations that have been in a region longer typically show greater genetic diversity, as they have had more time for mutations to accumulate. Indian populations show high levels of genetic diversity that are consistent with very early settlement and long-term population continuity.

The Toba Bottleneck Connection: Genetic analysis has also revealed evidence of a population bottleneck in early human populations around 70,000 years ago, possibly connected to the massive Toba volcanic eruption in Indonesia. The genetic patterns in Indian populations suggest that the founding populations of India may have been among those who survived this bottleneck, further supporting the early timing of migration to India.

Why India? Environmental and Strategic Advantages

The choice of India as a destination for early human migration was not random but reflected the subcontinent's exceptional advantages for human settlement:

Climate Stability: India's monsoon climate system provided predictable seasonal patterns that enabled reliable resource planning. Unlike many other regions that experienced extreme climatic variability, the monsoon system created conditions where human populations could develop long-term strategies for survival and growth.

Geographic Protection: The subcontinent's natural boundaries—the Himalayas to the north and oceans on three sides—provided protection from many of the environmental and population pressures that affected other regions. This geographic isolation allowed for continuous cultural development without constant external disruption.

Resource Abundance: India's diverse ecosystems provided abundant resources for human populations. Coastal areas offered marine resources, river valleys provided fresh water and fertile soils, and forested regions supplied materials for tools and shelter. This resource diversity enabled populations to thrive and grow.

Strategic Position: India's location at the crossroads between Africa, Asia, and Southeast Asia made it a natural hub for further human expansion. Populations established in India could serve as launching points for further migrations to Southeast Asia, East Asia, and beyond.

The migration to India, occurring in multiple waves over many thousands of years, was particularly significant because the Indian subcontinent provided conditions that were exceptionally favorable for the continued development and elaboration of the foundational knowledge brought from Africa. The genetic evidence confirms that these early migrants not only reached India but established thriving populations that would maintain continuous occupation for tens of thousands of years, creating the foundation for one of the world's longest continuous civilizations.

The settlement of the Indian subcontinent beginning over 60,000 years ago provided human civilization with an unprecedented opportunity for continuous development. Unlike many other regions that experienced repeated disruptions from climate change, natural disasters, or population movements, the Indian subcontinent offered remarkable stability and continuity that allowed for the uninterrupted accumulation of knowledge and cultural sophistication over tens of thousands of years.

This extraordinary length of continuous habitation created conditions unlike anywhere else on Earth. Each generation could build upon the accumulated wisdom of their predecessors without the disruptions that forced other populations to repeatedly restart their civilizational development. This continuity allowed for the gradual refinement and sophistication of knowledge systems that would have been impossible in less stable environments.

The migrants who reached India brought with them the full complement of foundational knowledge from Africa, but they encountered environmental conditions that stimulated further innovation while providing the stability necessary for long-term cultural development. The subcontinent's diverse ecosystems—from tropical coastlines to temperate highlands, from river valleys to desert regions—provided a natural laboratory for experimenting with different approaches to survival and social organization.

The Indian subcontinent's unique geographic features created exceptionally favorable conditions for civilizational development. Protected by the towering Himalayas to the north and surrounded by oceans on three sides, India formed a natural geographic unit that provided both security and accessibility. This geographic configuration protected early inhabitants from many of the disruptions that affected other regions while facilitating trade and cultural exchange with neighboring areas.

The monsoon climate system provided reliable seasonal patterns that enabled sophisticated agricultural planning and development. Unlike regions dependent on unpredictable rainfall or subject to extreme climatic variations, the monsoon system created conditions where agricultural communities could develop long-term strategies for food production and population growth.

The subcontinent's river systems—particularly the Indus, Ganges, and their tributaries—provided abundant water resources, fertile soils, and natural transportation networks. These rivers enabled the development of large settled communities and facilitated communication and trade between different regions.

The diverse mineral resources available in different parts of the subcontinent provided raw materials for increasingly sophisticated technologies. Rich deposits of iron, copper, gold, and precious stones enabled the development of advanced metallurgy and craftsmanship that would become renowned throughout the ancient world.

The Mehrgarh Revolution: Agricultural Foundations (9000-7000 BCE)

The development of agriculture at Mehrgarh, in present-day Pakistan, around 9000-7000 BCE represents one of the earliest and most successful transitions from hunter-gatherer societies to settled agricultural communities anywhere in the world. This transition was not a sudden shift but a gradual process that built upon thousands of years of accumulated knowledge about plant and animal behavior, seasonal patterns, and environmental management.

The Mehrgarh culture developed sophisticated techniques for crop cultivation, including the domestication of wheat, barley, and other grains that would become staples of agricultural societies throughout the region. They also domesticated cattle, water buffalo, sheep, and goats, creating integrated agricultural systems that combined crop production with animal husbandry.

The agricultural innovations at Mehrgarh were not limited to food production but extended to all aspects of material culture. The development of pottery, textile production, and tool-making reached new levels of sophistication. The creation of permanent settlements enabled the accumulation of material goods and the development of specialized crafts that would have been impossible in nomadic societies.

Perhaps most importantly, the agricultural revolution at Mehrgarh created the economic foundation for population growth and social complexity. Reliable food production enabled communities to support larger populations and to develop specialized roles for different members of society. This specialization was crucial for the later development of more complex forms of social organization and cultural achievement. The Mehrgarh culture also demonstrates early evidence of long-distance trade networks. Archaeological evidence shows the presence of materials and artifacts from distant regions, indicating that these early agricultural communities were not isolated but were part of broader networks of exchange and communication.

Urban Sophistication: The Hindus Valley Civilization Network (3300 BCE)

The emergence of the Hindus Valley Civilization around 3300 BCE represents one of the most remarkable achievements in human urban development. What makes this civilization truly extraordinary is not just the famous sites of Harappa and Mohenjo-daro, but the vast network of over 1,400 settlements that have been discovered across the Hindus Valley region, spanning from present-day Afghanistan to Gujarat in India—covering an area larger than Egypt and Mesopotamia combined.

The discovery of these numerous sites reveals that the Hindus Valley was not the birthplace of urban civilization in this region, but rather the culmination of thousands of years of earlier urban experimentation and development. Archaeological evidence shows that sophisticated urban settlements existed in the region centuries before the peak Harappan period, with sites like Rehman Dheri (3300 BCE) and Kot Diji (3300-2600 BCE) demonstrating advanced urban planning and craftsmanship that predated the classical Harappan cities.

Sites such as Dholavira, Kalibangan, Lothal, Banawali, and Rakhigarhi each demonstrate unique innovations and specializations while maintaining the remarkable consistency in urban planning and material culture that characterized the entire civilization. Dholavira, for example, showcased sophisticated water management systems with elaborate reservoirs and dams. Lothal featured advanced port facilities and dockyards that connected the inland cities to maritime trade networks. Kalibangan revealed evidence of the world's earliest known ploughed agricultural field.

The sheer scale of this urban network is staggering. Rakhigarhi, recently determined to be larger than Harappa itself, spans over 350 hectares and may have housed over 40,000 people. These weren't isolated city-states but interconnected urban centers that maintained standardized systems of weights, measures, brick sizes, and urban planning principles across thousands of kilometers and hundreds of years.

What's particularly significant is that these weren't the first urban experiments in the region. Earlier settlements like Mehrgarh had already established sophisticated agricultural and craft traditions. The site of Kunal (dating to 4500 BCE) shows evidence of advanced metallurgy and urban planning that preceded the classical Harappan period by over a millennium. The gradual evolution from these earlier settlements to the mature Harappan cities demonstrates a continuous process of urban innovation and refinement spanning several millennia.

The Harappan cities themselves were not haphazard collections of buildings but carefully planned urban environments that incorporated sophisticated understanding of hydraulic engineering, waste management, and public health. The famous grid-pattern streets, advanced drainage systems, and standardized brick construction demonstrated remarkable consistency and coordination across this vast network of settlements.

The urban planning of Harappan cities reflected sophisticated understanding of social organization and public administration. The presence of public baths, granaries, and other community facilities suggested complex systems for managing community resources and maintaining public welfare. The standardization of weights, measures, and currency across the entire civilization indicated high levels of administrative sophistication and inter-regional coordination.

The Harappan civilization also demonstrated remarkable achievements in craftsmanship and technology. Harappan artisans produced sophisticated bronze work, precision-carved seals, and textiles of exceptional quality. The development of a standardized writing system, though not yet fully deciphered, indicates sophisticated systems for recording and transmitting information.

Perhaps most impressively, this vast urban network maintained high standards of urban development and social organization for over a thousand years, far longer than most other early urban civilizations. The consistency across such a vast area and long time period suggests sophisticated systems for maintaining social cohesion, managing resources, and adapting to changing conditions. The discovery of weights and measures that remained standardized across the entire civilization indicates administrative sophistication that could coordinate activities across hundreds of urban centers.

Recent archaeological discoveries continue to reveal new aspects of this remarkable civilization. Sites like Bhirrana and Girawad have pushed back the dating of Hindus Valley settlements even further, while underwater archaeology off the coast of Gujarat has revealed submerged Harappan sites that suggest the civilization was even more extensive than previously imagined. Each new discovery reinforces the understanding that the Hindus Valley Civilization was not an isolated phenomenon but the culmination of thousands of years of continuous urban development and innovation in the Indian subcontinent.

Continuous Mathematical and Philosophical Development

Throughout this entire period of settlement and development, Indian intellectual traditions were continuously evolving and becoming increasingly sophisticated. The mathematical innovations that would later astonish the world—including the concept of zero, the decimal system, and advanced geometric principles—were not sudden discoveries but the culmination of thousands of years of accumulated mathematical thinking.

The development of these mathematical concepts required not only individual genius but also cultural traditions that valued precision, abstraction, and systematic thinking. The long period of continuous civilizational development in India created conditions where mathematical knowledge could be gradually refined, tested, and improved upon over many generations.

Similarly, the philosophical traditions that would become central to Indian civilization—including detailed investigations of consciousness, systematic approaches to ethical reasoning, and sophisticated metaphysical systems—developed through thousands of years of accumulated wisdom and investigation. These traditions represented not merely abstract speculation but systematic investigations of fundamental questions about reality, consciousness, and human existence.

The integration of mathematical and philosophical thinking in Indian traditions also reflects the long period of continuous development that allowed for the synthesis of different approaches to knowledge. Rather than developing in isolation, mathematical and philosophical investigations influenced each other, creating integrated systems of understanding that would prove remarkably sophisticated and enduring.

The Accumulation of Practical Knowledge

The long period of continuous development in India also enabled the accumulation of sophisticated practical knowledge in areas such as medicine, metallurgy, agriculture, and craftsmanship. Indian medical traditions developed detailed understanding of anatomy, physiology, and therapeutic principles through thousands of years of careful observation and experimentation.

The metallurgical achievements of ancient India, including the production of high-quality steel and sophisticated alloys, represented the culmination of generations of accumulated knowledge about materials, processes, and techniques. The famous iron pillar in Delhi, which has resisted corrosion for over 1,500 years, demonstrates the remarkable sophistication of Indian metallurgical knowledge.

Agricultural techniques developed over thousands of years enabled Indian farmers to achieve some of the highest crop yields in the ancient world. The development of sophisticated irrigation systems, crop rotation practices, and plant breeding techniques created agricultural systems that could support large populations while maintaining soil fertility over many generations.

Cultural and Linguistic Sophistication

The long period of continuous development in India also enabled the evolution of sophisticated cultural and linguistic traditions. The development of Sanskrit as a language of scholarly and religious discourse created a medium for preserving and transmitting complex knowledge with remarkable precision.

The oral traditions that developed in India demonstrated extraordinary sophistication in the preservation of complex texts. The techniques developed for memorizing and accurately transmitting lengthy compositions enabled the preservation of vast bodies of knowledge for thousands of years before the development of writing systems.

The cultural traditions that emerged during this period also demonstrated sophisticated understanding of human psychology, social organization, and ethical reasoning. The development of complex ritual systems, social structures, and moral codes reflected deep thinking about human nature and social requirements.

The Foundation for Global Influence

Knowledge Networks and Cultural Exchange

By the time other major civilizations began to emerge elsewhere in the world, India had already accumulated thousands of years of sophisticated knowledge and cultural development. This head start positioned Indian civilization to become a major source of knowledge and cultural influence for emerging civilizations throughout Asia and beyond.

The extensive trade networks that developed from Indian ports carried not only goods but also ideas, techniques, and cultural practices to distant regions. Indian merchants, scholars, and travelers became conduits for the transmission of mathematical, philosophical, and technological knowledge to other civilizations.

The influence of Indian knowledge systems can be traced in the development of civilizations throughout Southeast Asia, Central Asia, and even parts of the Mediterranean world. The spread of Indian numerical systems, philosophical concepts, and cultural practices demonstrates the remarkable sophistication and attractiveness of knowledge systems that had been refined over thousands of years.

The Preservation and Transmission Advantage

The long period of continuous development in India also created sophisticated systems for preserving and transmitting knowledge. The development of detailed techniques for memorization and accurate transmission enabled the preservation of vast bodies of knowledge across many generations.

These preservation systems proved crucial for maintaining cultural continuity during periods of political change or social disruption. Unlike civilizations that lost significant knowledge during periods of instability, Indian traditions developed robust methods for maintaining cultural and intellectual continuity.

The sophisticated systems for knowledge preservation and transmission also enabled rapid recovery and renewal during periods of cultural renaissance. The accumulated knowledge preserved through traditional methods could be quickly accessed and built upon when conditions were favorable for intellectual development.

Conclusion: The Significance of India's Head Start

The 60,000-year head start that Indian civilization enjoyed over most other major civilizations created conditions for intellectual and cultural development that were unique in human history. This extraordinary period of continuous development enabled the accumulation of sophisticated knowledge systems, the refinement of cultural practices, and the development of social organizations that would influence human civilization for thousands of years.

The mathematical innovations, philosophical insights, technological achievements, and cultural sophistication that emerged from this long period of development would eventually spread throughout the world, influencing the development of civilizations on every continent. The decimal system and the concept of zero, the philosophical investigations of consciousness and reality, the medical and metallurgical achievements, and the sophisticated social and cultural systems that developed in India all bear the mark of this unprecedented period of continuous civilizational development.

Understanding India's head start helps explain not only the remarkable achievements of Indian civilization but also the broader patterns of human cultural development. It demonstrates the crucial importance of stability and continuity for the accumulation of knowledge and the development of sophisticated cultural systems. It also illustrates how the foundational achievements of one civilization can eventually benefit all of humanity through the processes of cultural exchange and knowledge transmission.

The African foundation layer provided humanity with the essential capabilities for civilization, but it was India's unique conditions and unprecedented head start that enabled these foundational capabilities to develop into the sophisticated knowledge systems that would eventually transform human civilization worldwide.

2
Cultural Evolution

The Unbroken Chain

In the rugged hills of central India, deep within the sandstone shelters of Bhimbetka, ancient hands once pressed ochre and charcoal against stone walls, creating images that would endure for fifteen millennia.These paintings—depicting dancing figures, hunting scenes, and ritualistic gatherings—represent not merely prehistoric art, but the earliest visible threads of a cultural tapestry that has never truly been severed. From these Paleolithic caves to the sophisticated urban centers of the Indian civilization, from the sacred verses of the Rigveda to the bustling cities of contemporary India, we witness an extraordinary phenomenon: the longest continuous thread of human civilization on Earth.

This continuity is not merely chronological but profoundly cultural, manifesting in recurring themes, persistent symbols, and enduring practices that transcend the conventional boundaries of historical periods. The dancing figures of Bhimbetka find their echo in the cosmic dance of Shiva; the urban planning principles of Harappa resonate in the spatial concepts of later temple architecture; the ritual symbolism of the Indian cities emerges transformed but recognizable in Vedic literature. This chapter explores how fifteen millennia of human creativity, innovation, and spiritual seeking have woven together to create one of humanity's most remarkable stories of cultural persistence within the Indian subcontinent.

Cave Painting Traditions (15,000 BCE)

The Dawn of Expression

The rock shelters scattered across the Vindhya Range, particularly at Bhimbetka in Madhya Pradesh, preserve humanity's longest continuous artistic tradition. Carbon dating reveals that humans have been painting on these walls for over 15,000 years, with the most recent additions dating to the medieval period. This represents not just an archaeological curiosity, but the world's oldest continuously active art gallery—a sacred space where generation after generation added their vision to an ever-evolving visual narrative.

The earliest paintings, created during the Upper Paleolithic period, demonstrate sophisticated artistic sensibilities. Using natural pigments—red and yellow ochre, white clay, charcoal, and plant-based dyes— prehistoric artists created dynamic compositions that capture both the physical and spiritual worlds of their creators. The techniques employed show remarkable consistency across millennia: finger painting for broad areas, fine brushwork using split twigs for details, and blow-pipe stenciling for handprints and geometric patterns.

What makes the Bhimbetka paintings extraordinary is not just their antiquity, but the persistence of certain themes across vast spans of time. The earliest paintings focus on large animals—bison, elephants, tigers, and rhinoceros—depicted with naturalistic accuracy that suggests intimate knowledge of animal behavior. These creatures are not merely hunted prey but seem to embody spiritual significance, their massive forms dominating the cave walls like prehistoric deities.

As the paintings evolve through the Mesolithic period (10,000-5,000 BCE), human figures become more prominent and stylized. Dancing scenes emerge as a central theme, with figures arranged in complex choreographies that suggest communal rituals. The famous "Bhimbetka dancers" show groups of elongated human forms with arms raised, bodies in motion, creating visual rhythms that seem to pulse with life even today. These dance scenes establish a motif that will resonate through Indian culture for millennia to come.

The Neolithic paintings (5,000-3,000 BCE) introduce new elements that bridge the prehistoric and historic periods. Geometric patterns become more elaborate, agricultural scenes appear, and most significantly, proto-religious symbols emerge. Circular designs that may represent the sun, intricate patterns that suggest early mandalas, and stylized human figures in poses remarkably similar to later yogic positions all point toward the development of complex spiritual concepts.

Perhaps most remarkable is the appearance of symbols that will persist throughout India cultural history. The swastika, one of humanity's oldest and most widespread symbols, appears in these caves in various forms—as a solar symbol, a representation of cosmic order, and a sign of auspiciousness. The trishul (trident) appears in stylized form, often associated with powerful animal figures, prefiguring its later association with Shiva. Hand stencils, created by blowing pigment around hands pressed against the rock face, establish a tradition of ritual handprints that continues in contemporary folk art and religious practices.

The persistence of certain color symbolism is equally striking. Red ochre, the dominant pigment in the earliest paintings, carries associations with life force, fertility, and sacred power that continue in Indian tradition today. White clay, used for ceremonial designs and ghostly spirit figures, maintains its association with purity and the divine. This continuity of symbolic meaning across such vast periods suggests not just artistic tradition, but the preservation of fundamental spiritual concepts.

Sites Beyond Bhimbetka

While Bhimbetka represents the most famous and extensively studied site, cave painting traditions flourished across the Indian subcontinent. In the Western Ghats, sites like Elephanta and Ajanta (much later Buddhist caves build upon earlier painting traditions. In the Deccan plateau, hundreds of rock art sites reveal regional variations on common themes. The Chhattisgarh region, Karnataka's granite outcrops, and even sites in present-day Pakistan and Afghanistan all contribute to a vast network of prehistoric artistic expression.

Each region developed distinctive styles while maintaining connection to broader themes. The Deccan paintings often emphasize geometric patterns and abstract designs that seem to prefigure later temple architecture. Sites in the northwest show influences from Central Asian artistic traditions, suggesting early cultural exchanges that would characterize the region throughout history. Yet all these regional variations share fundamental elements: the celebration of dance and ritual, the reverence for natural forces, and the use of art as a means of connecting with the spiritual realm.

The Living Tradition

What distinguishes Indian cave art from other prehistoric painting traditions is its continuous evolution rather than abandonment. While European cave art represents a closed chapter—the artistic traditions of Lascaux and Altamira ended with the Paleolithic period—Indian cave painting traditions adapted and evolved. Medieval additions to Bhimbetka caves show clear stylistic connections to their prehistoric predecessors, while incorporating new themes influenced by established religions.

Contemporary tribal communities in central India maintain artistic traditions that show clear connections to the ancient cave paintings. The Bhil, Gond, and other indigenous groups create art that employs similar techniques, symbols, and themes to their prehistoric predecessors. Their ritual paintings, created during festivals and ceremonies, demonstrate that the cave painting tradition never truly ended but simply moved from permanent rock faces to temporary ceremonial contexts.

This continuity suggests something profound about the relationship between art, spirituality, and cultural identity in Indian civilization. The caves were not merely decorated surfaces but sacred spaces where the boundary between the physical and spiritual worlds became permeable. Each generation that added to these galleries participated in a conversation spanning millennia, contributing their voice to an eternal dialogue about the nature of existence, the power of the divine, and the human place in the cosmic order.

The Foundation Stones - Settlement Development (8000 BCE 3000 BCE)

From Nomads to Villagers

The transition from the mobile hunting-gathering lifestyle depicted in early cave paintings to settled agricultural communities represents one of humanity's most significant transformations. In India, this transition occurred gradually over several millennia, beginning around 8000 BCE with the establishment of seasonal camps that eventually evolved into permanent settlements. This process was not uniform across the region but occurred at different rates in different areas, creating a complex mosaic of cultural developments that would eventually coalesce into the sophisticated urban civilizations of the Bronze Age.

The earliest permanent settlements appeared in the hills and river valleys where resources were abundant and reliable. Sites like Mehrgarh in present-day Pakistan, dating to around 7000 BCE, represent some of the world's earliest farming communities outside the Fertile Crescent. These settlements reveal a sophisticated understanding of agriculture, animal domestication, and craft production that would form the foundation for all subsequent South Asian civilizations.

Mehrgarh: The Dawn of Agriculture

Mehrgarh stands as perhaps the most significant early settlement in South Asia, representing a crucial link between the hunting-gathering traditions of the Paleolithic period and the urban sophistication of the Indus Valley Civilization. Archaeological excavations have revealed a continuous sequence of occupation spanning over 4,000 years, from approximately 7000 BCE to 2500 BCE, providing unprecedented insight into the development of agricultural society in South Asia.

The earliest levels of Mehrgarh show evidence of wheat and barley cultivation using varieties that were likely domesticated locally rather than imported from the Middle East. This suggests that Indian agricultural development was largely independent, arising from indigenous experimentation with local plant species. The discovery of early cotton cultivation at Mehrgarh is particularly significant, as it represents the world's first known production of cotton textiles—an industry that would become central to Indian economy and culture for millennia to come.

Animal domestication at Mehrgarh followed a similar pattern of indigenous development. Cattle, water buffalo, goats, and sheep were all domesticated locally, with evidence suggesting that zebu cattle—the humped cattle species that remains central to Indian agriculture—were first domesticated in this region. The relationship between humans and cattle evident at Mehrgarh establishes patterns of reverence and utility that continue to characterize Indian culture today.

As settlements grew and stabilized, craft specialization emerged as a defining characteristic of South Asian village life. Mehrgarh and contemporary sites reveal sophisticated pottery traditions, with evidence of the potter's wheel appearing around 4000 BCE. The pottery shows remarkable artistic sophistication, with geometric patterns and animal motifs that echo the symbolic systems of cave art while developing new forms of expression.

Metallurgy represents another crucial development during this period. Copper working began around 4500 BCE, with evidence of both functional tools and decorative objects. The early metalworkers showed remarkable skill, producing delicate ornaments and sophisticated alloys that demonstrate advanced understanding of metallurgical processes. This technical knowledge would provide the foundation for the bronze-working traditions that would characterize the later Indus Valley Civilization.

Perhaps most significantly, these early settlements established trade networks that would connect India to the broader world for millennia to come. Lapis lazuli from Afghanistan, shells from the Arabian Sea coast, and turquoise from Central Asia all appear in settlements hundreds of miles from their sources, indicating sophisticated trade relationships and cultural exchange. These networks established India as a crucial link between Central Asia, the Middle East, and Southeast Asia—a role it would maintain throughout its history.

The organization of early settlements reveals the emergence of complex social structures that would characterize South Asian civilization. Houses were arranged in planned layouts with clear distinctions between residential, craft production, and storage areas. Public spaces, possibly used for community gatherings and rituals, appear in most settlements, suggesting the development of shared community identity beyond kinship groups.

Evidence of ritual activity becomes increasingly sophisticated throughout this period. Elaborate burials with grave goods, including pottery, ornaments, and tools, suggest beliefs about afterlife and social status. Figurines of animals and humans, often with emphasized sexual characteristics, point toward fertility cults and goddess worship that would become central to later Indian religious traditions.

The appearance of seals and standardized weights and measures during the later phases of this period indicates the development of administrative systems and long-distance trade regulation. These innovations represent crucial steps toward the complex urban administration that would characterize the Indus Valley Civilization.

While Mehrgarh represents the most thoroughly studied early settlement, similar developments occurred across India with regional variations that reflect local adaptations to different environmental conditions. In the Ganges valley, settlements like Lahuradewa show evidence of rice cultivation as early as 8000 BCE,

establishing the agricultural foundation for later Gangetic civilizations. In South India, sites like Sanganakallu reveal the development of distinctive architectural traditions using local granite, while maintaining connections to broader Indian cultural patterns.

The interaction between these regional traditions created a dynamic cultural landscape where innovations spread rapidly while local characteristics were maintained. This pattern of unity within diversity would become a defining characteristic of Indian civilization, allowing for remarkable cultural continuity while accommodating tremendous regional and temporal variation.

Urban Precursors - 4000 BCE

By 4000 BCE, some settlements had grown to substantial size and complexity, prefiguring the urban developments that would follow. Sites like Kot Diji show evidence of planned layouts, defensive walls, and craft specialization that represent clear precursors to Harappan urbanism. The pottery traditions, artistic motifs, and technological innovations of these late Neolithic settlements provide clear continuity with the Harappan Civilization, demonstrating that Harappan culture did not emerge suddenly but developed gradually from indigenous Indian foundations.

The writing systems that would later characterize the Harappan Civilization also show precursors in these early settlements. Simple marks and symbols on pottery evolve gradually into more complex sign systems, suggesting that literacy developed slowly and organically rather than being imported from elsewhere. This indigenous development of writing represents another crucial element in the continuous thread of Indian cultural development.

The Urban Revolution - The Civilization Across India (3300 BCE - 1300 BCE)

The Great Cities Rise

Around 3300 BCE, the scattered villages and towns across the Indian subcontinent began a remarkable transformation that would produce one of the world's most sophisticated ancient civilizations. The Civilization, stretching from the foothills of the Himalayas to the shores of the Arabian Sea and from the banks of the Ganges to the coasts of Gujarat, represented not just an advancement in urban planning and technology, but the culmination of millennia of cultural development that had been building since the first cave paintings and earliest settlements. What emerged was a civilization that unified the entire northern and western regions of India through shared cultural practices, standardized systems, and urban planning principles that reflected deep philosophical concepts about order, harmony, and the relationship between human society and the natural world.

The major cities of this pan-Indian civilization—Dholavira in Gujarat, Kalibangan in Rajasthan, Rakhigarhi in Haryana, Lothal in Gujarat, and Banawali in Haryana—were not merely large settlements but carefully planned urban environments that embodied sophisticated concepts of civic organization.

These cities shared remarkably consistent planning principles despite being separated by hundreds of miles across the Indian landscape, suggesting a unified cultural vision that guided urban development from the Thar Desert to the Gangetic plains.

Dholavira: The Desert Metropolis

Dholavira, located on the arid island of Khadir in Gujarat's Rann of Kutch, stands as perhaps the most spectacular example of Harappan urban planning adapted to challenging environmental conditions. This magnificent city, discovered relatively recently in 1967, reveals the extraordinary ingenuity of ancient Indian engineers who created a thriving metropolis in one of the subcontinent's most challenging environments.

The city's sophisticated water management system represents one of humanity's earliest examples of large-scale water conservation in arid regions. Dholavira's engineers constructed an elaborate network of reservoirs, dams, and channels that captured and stored every drop of the region's scarce rainfall. Sixteen massive reservoirs, carved into the living rock and lined with precisely fitted stone blocks, could store enough water to sustain a population of tens of thousands through multiple years of drought.

The famous Dholavira signboard, discovered at the site, contains ten large symbols of the stillundeciphered Harappan script, representing one of the world's largest ancient inscriptions. This monumental signboard, prominently displayed at the city's northern gateway, suggests that Dholavira served as a major administrative and cultural center for the entire Gujarat region, communicating its importance to travelers approaching from across the Thar Desert.

Kalibangan: The Sacred City of Rajasthan

Kalibangan, located on the banks of the now-dry Ghaggar River in Rajasthan, provides crucial insights into the ritual and religious practices that unified civilization across the Indian subcontinent. This ancient city, whose name means "black bangles" in reference to the numerous black glass bangles found at the site, represents one of the most important ceremonial centers of the Indus-Sarasvati world.

The most remarkable feature of Kalibangan is its elaborate fire altar complex, representing some of the earliest evidence of systematic fire worship in Indian civilization. These carefully constructed brick platforms, arranged in precise geometric patterns, were used for elaborate fire rituals that appear to prefigure the Vedic fire sacrifices that would later become central to Indian spiritual practice. The discovery of charred grains, animal bones, and ritual pottery around these altars suggests elaborate community ceremonies that brought together the entire population in shared spiritual practice.

The residential architecture of Kalibangan reveals a society with sophisticated concepts of privacy, comfort, and social organization adapted specifically to the harsh Rajasthani climate. Houses were built around central courtyards with thick walls and few external windows to minimize heat gain, while interior courtyards provided cooling through natural air circulation. Most houses had private wells and sophisticated drainage systems—innovations particularly crucial in the arid environment of Rajasthan.

Rakhigarhi: The Giant of Haryana

Recent excavations at Rakhigarhi in Haryana have revealed what may have been the largest city of the Indian civilization, covering over 350 hectares and representing a massive urban center that dominated the fertile plains of what is now northern India. This discovery has revolutionized our understanding of Indian civilization, demonstrating that the largest centers of this ancient culture were located not in the far west but in the heart of the Indian subcontinent.

Rakhigarhi's enormous size and sophisticated planning demonstrate the ability of Indus-Sarasvati civilization to support massive urban populations through advanced agricultural techniques adapted to the Indo-Gangetic plains. The city's location in the fertile alluvial plains of Haryana, with access to both the Ghaggar-Hakra river system and monsoon rainfall, made it an ideal center for the surplus agricultural production necessary to support large non-farming populations of craftsmen, traders, and administrators.

The recent discovery of sophisticated metallurgical workshops at Rakhigarhi reveals that this Indian heartland was a major center of technological innovation for the entire Indus-Sarasvati world. Advanced bronze-working techniques, sophisticated pottery kilns, and elaborate bead-making facilities all demonstrate that the interior regions of India were not merely agricultural suppliers but major centers of craft production and technological development.

The Indus-Sarasvati civilization was fundamentally connected across the Indian subcontinent and to the broader world through extensive trade networks that reached from the Himalayas to the southern Deccan and from the Arabian Sea to the Bay of Bengal. Indus-Sarasvati seals and artifacts have been found in locations across India, while goods from various regions of the subcontinent appear in Indus-Sarasvati cities, indicating sophisticated commercial relationships that unified diverse ecological and cultural zones.

The famous Indus-Sarasvati seals, with their undeciphered script and sophisticated animal imagery, served not only as trade markers but as carriers of cultural and religious concepts across the length and breadth of India. The recurring motifs on these seals—the "proto-Shiva" figure in yogic meditation, the sacred bull, the pipal tree, and various fertility symbols—establish iconographic traditions that would persist throughout Indian cultural history from Kashmir to Tamil Nadu.

Lothal, the great port city in Gujarat, demonstrates the sophisticated maritime technology that enabled far-flung trade connections. The city's dock, constructed with precisely fitted stone blocks and equipped with sophisticated locks and spillways, represents one of the world's earliest engineered harbors. The discovery of a ship channel connecting the dock to the Arabian Sea shows that Indus-Sarasvati engineers understood tidal patterns and seasonal variations, engineering solutions that accommodated natural cycles rather than fighting against them.

While the Indus-Sarasvati script remains undeciphered, the archaeological evidence from sites across India reveals a rich spiritual culture that established many themes that would persist throughout Indian religious traditions. The "Priest-King" statue from Pakistan, the fire altars of Kalibangan, and the sophisticated water management systems found at multiple sites across India all suggest a civilization where spiritual and temporal authority were closely linked—a pattern that would characterize Indian governance for millennia.

The famous seal depicting a horned figure seated in what appears to be a yogic posture, surrounded by animals, has been interpreted as a proto-Shiva figure, establishing connections between Indus-Sarasvati spiritual practices and later Hindu traditions that would spread across the entire subcontinent. The recurring bull imagery on seals found from Gujarat to Haryana suggests the sacred status of cattle that would become central to Indian culture, while the prominent goddess figurines found throughout Indus-Sarasvati sites from Rajasthan to Punjab indicate goddess worship traditions that would persist in various forms throughout Indian history.

The Great Bath-type structures and similar ritual bathing facilities found at multiple Indus-Sarasvati sites across India establish the centrality of ritual purification through water—a practice that remains fundamental to Indian religious traditions from the Ganges ghats of Varanasi to the temple tanks of South India. The sophisticated engineering of these facilities, with their perfect water-tight construction and elaborate drainage, suggests that ritual bathing was not merely personal hygiene but a central community practice requiring significant social investment.

The craftsmanship from sites across the Indian subcontinent represents a pinnacle of Bronze Age technical achievement. The civilization's metallurgists, working from workshops in Rakhigarhi, Kalibangan, and other centers, produced sophisticated bronze alloys for tools and weapons while creating delicate ornaments and sculptures that demonstrate advanced understanding of casting, forging, and finishing techniques. The famous "Dancing Girl" bronze, with its naturalistic proportions and confident posture, represents one of the world's earliest examples of realistic bronze sculpture and exemplifies the artistic sophistication achieved across the Indus-Sarasvati cultural sphere.

Indus-Sarasvati pottery from Gujarat to Haryana, while less decorated than that of contemporary civilizations, shows sophisticated understanding of ceramic technology and aesthetic principles. The standardized shapes and precise construction reflect cultural values emphasizing function and mathematical harmony over ornamental display. The distinctive red-on-buff painted pottery found across Indian Indus-Sarasvati sites establishes decorative traditions that would influence Indian ceramic arts for centuries to come.

The civilization's urban planning achievements, visible from Dholavira in the west to Rakhigarhi in the east, represent perhaps its greatest legacy to Indian culture. The sophisticated water management systems, precise grid layouts, and functional zoning of Indus-Sarasvati cities demonstrate urban planning principles that would influence Indian city design throughout history. These achievements were not merely technical but reflected deeper cultural concepts about the proper relationship between human society and natural order that remain central to Indian philosophical thought.

The Sacred Word - Vedic Literature and Rituals (1500 BCE - 500 BCE)

Around 1500 BCE, as the great cities were transforming and their populations dispersing across the subcontinent, a new form of cultural expression emerged that would provide the philosophical and spiritual foundation for Indian civilization for millennia to come. The Vedic tradition—centered on a vast corpus of hymns, rituals, and philosophical teachings preserved with extraordinary precision through oral transmission—represents not a break with earlier traditions but their transformation into sophisticated literary and spiritual forms.

The Vedas represent humanity's oldest continuously preserved religious literature, maintained through an unbroken oral tradition that has preserved not only the words but the precise pronunciation, intonation, and ritual contexts necessary for their proper performance. This oral preservation system, with its elaborate mnemonic techniques and cross-checking mechanisms, demonstrates cultural values emphasizing precision, continuity, and the sacred power of properly articulated sound that connect directly to the mathematical precision and cultural standardization.

The central Upanishadic concepts—Brahman (ultimate reality), Atman (individual consciousness), and their fundamental identity—establish philosophical frameworks that would influence not only Hindu philosophy but Buddhist and Jain thought as well. The sophisticated analysis of consciousness states, the nature of knowledge, and the relationship between appearance and reality found in texts like the Chandogya and Brihadaranyaka Upanishads represent philosophical achievements that continue to influence world philosophy today.

The development of meditation techniques and spiritual practices described in the Upanishads connects directly to the yogic traditions suggested by Harappan archaeological evidence. The detailed analysis of breath control, sense withdrawal, and contemplative absorption found in these texts establishes practical spiritual methodologies that would be further developed in later yoga and Buddhist meditation traditions. The Vedic tradition represents both continuity with earlier Indian cultural traditions and their transformation into new forms adapted to the changing conditions across the subcontinent.

Threads of Connection

As we trace the continuous thread of Indian cultural development from the first paintings at Bhimbetka to the sophisticated philosophy of the Upanishads remarkable patterns of continuity emerge that transcend conventional historical periodization. These continuities are not merely coincidental survivals but represent the persistence of fundamental cultural concepts and practices that have provided stability and identity across fifteen millennia of change and development.

The thread metaphor is particularly appropriate for understanding South Asian cultural continuity because, like a woven fabric, the strength of the tradition comes not from the persistence of individual elements but from the way different strands are woven together to create patterns that are both stable and adaptable. Individual practices, beliefs, and institutions may change dramatically over time, but the underlying patterns of relationship between them maintain continuity that provides cultural identity and meaning.

One of the most persistent threads connecting these diverse periods is the concept of sacred geography—the understanding that physical landscape embodies spiritual principles and that human settlement should harmonize with cosmic order. This concept appears in the cave paintings' careful placement within natural rock formations that enhance their spiritual power, develops through the Indus-Sarasvati cities' precise orientation and mathematical planning, and reaches sophisticated expression in Vedic concepts of ritual space and sacred geography.

The Bhimbetka caves were not randomly chosen locations for artistic expression but carefully selected sites where natural rock formations created acoustic and visual effects that enhanced the spiritual impact of the paintings. The curved walls amplify sound, creating natural amphitheaters for ritual performance, while the positioning of paintings in relation to natural light sources creates dramatic visual effects that change throughout the day and across seasons.

This sophisticated understanding of the relationship between natural environment and spiritual practice reaches full expression in Indus-Sarasvati urban planning, where cities were oriented to cardinal directions and planned according to mathematical principles that reflected cosmic order. The precise grid systems, functional zoning, and integration of water management systems all demonstrate understanding that human habitation should embody rather than oppose natural principles.

The Vedic tradition inherits and develops these concepts through elaborate theories of sacred geography that map cosmic principles onto terrestrial landscape. The positioning of ritual fires, the orientation of sacrificial altars, and the geographical knowledge embedded in the texts all demonstrate sophisticated understanding of the relationship between spiritual practice and physical environment that connects directly to earlier traditions.

Knowledge Transmission and Cultural Continuity

Perhaps most remarkably, all these periods demonstrate sophisticated systems for preserving and transmitting cultural knowledge across generations. From the long-term maintenance of cave painting sites through the standardization systems that maintained Indus-Sarasvati cultural unity to the elaborate oral tradition techniques that preserved Vedic literature, we see persistent cultural values emphasizing accurate knowledge transmission and cultural continuity.

The cave painting tradition maintained active sites for over ten millennia, with each generation adding to rather than replacing earlier work. This demonstrates cultural values emphasizing continuity and cumulative development rather than innovation through replacement—a pattern that would characterize South Asian cultural development throughout its history.

Indus-Sarasvati civilization maintained remarkable cultural standardization across vast geographical areas and long time periods through systems that ensured accurate transmission of technical knowledge, artistic traditions, and cultural practices. The consistency of brick ratios, pottery styles, and urban planning principles across hundreds of sites and over a millennium demonstrates sophisticated systems for maintaining cultural knowledge and training new generations of craftsmen and planners.

The Vedic tradition represents perhaps humanity's most sophisticated achievement in oral knowledge transmission, developing elaborate techniques that preserved not only textual content but precise pronunciation, ritual contexts, and philosophical interpretations across centuries of oral tradition. The cross-checking systems, mnemonic techniques, and family-based transmission methods ensured accuracy levels that rival or exceed written preservation systems.

Throughout these fifteen millennia, South Asian cultures demonstrated remarkable ability to adapt to environmental changes while maintaining cultural continuity. The drying of the Sarasvati River system, changes in monsoon patterns, and other environmental challenges were met with cultural adaptations that maintained essential continuities while allowing for necessary innovations.

The cave painting tradition adapted to changing climatic conditions by shifting artistic themes while maintaining core symbolic systems. The transition from large animal depictions to human-centered scenes reflects changing environmental conditions and hunting patterns, while the persistence of dance scenes and ritual imagery maintains cultural continuities across environmental changes.

Indus-Sarasvati civilization's response to environmental challenges demonstrates sophisticated understanding of adaptation strategies that maintain cultural identity while accommodating necessary changes. The gradual eastward movement of populations, the development of new agricultural techniques, and the evolution of urban planning principles all represent successful adaptations to changing conditions that maintained cultural continuity.

The Vedic tradition's geographical knowledge and agricultural practices demonstrate sophisticated understanding of environmental cycles and adaptation strategies. The detailed seasonal observations, the agricultural rituals timed to environmental patterns, and the sacred geography that encompasses diverse ecological zones all demonstrate cultures that understood adaptation as maintaining harmony with rather than opposition to natural cycles.

The development of philosophical and spiritual concepts across these periods reveals remarkable integration of practical knowledge with metaphysical speculation. From the symbolic systems of cave art through the ritual technologies of Indus-Sarasvati culture to the sophisticated philosophy of the Upanishads, we see persistent attempts to understand the relationship between material existence and spiritual reality.

The cave paintings integrate naturalistic observation with symbolic representation, demonstrating early attempts to understand the relationship between physical appearance and spiritual essence. The careful observation of animal behavior combined with symbolic representation suggests philosophical concepts about the nature of reality that would be developed in later traditions.

Indus-Sarasvat culture demonstrates sophisticated integration of practical technology with spiritual purpose through urban planning, ritual architecture, and craftsmanship that embody mathematical and spiritual principles. The precision of construction, the symbolism of decorative motifs, and the integration of practical and ceremonial functions all suggest cultures that understood material construction as spiritual practice.

The Vedic tradition represents the full philosophical development of these earlier integrative approaches through sophisticated metaphysical systems that understand material existence as manifestation of spiritual principles. The elaborate ritual technologies, the detailed philosophical speculation, and the integration of practical knowledge with spiritual instruction all demonstrate the culmination of millennia of cultural development.

Conclusion: The Living Tradition

As we reach the end of this exploration of fifteen millennia of cultural continuity, the metaphor of the continuous thread reveals its full significance. What we have traced is not merely the persistence of isolated cultural elements but the dynamic weaving together of diverse strands into patterns that maintain identity while allowing for constant adaptation and development.

The thread that connects the first handprint pressed into ochre at Bhimbetka to the sophisticated philosophy of the Chandogya Upanishad is not a simple linear progression but a complex weaving of multiple traditions, innovations, and adaptations that create patterns of remarkable resilience and creativity. Like a master weaver working with diverse fibers, South Asian cultures have integrated influences from multiple sources while maintaining distinctive patterns that provide identity and meaning across vast spans of time and space.

This continuous thread is not merely historical curiosity but living tradition that continues to influence contemporary South Asian culture and world civilization. The urban planning principles developed by Indus-Sarasvati engineers influence contemporary sustainable city design. The ritual technologies preserved in Vedic tradition continue to provide spiritual practices for millions of people. The artistic traditions established in prehistoric caves continue to inspire contemporary artists and spiritual seekers.

The philosophical concepts developed across these millennia—the understanding of consciousness and reality explored in the Upanishads, the integration of material and spiritual life demonstrated throughout these traditions, the sophisticated approaches to environmental adaptation and community organization—all continue to offer insights relevant to contemporary global challenges.

Perhaps most significantly, this fifteen-thousand-year story demonstrates the possibility of cultural continuity that maintains identity while accommodating constant change and development. In an era when rapid technological and social change often seems to threaten cultural identity and community cohesion, the South Asian example offers hope that human communities can maintain meaningful continuity while adapting successfully to changing conditions.

The continuous thread of South Asian civilization reminds us that culture is not a museum artifact to be preserved unchanged but a living tradition that maintains identity through constant adaptation and creative development. The cave painters of Bhimbetka, the urban planners of the Indus-Sarasvati cities, and the philosopher-poets of the Vedic tradition all contributed to an ongoing conversation about the nature of human existence and the possibility of creating meaningful community in harmony with cosmic principles.

This conversation continues today, as contemporary South Asian communities and cultures around the world inspired by South Asian traditions continue to weave new patterns while maintaining connection to the threads established by their predecessors. The continuous thread remains unbroken, connecting past achievements to present possibilities and future potential in an eternal weave that demonstrates the remarkable capacity of human culture to maintain identity while embracing change.

In studying this remarkable story of cultural continuity, we gain not only knowledge of the past but inspiration for the future. The fifteen-thousand-year thread reminds us that human cultures can maintain meaning and identity across vast spans of time and dramatic changes in circumstances. It suggests that the challenges facing contemporary global civilization—environmental crisis, social fragmentation, spiritual emptiness—can be addressed through approaches that integrate practical wisdom with spiritual insight, individual development with community welfare, and local identity with universal principles.

The continuous thread of South Asian civilization stands as testimony to the remarkable capacity of human culture to maintain meaningful patterns across time while adapting creatively to changing circumstances. It offers hope that contemporary global civilization can learn to weave together diverse traditions and innovations into patterns that maintain identity while embracing the changes necessary for survival and flourishing in an interconnected world.

As we conclude this exploration, we are reminded that we too are part of this continuous thread, adding our own contributions to patterns established by countless predecessors and influencing patterns that will guide countless successors. The thread continues, and we are both its inheritors and its weavers, responsible for maintaining its integrity while adapting it to meet the challenges and opportunities of our own time.

3
The Rigvedic World

The Rigveda, composed between approximately 1500-1200 BCE, provides our earliest and most substantial window into the social organization of ancient India. This collection of 1,028 hymns reveals a society in transition, where tribal structures were evolving into more complex forms of organization that would eventually shape the contours of classical Indian civilization. The Rigvedic world was one of dynamic change, where pastoral and semi-nomadic communities were gradually settling into agricultural patterns, developing sophisticated political institutions, and establishing social hierarchies that would endure for millennia.

Understanding Rigvedic society requires careful interpretation of hymnic literature that was primarily religious in nature, yet contains abundant references to social, political, and economic life. The composers of these hymns were primarily priests and poets who served the needs of tribal chiefs and warriors, and their perspective inevitably colors our understanding of this formative period. Nevertheless, through careful analysis of the Rigvedic corpus, we can reconstruct the broad outlines of a society that was laying the foundations for one of the world's great civilizations.

Tribal Organization and Leadership

The fundamental unit of Rigvedic society was the tribe, known as *jana* or *vis*. These terms, which appear frequently throughout the Rigvedic hymns, denote groups of people bound together by kinship, shared ancestry, and common religious practices. The concept of *jana* was particularly significant, as it encompassed not merely a political entity but a cultural and ethnic identity that would remain central to Indian thought throughout antiquity.

The tribal organization of the Rigvedic period represented a sophisticated form of social arrangement that balanced individual autonomy with collective security and identity. Unlike the highly centralized states that would later emerge in the Gangetic plain, Rigvedic tribes maintained a relatively egalitarian structure where leadership was based on personal qualities such as valor, wisdom, and religious knowledge rather than hereditary privilege alone. This system allowed for considerable social mobility and provided mechanisms for capable individuals to rise to positions of authority regardless of their birth circumstances.

Archaeological evidence from sites associated with the Painted Grey Ware culture, which many scholars connect with the later Vedic period, suggests that Rigvedic tribes were organized around fortified settlements that served as centers for both defense and administration. These settlements, referred to as *pur* in the Rigveda, were typically located on elevated ground and surrounded by earthen ramparts or wooden palisades. The strategic placement of these settlements indicates a society that was both militarily sophisticated and economically prosperous, capable of supporting specialized craftsmen, warriors, and religious specialists.

The archaeological record reveals an extensive distribution of Vedic settlements across the Indian subcontinent. Excavations conducted over the last forty years have unearthed numerous post-Harappan settlements in Punjab, Uttar Pradesh, and northern Rajasthan, particularly along the Indus and Ghaggar rivers. Important archaeological sites include Hastinapur, Alamgirpur, Ahichchhatra, Allahpur, Mathura,

Kampil, Kaushambi and Shravasti in Uttar Pradesh; Noh, Jodhpura and Jakhera in Rajasthan; and Bhagwanpura in Haryana. At sites like Bhagwanpura as well as Dadheri and Katpalon in Punjab, archaeological layers show the transition between different cultural phases, providing evidence for the continuity and evolution of Vedic civilization.

Archaeological excavations have revealed evidence of substantial technological developments during the Iron Age, with the Painted Grey Ware Culture emerging between 1,100 and 800 BC, including not only the distinctive painted pottery but also a wide range of tools and craftworks in ceramics, iron, copper, glass and bone. Thousands of Painted Grey Ware sites have now been located along the rivers in the IndoGangetic divide, indicating the widespread distribution of Vedic settlements across northern India.

The geographical spread of these archaeological sites corresponds remarkably with the river systems mentioned in the Rigveda. The river Saraswati (modern Ghagghar-Hakra river) is recorded at least 71 times in the Rigvedic text, and during archaeological excavations, a majority of Harappan and postHarappan settlements were discovered along the banks of this river system. This archaeological evidence supports the historical accuracy of Vedic geographical references and demonstrates the continuity of settlement patterns from the Harappan period into the Vedic age.

The tribal structure was hierarchical but flexible, with various sub-groups or clans (*kula* or *gotra*) forming the constituent elements of the larger tribal entity. Each clan traced its ancestry to a common ancestor, often mythologized as a great sage or hero, and maintained its own traditions, rituals, and territorial claims. This segmentary structure provided the tribe with considerable resilience, as the loss or displacement of one segment did not necessarily threaten the survival of the whole. It also facilitated the absorption of new groups through adoption, marriage alliances, or voluntary association.

The economic foundation of tribal life was primarily pastoral, centered on cattle herding supplemented by agriculture and trade. Cattle represented not merely economic wealth but social status and religious significance, as they were essential for the elaborate sacrificial rituals that formed the core of Rigvedic religious practice. The importance of cattle is reflected in the frequent use of *go* (cow) as a term for wealth and prosperity, and in the elaborate metaphors that compare various aspects of cosmic and social order to cattle herding.

Warfare played a central role in tribal life, not merely as a means of defense but as a mechanism for acquiring wealth, prestige, and territory. The Rigvedic hymns contain numerous references to cattle raids, tribal conflicts, and the division of spoils among warriors. These military activities were highly ritualized, with elaborate ceremonies performed before and after battles to ensure divine favor and to integrate the social and cosmic consequences of warfare into the broader religious worldview.

The mobility of Rigvedic tribes was facilitated by their mastery of horse-drawn chariots, a technology that gave them decisive advantages in both warfare and transportation. The chariot represented the pinnacle of Rigvedic technology and craftsmanship, requiring sophisticated knowledge of metallurgy, woodworking, and animal training. The social prestige associated with chariot ownership is evident from the frequent references to chariots in royal epithets and the elaborate descriptions of divine chariots in mythological contexts.

The Raja (Chief) and Tribal Assemblies

At the apex of tribal organization stood the *raja*, a term that would eventually evolve to mean "king" but in the Rigvedic context denoted something closer to a chief or war leader. The position of *raja* represented a fascinating balance between individual authority and collective governance that distinguished early Vedic society from both the egalitarian societies that preceded it and the monarchical states that would follow.

The *raja* was not an absolute ruler but rather a leader whose authority derived from multiple sources: military prowess, religious sanction, tribal consensus, and personal charisma. This multifaceted basis of authority required the *raja* to maintain the support of various constituencies within the tribe, including warriors, priests, wealthy cattle owners, and the broader tribal assembly. The result was a form of leadership that was both effective and accountable, capable of providing decisive action in times of crisis while remaining responsive to the needs and wishes of the tribal community.

The selection of a *raja* appears to have involved a combination of hereditary succession and electoral confirmation. While sons of previous *rajas* had advantages in terms of training, resources, and name recognition, they still required the approval of the tribal assembly to assume leadership. This system prevented the automatic succession of incompetent heirs while preserving the benefits of continuity and established relationships. In cases where the hereditary line was broken or disputed, the assembly could select new leaders from among the prominent families of the tribe.

The religious dimensions of royal authority were crucial to understanding the *raja's* position in Rigvedic society. The king was not merely a secular leader but served as the focal point for the tribe's relationship with the divine realm. Through his performance of sacrifices, his protection of dharma, and his maintenance of cosmic order, the *raja* ensured the continued prosperity and security of his people. This religious role gave the king considerable moral authority but also imposed significant obligations and constraints on his behavior.

The institution of the *sabha* and *samiti* represented the collective dimension of Rigvedic governance. These assemblies, mentioned frequently in the hymns, provided forums for discussion, debate, and decision-making that complemented and constrained royal authority. The *sabha* appears to have been a smaller, more select body composed of the tribal elite, including prominent warriors, wealthy cattle owners, and respected elders. The *samiti* was a broader assembly that included all adult male members of the tribe and served as the ultimate source of tribal consensus on major issues.

The functioning of these assemblies reflected sophisticated understanding of collective decision-making processes. Debates were conducted according to established procedures, with speakers recognized by the assembly president and given opportunities to present their views. Decisions were reached through discussion and consensus-building rather than formal voting, with the aim of achieving solutions that could command broad support rather than simple majorities. This emphasis on consensus reflected the recognition that tribal survival depended on unity and cooperation that could not be achieved through coercion alone.

The relationship between the *raja* and the assemblies was dynamic and contextual, varying according to circumstances and the personalities involved. In times of war or external threat, the king's authority was enhanced and the assemblies might defer to his judgment on tactical and strategic matters. During periods of peace and prosperity, the assemblies played more active roles in governance, particularly in matters relating to law, resource allocation, and internal disputes. This flexibility allowed the political system to adapt to changing circumstances while maintaining its essential character.

The *raja's* court (*rajasabha*) served as the administrative center of tribal governance, where the king met with advisors, received petitioners, and conducted the daily business of leadership. The court included various specialized officials, including the *purohita* (chief priest), *senapati* (military commander), and other functionaries who assisted in specific aspects of governance. The development of these specialized roles indicates the growing complexity of tribal administration and the emergence of bureaucratic institutions that would later characterize classical Indian statecraft.

The *raja's* responsibilities encompassed military leadership, judicial functions, religious duties, and economic management. As military leader, he was expected to protect the tribe from external enemies, lead successful raids against rival groups, and ensure the fair distribution of war spoils. His judicial role involved resolving disputes between tribal members, punishing crimes, and maintaining social order according to customary law. Religiously, he served as the patron of sacrificial rituals and the protector of dharma, ensuring that the tribe maintained proper relationships with the gods and ancestors.

Social Structure: Emerging Hierarchy

The social structure of Rigvedic society represented a critical phase in the development of the Indian caste system, though the elaborate hierarchies of later periods were still in embryonic form. The emerging social stratification was based on a combination of occupational specialization, ritual status, and economic differentiation that created distinct but not yet rigid social categories.

The earliest and most fundamental division in Rigvedic society was between the *arya* (noble or free) and the *dasa* or *dasyu* (servants or slaves). This distinction appears to have originated in the complex interactions between different tribal groups and the incorporation of various populations during the Vedic period, though the reality was undoubtedly more nuanced than simple conquest narratives would suggest. Over time, this basic division evolved into a more nuanced system that recognized degrees of status and different types of social relationships.

Among the *arya*, three primary social categories began to emerge: the *brahma* (priests), *kshatra* (warriors), and *vis* (common people). These groups, which would later crystallize into the brahmin, kshatriya, and vaishya varnas, were distinguished primarily by their occupational roles and their positions in the ritual hierarchy. However, in the Rigvedic period, these categories remained relatively fluid, with individuals sometimes moving between them based on their abilities, circumstances, and life choices.

The *brahma* represented the priestly class whose members possessed the sacred knowledge necessary for conducting sacrificial rituals. These individuals were distinguished not merely by their ritual functions but by their mastery of the complex oral traditions that preserved and transmitted Vedic knowledge. The brahmin's social status derived from their exclusive access to sacred power and their role as intermediaries between human and divine realms. However, the priestly class was not uniformly wealthy or powerful, and many brahmins served as household priests for individual families rather than occupying positions of great influence.

The *kshatra* encompassed the warrior aristocracy, including the *raja* and other military leaders who bore primary responsibility for tribal defense and expansion. This group's social position was based on their military prowess, their control of weapons and chariots, and their leadership roles in warfare. The kshatriya ideal emphasized physical courage, martial skill, and the protection of dharma through force when necessary. However, the warrior class also included individuals of varying economic circumstances, from powerful chiefs who controlled vast herds to minor warriors who served in the retinues of greater leaders.

The *vis* represented the bulk of the tribal population, including farmers, herders, craftsmen, and traders who formed the economic foundation of society. This group was internally diverse, ranging from wealthy cattle owners who rivaled the warrior aristocracy in economic terms to small farmers and artisans who lived more modest lives. The vis were distinguished from the upper varnas not by poverty or low status but by their primary focus on productive rather than ritual or military activities.

The integration of *dasa* populations into Rigvedic society created additional complexity in the social hierarchy. Some *dasas* appear to have been incorporated as servants or slaves, while others may have been adopted into the tribe as members of the *vis* category. Over time, the distinction between *arya* and *dasa* became less important than the functional distinctions between different occupational groups, though the memory of this original division persisted in later social thought.

The economic foundations of social stratification were complex and multifaceted. Wealth was measured primarily in cattle, but also included horses, gold ornaments, textiles, and other valuable goods. The accumulation of wealth enabled individuals and families to sponsor elaborate sacrifices, which enhanced their ritual status and social prestige. However, wealth alone was not sufficient to determine social position; ritual knowledge, martial prowess, and family lineage all played important roles in establishing and maintaining social rank.

The relationship between social status and occupational specialization was becoming increasingly important during the Rigvedic period. Skilled craftsmen, including metalworkers, carpenters, and textile producers, occupied ambiguous positions in the social hierarchy. Their technical expertise was valued and well-rewarded, but their status relative to the emerging varna system was unclear. Similarly, merchants and traders, who were becoming increasingly important as tribal settlements engaged in long-distance commerce, did not fit neatly into traditional social categories.

The religious dimensions of social hierarchy were particularly significant in shaping the emerging varna system. The elaborate sacrificial rituals that formed the core of Rigvedic religion required the cooperation of different social groups, each contributing their specialized skills and resources. The brahmins provided ritual knowledge, the kshatriyas sponsored the ceremonies and provided protection, and the vis contributed the wealth necessary to purchase sacrificial animals and materials. This ritual interdependence created bonds between social groups that transcended simple relationships of dominance and subordination.

Social mobility, while limited, was not impossible in Rigvedic society. Exceptional individuals could rise in status through military achievement, acquisition of sacred knowledge, or accumulation of wealth. Conversely, families could lose status through poverty, defeat in warfare, or ritual pollution. This fluidity distinguished Rigvedic social structure from the more rigid caste system that would later emerge, though the trend toward hereditary transmission of occupational roles was already becoming evident.

Family Life and Kinship Patterns

The family (*kula*) served as the fundamental building block of Rigvedic society, providing the primary context for socialization, economic production, and ritual practice. Rigvedic family structure was patriarchal and patrilineal, with descent traced through the male line and authority concentrated in the hands of male household heads. However, the system was more flexible and egalitarian than the rigid patriarchal structures that would later characterize classical Indian society.

The typical Rigvedic household was an extended family unit that included multiple generations living together under the authority of the eldest male (*grihapati*). This arrangement provided economic advantages through the pooling of labor and resources, as well as social benefits through the maintenance of family traditions and the care of elderly members. The joint family system also facilitated the transmission of specialized knowledge, whether relating to ritual practice, craft techniques, or agricultural methods.

Marriage patterns in Rigvedic society were complex and varied, reflecting both practical considerations and religious requirements. The preferred form of marriage was *anuloma*, in which a man married a woman of equal or lower social status. However, various other forms of marriage were recognized and practiced, including love marriages (*gandharva*), marriages by capture (*rakshasa*), and marriages involving the payment of bride-price (*asura*) . The diversity of marriage forms indicates a society that was adaptable and pragmatic in its approach to family formation.

The marriage ceremony itself was an elaborate ritual affair that involved both families and served to create lasting alliances between kinship groups. The exchange of gifts, the performance of sacrificial rituals, and the public recognition of the union all served to integrate the new couple into the broader social fabric. The marriage ceremony also had cosmic significance, as it was seen as a reenactment of divine marriages and a contribution to the maintenance of cosmic order.

The kinship system extended far beyond the immediate family to include complex networks of relatives traced through both paternal and maternal lines. While descent was patrilineal, maternal relatives (*matamaha*, *matulamaha*) maintained important roles in individual and family life. The extended kinship network provided social security, economic cooperation, and political alliance that were essential for survival in a competitive tribal environment.

The concept of *gotra*, which would later become central to Hindu marriage law, was beginning to emerge during the Rigvedic period. The *gotra* represented a patrilineal clan or lineage group that traced its descent to a common ancestral sage. Members of the same *gotra* were considered siblings and were prohibited from intermarrying, a practice that served both to maintain genetic diversity and to strengthen social bonds through marriage alliances with other groups.

Property rights within the family were complex and varied according to the type of property involved. Land, cattle, and other productive assets were typically controlled by the male household head, who had the authority to dispose of them as he saw fit. However, women and younger males often had usufructuary rights that allowed them to benefit from family property even if they could not dispose of it independently. The inheritance system favored male heirs, but women could inherit property in the absence of male relatives and could maintain control over their personal possessions and jewelry.

The religious dimensions of family life were pervasive and significant. The household was the primary site for many ritual activities, including daily offerings to household deities, seasonal festivals, and life-cycle ceremonies. The male household head served as the family priest for many of these activities, though professional brahmins were employed for the more elaborate sacrificial rituals. The family's religious obligations extended beyond ritual performance to include hospitality to guests, charity to the poor, and maintenance of ancestral cult practices.

Child-rearing practices reflected the values and priorities of Rigvedic society, with different expectations for boys and girls. Boys were prepared for their future roles as warriors, priests, or householders through education in military skills, sacred knowledge, and economic activities. The *upanayana* ceremony, which marked the beginning of formal education, was a crucial rite of passage that transformed boys into full members of their *varna*. Girls received education appropriate to their future roles as wives and mothers, including training in household management, textile production, and religious observances.

The relationship between family life and the broader tribal community was intimate and reciprocal. Families depended on the tribe for protection, legal redress, and economic opportunities, while the tribe relied on families to provide warriors, tribute, and labor for communal projects. This interdependence created a stable social system that could adapt to changing circumstances while maintaining its essential character.

Conflict resolution within families typically followed established hierarchical patterns, with disputes resolved by the household head or, in more serious cases, referred to tribal assemblies or the *raja*. The emphasis was on restoration of harmony and maintenance of family unity rather than punishment or retribution. This approach reflected the recognition that family cohesion was essential for both individual and collective survival.

Role of Women in Early Vedic Society

The status and role of women in Rigvedic society present one of the most complex and debated aspects of early Indian social history. The evidence from the hymns reveals a society in which women occupied positions that were simultaneously privileged and constrained, where female agency was both recognized and limited by patriarchal structures. Understanding women's roles requires careful attention to the multiple contexts in which they appear in the Rigvedic corpus, including domestic, religious, and public spheres.

In the domestic sphere, women held positions of considerable authority and responsibility as managers of household affairs. The term *grihini* (mistress of the house) indicates a role that encompassed far more than simple domesticity, including oversight of household production, management of servants and dependents, and maintenance of family religious observances. The *grihini* worked in partnership with the *grihapati* to ensure the smooth functioning of the extended family unit, and her consent was required for major household decisions.

The economic roles of women were diverse and significant. Women participated actively in agricultural work, cattle herding, and various craft activities including textile production, pottery making, and food processing. The Rigveda contains references to women traders and merchants, indicating that some women engaged in commercial activities beyond the household level. The economic contributions of women were recognized and valued, and women appear to have had rights to personal property including jewelry, clothing, and sometimes livestock.

In the religious sphere, women occupied positions of remarkable prominence and authority. Female deities played central roles in the Rigvedic pantheon, with goddesses like Ushas (Dawn), Aditi (Infinity), and Sarasvati (River and Wisdom) receiving elaborate hymns of praise and worship. More significantly, some of the Rigvedic hymns are attributed to female *rishis* (sages), including Ghosa, Apala, and Lopamudra, indicating that women could achieve the highest levels of spiritual authority and sacred knowledge.

The institution of *brahmavadini* (women knowledgeable in Brahman) represented the pinnacle of female religious achievement in Rigvedic society. These women were distinguished not merely by their piety but by their mastery of sacred knowledge and their ability to compose and recite hymns. The existence of *brahmavadinis* indicates that access to spiritual education was not absolutely restricted by gender, though it was certainly limited by social class and family circumstances.

Women's participation in sacrificial rituals was extensive and essential. The wife (*patni*) of the sacrificial sponsor played crucial roles in many ceremonies, and her presence and participation were required for the rituals to be effective. This religious partnership between husband and wife was seen as a reflection of cosmic harmony and was necessary for maintaining proper relationships with the divine realm. The importance of women's ritual roles gave them considerable influence within families and communities.

Marriage represented both opportunity and constraint for Rigvedic women. On one hand, marriage provided access to adult status, economic security, and spiritual fulfillment through participation in household religious life. The ideal of the devoted wife who supported her husband's dharmic obligations was highly valued, and such women received considerable respect and honor. On the other hand, marriage typically involved leaving one's birth family and adapting to new circumstances, and the emphasis on chastity and fidelity created pressures and restrictions that limited female autonomy.

The practice of *svayamvara* (self-choice of husband) mentioned in some Rigvedic contexts suggests that women of high status could exercise significant agency in marriage decisions. However, this practice appears to have been limited to exceptional circumstances and was not available to women of ordinary families. Most marriages were arranged by families for economic, political, or social reasons, though the consent of the bride was generally considered desirable if not absolutely necessary.

Educational opportunities for women varied considerably according to social class and family circumstances. While most women received informal education in household management and religious observances, some had access to more formal instruction in sacred knowledge, poetry, and music. The existence of learned women who could compose hymns and engage in philosophical discussions indicates that intellectual achievement was not absolutely barred to women, though it was certainly more difficult for them to achieve than for men.

The legal status of women in Rigvedic society was complex and contextual. Women appear to have had rights to personal property and could inherit from their families in the absence of male heirs. However, their legal capacity was generally exercised through male relatives, and they rarely acted as independent legal agents. The emphasis on family honor and the collective responsibility of kinship groups meant that women's actions reflected on their families and could have consequences beyond their individual circumstances.

Widowhood presented particular challenges and opportunities for women in Rigvedic society. While some evidence suggests that *sati* (widow immolation) was practiced in exceptional circumstances, this was not the normal expectation for widows. Most widows appear to have remained with their husband's family, where they could continue to play important roles in household management and religious observances. Wealthy widows might exercise considerable authority within their families, particularly if they had adult sons who recognized their wisdom and experience.

The representation of women in Rigvedic literature reveals both respect for female agency and acceptance of patriarchal limitations. Female characters in the hymns are portrayed as intelligent, resourceful, and spiritually powerful, capable of achieving great things when circumstances permit. However, these same texts also reflect assumptions about gender roles that limited women's opportunities and subordinated their interests to those of male relatives and the broader patriarchal order.

The diversity of women's experiences in Rigvedic society is perhaps its most striking characteristic. While most women lived lives constrained by domestic responsibilities and social expectations, some achieved remarkable prominence as religious teachers, poets, and household managers. The variation in women's status appears to have depended on factors including family wealth, social class, personal abilities, and individual circumstances that could create opportunities for exceptional women to transcend normal gender limitations.

The transition from Rigvedic to later Vedic society would see significant changes in women's status, with many of the opportunities and freedoms evident in the early period being gradually restricted. However, the Rigvedic evidence demonstrates that patriarchal structures in ancient India were neither uniform nor unchanging, and that women found ways to exercise agency and achieve recognition within the constraints of their social circumstances.

Conclusion

The Rigvedic world represents a crucial formative period in Indian social history, when the foundations of classical Indian civilization were being established through the complex evolution and interaction of various cultural traditions during the early Vedic age. The society revealed in the hymns was dynamic and adaptable, characterized by sophisticated political institutions, flexible social hierarchies, and rich cultural traditions that would profoundly influence the subsequent development of Indian civilization.

The tribal organization of Rigvedic society provided a stable framework for social life while allowing for considerable individual mobility and adaptation to changing circumstances. The balance between individual authority and collective governance, exemplified in the relationship between the *raja* and the tribal assemblies, created political institutions that were both effective and accountable. The emerging social hierarchy, while increasingly stratified, remained sufficiently flexible to accommodate social mobility and occupational change.

Family life and kinship patterns provided the primary context for individual socialization and economic production, while also serving as the foundation for broader social and political networks. The complex patterns of marriage alliance and kinship obligation created bonds that transcended immediate family interests and contributed to tribal cohesion and stability. The roles of women, while constrained by patriarchal structures, were nevertheless significant and varied, encompassing domestic, economic, and religious responsibilities that were essential for family and tribal prosperity.

The religious dimensions of social life were pervasive and fundamental, providing not merely spiritual guidance but practical frameworks for social organization and political authority. The elaborate sacrificial rituals that formed the core of Rigvedic religion required the cooperation of different social groups and created bonds of interdependence that strengthened social cohesion while legitimizing social hierarchy.

The Rigvedic world was one of transition and transformation, where older tribal traditions were being adapted to new circumstances and challenges. The society revealed in the hymns was neither primitive nor static, but rather sophisticated and dynamic, capable of supporting complex political institutions, diverse economic activities, and rich cultural traditions. The foundations established during this period would prove remarkably enduring, providing the structural principles that would shape Indian society for millennia to come.

Understanding Rigvedic society remains crucial for comprehending the broader patterns of Indian social development and for appreciating the complexity and sophistication of ancient Indian civilization. The world revealed in these ancient hymns was one of remarkable creativity and adaptability, where human communities were working out solutions to fundamental problems of social organization that would influence not merely their own descendants but the broader course of human social evolution. The legacy of Rigvedic social innovations continues to resonate in contemporary India, where many of the institutions, values, and practices first articulated in these ancient texts remain relevant to modern social life.

4
Pastoral Beginnings

Introduction

The economic foundations of Rigvedic society reveal a civilization in transition, where the pastoral traditions of tribes were gradually giving way to more diverse and settled patterns of livelihood. This transformation,spanning roughly from 1500 to 1100 BCE, represents one of the most significant economic developments in the history of the Indian subcontinent. The Rigveda, with its rich vocabulary of economic terms and detailed descriptions of material life, provides us with an unprecedented window into the daily experiences of these ancient peoples.

The economy of the Rigvedic period was fundamentally different from both the urban commercial systems of the preceding Indus Valley Civilization and the complex agricultural economies that would emerge in later Vedic times. It was characterized by a unique blend of pastoralism and emerging agriculture, supplemented by specialized crafts and limited trade networks. This economic system was intimately connected to the social and religious structures of the time, with wealth serving not merely as a means of subsistence but as a marker of social status, political power, and divine favor.

Understanding the economic life of the Rigvedic period is crucial for comprehending the broader patterns of social organization and cultural development that characterized this formative era. The distribution of wealth, the organization of labor, and the systems of exchange all played vital roles in shaping the hierarchical structures that were emerging in Rigvedic society. Moreover, the economic practices of this period established patterns and preferences that would influence Indian civilization for millennia to come.

The economic vocabulary of the Rigveda reveals a society that was already developing sophisticated concepts of value, exchange, and property. Terms related to cattle, agriculture, crafts, and trade appear frequently throughout the hymns, often in contexts that reveal the complex relationships between economic activity and social identity. The frequent references to wealth in prayers and praise songs indicate that prosperity was seen as a divine blessing, while poverty was often viewed as a sign of divine displeasure or personal failure.

This chapter examines the multifaceted economic life of Rigvedic society, exploring how these ancient peoples sustained themselves, organized their productive activities, and created the material foundations for their emerging civilization. We will investigate the central role of cattle in their economic system, the development of agricultural practices, the emergence of specialized crafts, the evolution of trade networks, and the rich material culture that archaeologists have uncovered from this period.

Cattle-Based Economy

The economic foundation of Rigvedic society rested upon cattle, which served simultaneously as the primary measure of wealth, the basic unit of exchange, and the source of numerous essential products. The centrality of cattle in Rigvedic life cannot be overstated—they were not merely animals but the very foundation of economic security, social prestige, and religious practice. The Sanskrit word "go," meaning cow, appears over 700 times in the Rigveda, more frequently than almost any other noun, reflecting the overwhelming importance of cattle in the minds and lives of the Rigvedic people.

The cattle economy was built around several species of bovines, with cows being the most prized, followed by bulls, oxen, and water buffalo. Each type of animal served specific functions within the economic system. Cows were valued primarily for their milk and reproductive capacity, bulls for their strength in plowing and transportation, and oxen for their docility and usefulness in heavy labor. The Rigveda also mentions horses, though these appear to have been more associated with warfare and prestige than with everyday economic activities.

The measurement of wealth in terms of cattle created a unique economic system where value was determined by the number and quality of animals owned. A wealthy individual was described as "gomat" (possessing many cows), while poverty was often characterized by the absence of cattle. This system of wealth measurement had profound implications for social organization, as it meant that wealth was mobile and could be increased through successful cattle raids or lost through disease, drought, or enemy attacks.

The management of cattle herds required sophisticated knowledge of animal husbandry, pasture management, and seasonal migration patterns. The Rigvedic people developed detailed understanding of cattle breeding, with specific terms for animals of different ages, sexes, and qualities. The hymns reveal knowledge of cattle diseases and treatments, indicating that veterinary practices were already welldeveloped. The importance of cattle led to the emergence of specialized roles within society, including cowherd chiefs, veterinarians, and experts in cattle breeding.

The daily routine of cattle management shaped the rhythm of Rigvedic life. The day began with the milking of cows, a task that was often performed by women and was surrounded by ritual significance. The Rigveda contains numerous hymns celebrating the cow and her gifts, with milk being seen as a divine blessing that sustained human life. The care and protection of cattle required constant vigilance, as herds were vulnerable to wild animals, thieves, and enemy raiders.

The seasonal movement of cattle in search of pasture was a defining feature of Rigvedic economic life. These migrations, known as "gochara," followed well-established routes that took advantage of seasonal variations in grass growth and water availability. The timing and routes of these migrations were carefully planned, with tribal councils making collective decisions about when and where to move the herds. This semi-nomadic lifestyle required portable possessions and temporary shelters, influencing the material culture of the period.

Cattle raids were a prominent feature of Rigvedic economic life, serving both as a means of acquiring wealth and as a way of demonstrating martial prowess. The hymns are filled with references to successful cattle raids, which were seen as legitimate means of increasing one's herd and achieving social recognition. The protection of one's own cattle and the capture of enemy herds were primary motivations for warfare, with successful warriors being rewarded with shares of captured cattle.

The religious significance of cattle in Rigvedic society was intimately connected to their economic importance. Cattle were essential for sacrificial rituals, with cows, bulls, and other animals being offered to the gods in elaborate ceremonies. The sacrifice of cattle was seen as the ultimate expression of devotion and generosity, demonstrating the sacrificer's willingness to give up valuable possessions for divine favor. This religious dimension of cattle ownership reinforced their economic importance and created additional incentives for accumulating large herds.

The products derived from cattle were essential for daily life and formed the basis of numerous economic activities. Milk was consumed fresh, converted into various dairy products, and used in religious ceremonies. Butter, particularly clarified butter (ghee), was highly valued both for its nutritional properties and its ritual significance. The Rigveda contains detailed descriptions of butter-making processes, indicating that dairy technology was well-developed.

Cattle hides were processed into leather for various purposes, including clothing, containers, and equipment. The bones and horns of cattle were used to make tools, ornaments, and household items. Even cattle dung was valuable, being used as fuel for fires and as a building material when mixed with clay. This comprehensive utilization of cattle products demonstrates the efficiency of the pastoral economy and the ingenuity of the Rigvedic people in maximizing the value of their most important resource.

The cattle-based economy also influenced patterns of social organization and political structure. Wealth in cattle was relatively easy to assess and compare, making it a natural basis for social ranking. The number of cattle owned by an individual or family determined their position in the social hierarchy and their ability to participate in expensive religious ceremonies. This created a system where economic success translated directly into social status and political influence.

The vulnerability of cattle to disease, predation, and environmental factors created risks that shaped Rigvedic economic strategies. Diversification of herds across different species and age groups was one way of managing these risks. The development of mutual support networks among pastoralists was another important adaptation, with communities sharing resources during times of hardship and cooperating in the protection of herds.

The transition from a purely pastoral economy to one that included agriculture and other activities was gradual and uneven. Even as farming became more important, cattle remained central to Rigvedic economic life. The integration of cattle herding with crop cultivation created new economic opportunities and challenges, as farmers needed to balance the needs of their animals with the requirements of their crops.

Agriculture: Early Practices and Crops

The agricultural practices of the Rigvedic period represent a crucial transition from the primarily pastoral economy of the early Indo-Aryan settlers to the more diverse and settled agricultural systems that would characterize later Vedic civilization. While cattle remained the cornerstone of economic life, the gradual adoption and development of farming techniques provided new sources of food security and economic stability that would prove essential for the growth of more complex social and political structures.

The Rigveda contains numerous references to agricultural activities, using a rich vocabulary that reveals sophisticated understanding of farming techniques, crop cycles, and agricultural tools. The word "krishi" (agriculture) appears in various forms throughout the hymns, often in contexts that suggest farming was becoming an increasingly important economic activity. However, the agricultural practices described in the Rigveda were still relatively simple compared to the intensive cultivation systems that would develop in later periods.

The primary grain crop mentioned in the Rigveda is barley (yava), which appears to have been the staple cereal of the period. Barley was well-suited to the semi-arid conditions of the northwestern regions where the Rigvedic people initially settled, and its relatively short growing season made it compatible with the semi-nomadic lifestyle of the early Indo-Aryans. The grain was used for various purposes, including the preparation of food, the brewing of alcoholic beverages, and offerings in religious ceremonies.

Wheat (godhuma) is also mentioned in the Rigveda, though less frequently than barley. The cultivation of wheat may have been adopted from the indigenous populations of the subcontinent, as it was already being grown in the region by the time of the Indus Valley Civilization. The adoption of wheat cultivation represents one of the ways in which the Indo-Aryan settlers adapted to local conditions and incorporated indigenous agricultural knowledge into their economic system.

Rice (vrihi) is mentioned in the later hymns of the Rigveda, indicating that its cultivation was beginning to spread into the areas occupied by the Rigvedic people. However, rice cultivation was still relatively limited during this period, and it would not become a major crop until the later Vedic period when the IndoAryans expanded into the more humid regions of the Ganges valley where rice could be grown more successfully.

The agricultural techniques described in the Rigveda were relatively simple but effective. The primary tool for cultivation was the plow (hal), which was typically drawn by oxen or bulls. The Rigvedic plow was probably a simple wooden implement with a metal share, capable of breaking up soil and creating furrows for planting. The use of animal traction for plowing was a significant advancement over purely manual cultivation techniques and allowed for the cultivation of larger areas of land.

The preparation of fields for cultivation involved several steps, beginning with the clearing of vegetation and the breaking up of soil. The Rigveda mentions various tools used in field preparation, including hoes, digging sticks, and other implements. The timing of plowing and planting was carefully coordinated with seasonal patterns, with most crops being planted at the beginning of the monsoon season when soil moisture was adequate for germination.

Irrigation was practiced on a limited scale during the Rigvedic period, primarily through the diversion of streams and the construction of simple channels to direct water to cultivated fields. The Rigveda contains references to irrigation channels (kulya) and the importance of water management in ensuring successful crops. However, the irrigation systems of this period were relatively simple compared to the elaborate canal networks that would be developed in later periods.

The harvesting of crops was a community activity that brought together families and neighbors to complete the work quickly and efficiently. The Rigveda describes various aspects of the harvest, including the cutting of grain, the gathering of sheaves, and the processing of harvested crops. Sickles (srini) made of metal were the primary tools used for harvesting, and the grain was typically processed using simple techniques such as threshing with sticks or having animals trample the harvested crop.

The storage of grain was an important consideration in Rigvedic agriculture, as successful preservation of harvested crops was essential for food security throughout the year. The Rigveda mentions various types of storage containers and techniques, including large ceramic vessels, woven baskets, and underground storage pits. The proper storage of grain required knowledge of techniques to prevent spoilage from moisture, pests, and rodents.

The integration of agriculture with pastoralism created synergies that enhanced the efficiency of both activities. Cattle provided draft power for plowing and transportation, while crop residues and agricultural by-products provided supplementary feed for animals. The manure from cattle was used to fertilize fields, improving soil fertility and crop yields. This integration of crop and livestock production would become a defining feature of Indian agriculture for millennia to come.

The development of agriculture during the Rigvedic period was not uniform across all regions or communities. Some groups remained primarily pastoral, while others adopted farming as their primary economic activity. The choice between pastoralism and agriculture was influenced by various factors, including environmental conditions, population density, and contact with indigenous farming communities. This diversity in economic strategies allowed Rigvedic society to adapt to different ecological niches and exploit a wider range of resources.

The religious significance of agriculture in Rigvedic society was considerable, with numerous hymns celebrating the earth, the rains, and the fertility of crops. The goddess Prithvi (Earth) was revered as the mother of all life, while various other deities were associated with different aspects of agricultural productivity. The performance of agricultural rituals at key points in the farming cycle was believed to ensure divine favor and successful harvests.

The economic impact of agriculture on Rigvedic society was profound, providing a more reliable source of food than could be obtained through pastoralism alone. The development of farming created new opportunities for economic specialization, as some individuals could focus on agricultural production while others engaged in crafts, trade, or other activities. The surplus production made possible by agriculture also supported the growth of non-productive classes, including priests, warriors, and political leaders.

The gradual expansion of agriculture during the Rigvedic period laid the foundation for the more intensive farming systems that would characterize later Vedic civilization. The techniques, crops, and practices developed during this period would be refined and expanded in subsequent centuries, ultimately supporting the growth of large urban centers and complex political structures. The transition from pastoralism to agriculture was thus a crucial step in the development of Indian civilization.

Crafts and Specialized Occupations

The emergence of specialized crafts and occupations during the Rigvedic period represents a crucial development in the evolution of economic complexity and social stratification. While the society remained primarily pastoral and agricultural, the growing need for tools, weapons, ornaments, and other manufactured goods led to the development of various specialized skills and the emergence of craftspeople who dedicated their lives to particular trades. This occupational specialization was both a cause and consequence of increasing economic sophistication and social differentiation.

The Rigveda contains numerous references to different types of craftspeople and their products, revealing a society that was already developing considerable technical expertise in various areas. The hymns mention carpenters, metalworkers, potters, weavers, leatherworkers, and numerous other specialists, each with their own techniques, tools, and products. The existence of these specialized occupations indicates that Rigvedic society had progressed beyond simple subsistence economy to a more complex system where individuals could focus on particular skills and exchange their products for other necessities.

Metalworking was one of the most important and prestigious crafts in Rigvedic society. The smith (karmara) held a special position due to his ability to transform raw materials into essential tools and weapons. The Rigveda mentions various types of metalworkers, including those who specialized in working with copper, bronze, and iron. The techniques of smelting, forging, and casting were welldeveloped, with smiths producing a wide range of items including agricultural tools, weapons, cooking utensils, and ornaments.

The transition from bronze to iron working during the later Rigvedic period represents one of the most significant technological developments of the era. Iron tools and weapons were superior to their bronze counterparts in terms of durability and effectiveness, and the adoption of iron technology had profound implications for both economic productivity and military capability. The Rigveda contains references to iron (ayas) and describes its superior qualities, indicating that the Indo-Aryans were among the early adopters of this revolutionary technology.

Carpentry was another highly skilled craft that was essential for the construction of houses, vehicles, and various tools and implements. The carpenter (takshan) was skilled in working with different types of wood, using various tools including axes, adzes, chisels, and saws. The Rigveda describes the construction of houses, chariots, and boats, revealing sophisticated knowledge of woodworking techniques and joinery. The chariot makers were particularly skilled craftspeople, as the construction of these vehicles required precise engineering and craftsmanship.

Pottery making was a widespread craft that was practiced at various levels of skill and specialization.

While basic pottery was probably made by most households for their own use, specialized potters (kumbhakara) produced higher-quality vessels for trade and ceremonial purposes. The Rigveda mentions

various types of ceramic vessels, including water jars, storage containers, and cooking pots. The techniques of pottery making included hand-building, wheel-throwing, and various decorative techniques.

Textile production was an important craft that was practiced primarily by women, though male specialists also existed. The Rigveda contains numerous references to weaving, spinning, and various textile processes. The weavers (vaya) produced cloth from various materials including wool, cotton, and possibly silk. The hymns describe the use of looms and various weaving techniques, indicating that textile production had already achieved considerable sophistication.

Leatherworking was a specialized craft that was closely connected to the pastoral economy. The leather worker (charman) processed hides and skins to produce various products including clothing, containers, harnesses, and armor. The techniques of tanning, dyeing, and leather working were well-developed, with craftspeople producing both utilitarian and decorative items. The close connection between leatherworking and the cattle economy made this craft particularly important in Rigvedic society.

The organization of crafts production varied depending on the type of craft and the level of specialization involved. Some crafts were organized around family workshops where skills were passed down from generation to generation. Others were practiced by individual specialists who traveled from place to place offering their services. The most skilled craftspeople may have been attached to the households of wealthy patrons or rulers, producing luxury items and specialized products.

The economic position of craftspeople in Rigvedic society was complex and varied. While they provided essential services and products, their social status was generally lower than that of warriors, priests, and wealthy cattle owners. However, skilled craftspeople could achieve considerable prosperity and social recognition through their expertise and the quality of their work. The Rigveda contains references to wealthy craftspeople who owned cattle and land, indicating that economic success was possible in these occupations.

The tools and techniques used by Rigvedic craftspeople were sophisticated for their time and represented the accumulation of generations of technical knowledge. The smiths used furnaces, bellows, hammers, and anvils, while carpenters employed axes, adzes, chisels, and measuring tools. Potters used wheels, kilns, and various forming and decorating tools. The quality of craftsmanship achieved by these ancient artisans is evidenced by the archaeological remains that have been discovered from this period.

The training of craftspeople was typically accomplished through apprenticeship systems where young people learned their trades by working alongside experienced masters. The Rigveda contains references to the transmission of technical knowledge from teacher to student, indicating that formal training systems existed for various crafts. The complexity of some crafts required years of training and practice before full competency was achieved.

The religious significance of certain crafts was considerable, with some craftspeople playing important roles in religious ceremonies and rituals. The construction of sacrificial altars, the making of ritual vessels, and the preparation of ceremonial objects all required specialized skills and knowledge. Some craftspeople were considered to have semi-sacred status due to their association with religious activities.

The geographic distribution of crafts production was influenced by the availability of raw materials and the location of markets. Metalworking was concentrated in areas where ores were available, while pottery making was widespread due to the universal availability of clay. The development of trade networks facilitated the distribution of craft products beyond their immediate areas of production, allowing for greater specialization and improved quality.

The impact of craft specialization on Rigvedic society was profound, contributing to economic growth, social differentiation, and technological advancement. The availability of specialized tools and products improved the efficiency of agricultural and pastoral activities, while the development of weapons and military equipment enhanced the military capabilities of the tribes. The emergence of a craft-producing class also contributed to the development of more complex social hierarchies and economic relationships.

Trade and Exchange Systems

The development of trade and exchange systems during the Rigvedic period represents a crucial step in the evolution of economic complexity and inter-regional connections. While the economy remained primarily based on pastoralism and agriculture, the growing need for resources that were not locally available, combined with the production of surplus goods, led to the emergence of various forms of exchange that connected different communities and regions. These early trade networks would lay the foundation for the more extensive commercial systems that would characterize later periods of Indian history.

The Rigveda contains numerous references to trade and exchange, using a vocabulary that reveals sophisticated understanding of commercial concepts and practices. The word "vanij" (trader) appears in various forms throughout the hymns, indicating that trade was already a recognized and important economic activity. The existence of specialized traders suggests that commercial exchange had progressed beyond simple barter between neighbors to more complex systems involving professional merchants and long-distance trade.

The primary form of exchange in Rigvedic society was barter, where goods were traded directly for other goods without the use of money. The most common medium of exchange was cattle, which served as a standard of value for measuring the worth of other goods. The Rigveda contains numerous references to transactions involving cattle, with various goods being valued in terms of cows, bulls, or other animals. This cattle-based system of exchange was well-suited to the pastoral economy of the period and provided a flexible medium for commercial transactions.

The development of standardized measures and weights was an important advancement in Rigvedic trade systems. The hymns mention various units of measurement for different types of goods, including grain, liquids, and other commodities. The existence of standardized measures facilitated trade by providing common standards for evaluating quantities and values. Archaeological evidence suggests that some form of standardized weights was already in use during this period, though the systems were probably less sophisticated than those of later periods.

The goods that were traded in Rigvedic commercial networks included both necessities and luxury items. Essential commodities such as grain, metal tools, and pottery were traded to meet basic needs that could not be satisfied through local production. Luxury goods including precious metals, ornaments, fine textiles, and exotic products were traded to satisfy the desires of the wealthy and powerful. The range of goods mentioned in the Rigveda suggests that trade networks were already quite extensive and sophisticated.

The organization of trade involved various types of merchants and trading arrangements. Some traders were probably part-time merchants who combined commercial activities with farming or other occupations. Others were professional traders who devoted their full time to commercial activities. The Rigveda mentions trading expeditions and commercial journeys, indicating that some merchants traveled considerable distances to conduct their business. The organization of these trading ventures required planning, resources, and knowledge of distant markets and routes.

The routes used by Rigvedic traders followed rivers, mountain passes, and established trails that connected different regions and communities. The major rivers of the region, including the Indus and its tributaries, served as important commercial highways, providing both transportation routes and sources of water for trading caravans. The development of these trade routes facilitated not only commercial exchange but also the movement of people, ideas, and cultural influences.

The role of rivers in Rigvedic trade was particularly significant, as they provided natural highways for the movement of goods and people. The Rigveda contains numerous references to river transportation, including the use of boats and rafts for carrying goods. The major rivers of the region were well-known to the Rigvedic people, and many of them are mentioned by name in the hymns. The seasonal nature of river transportation meant that trade patterns were influenced by monsoon cycles and water levels.

The security of trade routes was a major concern for Rigvedic merchants, as the constant warfare and tribal conflicts of the period made travel dangerous. The Rigveda contains references to the protection of traders and the importance of safe passage for commercial activities. Some rulers may have provided protection for merchants in exchange for tolls or other payments, while traders themselves sometimes traveled in armed groups for mutual protection.

The development of markets and trading centers was another important aspect of Rigvedic commercial systems. While the society was still primarily rural and pastoral, certain locations became recognized as places where traders gathered to exchange goods. These early markets were probably temporary affairs that coincided with religious festivals, tribal gatherings, or seasonal migrations. The concentration of traders and goods at these locations facilitated exchange and price discovery.

The relationship between trade and social stratification was complex and significant. Successful traders could accumulate considerable wealth and achieve high social status, while trade also provided opportunities for social mobility for individuals from lower social backgrounds. The Rigveda contains references to wealthy merchants who owned cattle and land, indicating that commercial success could lead to prosperity and social advancement.

The role of women in Rigvedic trade appears to have been more limited than in later periods, though some evidence suggests that women did participate in commercial activities. The hymns mention women who were involved in textile production and other crafts that were traded, and some women may have been independent traders or have assisted in family trading businesses. The extent of women's participation in trade was probably influenced by social norms and practical considerations related to travel and security.

The impact of trade on Rigvedic society was profound, contributing to economic growth, social differentiation, and cultural exchange. The availability of goods from distant regions enhanced the quality of life for those who could afford them, while the profits from trade provided resources for investment in other economic activities. Trade also facilitated the spread of ideas, technologies, and cultural practices between different communities and regions.

The development of credit and lending systems was another important aspect of Rigvedic commercial evolution. The hymns contain references to debt and repayment, indicating that some form of credit system existed to facilitate trade and other economic activities. The lending of cattle and other goods appears to have been common, with various arrangements for repayment and interest. These early credit systems were probably based on personal relationships and community standing rather than formal legal frameworks.

The seasonal nature of much Rigvedic economic activity influenced trade patterns and commercial relationships. The timing of harvests, the availability of pasture for cattle, and the seasonal movement of pastoral communities all affected the flow of goods and the organization of trade. Merchants had to adapt their activities to these seasonal patterns, timing their journeys and transactions to take advantage of the best opportunities.

The integration of trade with other economic activities was characteristic of Rigvedic commercial systems. Traders were often also farmers, herders, or craftspeople who engaged in commerce as a supplementary activity. This integration of commercial and productive activities created a more resilient economic system that could adapt to changing conditions and opportunities.

Material Culture: Pottery, Tools, Ornaments

The material culture of the Rigvedic period provides tangible evidence of the technological capabilities, artistic sensibilities, and daily life experiences of these ancient peoples. The archaeological record, combined with the detailed descriptions found in the Rigvedic hymns, reveals a society that had achieved considerable sophistication in the production of pottery, tools, ornaments, and other material goods. This material culture reflects not only the practical needs of daily life but also the social hierarchies, religious beliefs, and aesthetic values that characterized Rigvedic civilization.

The pottery of the Rigvedic period represents one of the most abundant and informative categories of material culture. The ceramic tradition of this era was characterized by considerable diversity in forms, functions, and decorative styles, reflecting both practical needs and aesthetic preferences. The Rigveda mentions various types of pottery vessels, including water jars (kumbha), cooking pots (sthali), storage containers (kostha), and ritual vessels (camasa), each designed for specific purposes and contexts.

The production techniques used by Rigvedic potters were sophisticated and varied. While some pottery was hand-built using coiling or pinching techniques, the potter's wheel was already in use for creating more regular and refined forms. The Rigveda contains references to the potter's wheel (chakra) and describes the skill required to create well-formed vessels. The use of the potter's wheel allowed for the production of more standardized and aesthetically pleasing pottery, contributing to the development of regional styles and traditions.

The decorative techniques employed by Rigvedic potters included painting, incision, and various surface treatments that enhanced both the appearance and functionality of ceramic vessels. Painted pottery was particularly common, with geometric patterns, animal motifs, and plant designs being popular decorative elements. The colors used in pottery decoration included red, black, white, and various earth tones, achieved through the use of iron oxides and other mineral pigments. The sophistication of these decorative techniques indicates that pottery making had evolved beyond purely utilitarian production to include artistic and aesthetic considerations.

The firing techniques used by Rigvedic potters were varied and reflect considerable technical knowledge. Both open firing and kiln firing were employed, with kilns allowing for better control of temperature and atmosphere. The achievement of different surface colors and textures through controlled firing demonstrates the potters' understanding of the relationship between firing conditions and final appearance. The production of high-quality pottery required not only technical skill but also knowledge of clay preparation, tempering materials, and firing procedures.

The tools and implements used in Rigvedic society were essential for daily life and economic activities, reflecting the technological capabilities and practical needs of the period. The tool kit of the Rigvedic people included implements for agriculture, hunting, warfare, crafts production, and domestic activities. The quality and sophistication of these tools varied considerably, with some being simple utilitarian objects while others were finely crafted items that demonstrated considerable technical skill.

Agricultural tools were among the most important implements in Rigvedic society, reflecting the growing importance of farming in the economic system. The plow (hal) was the most significant agricultural tool, typically made of wood with metal shares for cutting through soil. The Rigveda describes various types of plows and their use in different agricultural contexts. Other agricultural implements included hoes, sickles, and threshing tools, all of which were essential for successful crop production.

The metalworking technology of the Rigvedic period was advanced and produced a wide range of tools and weapons. Copper and bronze were the primary metals used in the early period, with iron becoming increasingly important during the later Rigvedic era. The smiths produced axes, knives, spears, swords, and various other implements that were essential for both practical and military purposes. The quality of Rigvedic metalwork was high, with some items showing sophisticated techniques such as inlay work and decorative patterning.

The woodworking tools used by Rigvedic carpenters included axes, adzes, chisels, and saws, all of which were necessary for the construction of houses, chariots, and various wooden implements. The Rigveda describes the skill of carpenters and the quality of their work, indicating that woodworking had achieved considerable sophistication. The construction of chariots, in particular, required precise engineering and craftsmanship, demonstrating the advanced technical capabilities of Rigvedic woodworkers.

The personal ornaments and decorative items of the Rigvedic period reveal much about the aesthetic preferences, social hierarchies, and religious beliefs of the society. The hymns contain numerous references to various types of ornaments, including necklaces, bracelets, earrings, and other personal adornments. These items were made from various materials including gold, silver, copper, precious stones, and organic materials such as shells and bones.

The production of ornaments required considerable skill and artistry, with craftspeople developing sophisticated techniques for working with precious metals and stones. The Rigveda mentions goldsmiths and jewelers who specialized in creating fine ornaments and decorative items. The techniques used included hammering, casting, wire-drawing, and various decorative processes such as granulation and filigree work. The quality of Rigvedic jewelry and ornaments was high, with some pieces showing remarkable artistic sophistication.

The social significance of ornaments in Rigvedic society was considerable, with different types of jewelry indicating social status, wealth, and personal identity. The wealthy and powerful wore elaborate ornaments made from precious materials, while common people wore simpler items made from less expensive materials. The Rigveda contains references to the ornaments worn by gods and goddesses, indicating that jewelry had important religious and symbolic significance as well as practical and aesthetic value.

The clothing and textiles of the Rigvedic period were another important aspect of material culture, though fewer physical remains have survived due to the perishable nature of organic materials. The Rigveda contains numerous references to different types of clothing and textiles, including garments made from wool, cotton, and other materials. The production of textiles was a skilled craft that involved spinning, weaving, dyeing, and various finishing techniques.

The household items and domestic equipment of the Rigvedic period included a wide range of objects designed for food preparation, storage, and other daily activities. These items included grinding stones, mortars and pestles, ladles, and various containers and vessels. The quality and sophistication of these household items varied considerably, with wealthy families possessing more elaborate and decorated objects while common people used simpler utilitarian items.

The weapons and military equipment of the Rigvedic period reflect the warlike nature of the society and the importance of military prowess. The hymns mention various types of weapons including spears, swords, bows and arrows, and shields. The quality of Rigvedic weapons was high, with some items showing sophisticated metallurgical techniques and decorative work. The production of weapons required considerable skill and knowledge of materials and techniques.

The religious and ceremonial objects of the Rigvedic period were another important category of material culture, reflecting the central role of religion in daily life. These items included ritual vessels, sacrificial implements, and various objects used in religious ceremonies. The production of religious objects required not only technical skill but also knowledge of religious requirements and symbolic significance.

The distribution and exchange of material goods in Rigvedic society was influenced by various factors including social status, economic relationships, and regional variations. The wealthy and powerful had access to the finest and most elaborate material goods, while common people used simpler and more utilitarian items. The development of trade networks facilitated the exchange of materials and finished goods between different regions and communities.

The technological traditions of the Rigvedic period were passed down through generations of craftspeople, with skills and techniques being transmitted from master to apprentice. The continuity of these traditions ensured that technical knowledge was preserved and refined over time, contributing to the gradual improvement of material culture. The integration of new technologies and techniques with existing traditions created a dynamic and evolving material culture that reflected both continuity and change.

Conclusion

The economic and material life of the Rigvedic period reveals a society in transition, where traditional pastoral nomadism was gradually giving way to more complex and diversified economic systems. The cattle-based economy that formed the foundation of Rigvedic life provided not only the material basis for survival but also the social framework for hierarchy, exchange, and cultural identity. The reverence for cattle evident throughout the Rigveda reflects their central importance in every aspect of life, from daily subsistence to religious ritual, from social status to political power.

The emergence of agriculture during this period represented a crucial development that would have profound implications for the future of Indian civilization. While still secondary to pastoralism in the early Rigvedic period, farming provided greater food security, supported larger populations, and enabled the development of more settled communities. The integration of agriculture with pastoralism created synergistic relationships that enhanced the efficiency of both activities and laid the foundation for the more complex agricultural systems that would characterize later periods.

The development of specialized crafts and occupations during the Rigvedic period demonstrates the increasing complexity of the economy and the growing sophistication of technological capabilities.

5
Religious Universe

The Vedic civilization stands as one of humanity's earliest and most sophisticated religious traditions, representing a profound attempt to understand and engage with the divine forces that govern existence. This ancient spiritual framework, with its deep roots in the Indian subcontinent's indigenous traditions and spiritual heritage, created a complex theological system that would fundamentally shape South Asian religious thought for millennia to come. The Vedic religious universe encompassed not merely a collection of deities and rituals, but a comprehensive worldview that sought to harmonize human existence with cosmic principles, establishing patterns of worship, sacrifice, and spiritual understanding that continue to influence religious practice today.

The Vedic Pantheon-Divine Forces of the Cosmos

The Vedic pantheon represents one of the most elaborate and sophisticated collections of deities in ancient religious traditions, embodying natural forces, cosmic principles, and abstract concepts that the Vedic peoples sought to understand and propitiate. Unlike later Hindu traditions that would develop anthropomorphic representations of divinity, the Vedic gods were primarily conceived as dynamic forces of nature and cosmic order, each possessing distinct attributes, powers, and spheres of influence that reflected the Indo-Aryan understanding of the natural world and its underlying principles.

Indra stands as perhaps the most prominent and frequently invoked deity in the Rigveda, appearing in over 250 hymns and representing the archetypal divine warrior and king of the gods. As the deity of storms, thunder, and war, Indra embodies the dynamic, aggressive forces of nature that both create and destroy, bringing life-giving rains while also wielding the destructive power of lightning and thunder. His most celebrated mythological achievement involves his cosmic battle against Vritra, the drought-demon who had imprisoned the waters of the world, a narrative that symbolizes the eternal struggle between order and chaos, fertility and barrenness, light and darkness.

The Vritra myth reveals Indra's fundamental role as a maintainer of cosmic order and a protector of both gods and humans. Armed with his thunderbolt weapon (vajra), crafted by the divine artificer Tvashtar, Indra shatters the serpentine demon and releases the imprisoned waters, allowing rivers to flow and rains to fall upon the earth. This mythological narrative serves multiple functions: it explains natural phenomena such as seasonal rains and droughts, establishes Indra's supremacy among the gods, and provides a cosmic model for human kingship and warfare. The parallels between Indra's divine battles and human conflicts are explicit throughout Vedic literature, with earthly rulers seeking his blessing and emulating his warrior virtues.

Indra's character reflects the values and concerns of the ancient Indian society that created these myths. As a deity who delights in soma, the sacred intoxicating beverage, and who leads the gods in their cosmic battles, Indra represents the idealized warrior-king who protects his people through strength, courage, and divine favor. His epithets—Maghavan (the generous one), Shakra (the mighty), Purandara (fortressdestroyer)—reveal the qualities most valued in leadership: generosity to followers, strength in battle, and the ability to overcome obstacles. The numerous hymns dedicated to Indra often emphasize his role as a generous patron who rewards his devotees with cattle, victory in battle, and protection from enemies.

The worship of Indra involved elaborate rituals and sacrifices, with devotees offering soma and other sacred substances to gain his favor. The Rigvedic hymns describe Indra's enormous appetite for soma, often depicting him as consuming vast quantities of the divine beverage before undertaking his cosmic battles. This association between Indra and soma reflects the central role of ritualistic consumption in Vedic religious practice, where the sharing of sacred substances created communion between the human and divine realms. The hymns also frequently invoke Indra's protection during warfare, suggesting that his worship was particularly important among the warrior classes who led the Indo-Aryan migrations and conquests.

Agni, the god of fire, occupies a unique and central position in the Vedic pantheon, serving simultaneously as a deity to be worshipped and as the medium through which worship reaches other gods. This dual nature makes Agni perhaps the most essential deity in Vedic religious practice, as every sacrifice requires his presence and participation. The name "Agni" itself derives from the Sanskrit root meaning "to burn" or "to shine," reflecting his fundamental association with fire in all its manifestations: the sacrificial fire, the domestic hearth, the lightning that flashes across the sky, and the digestive fire that burns within living beings.

As the divine messenger (duta) between humans and gods, Agni serves as the essential intermediary in Vedic religious practice. When offerings are placed into the sacrificial fire,

Agni consumes them and carries their essence to the appropriate deities, ensuring that human prayers and gifts reach their intended recipients. This role as messenger reflects a sophisticated understanding of the transformative power of fire, which changes solid matter into smoke and ethereal essence that can ascend to the heavenly realms. The Rigvedic hymns frequently address Agni as the "mouth of the gods" (devānām mukham), emphasizing his role as the divine consumer of offerings and the pathway through which human devotion reaches the celestial realms.

Agni's triple nature—existing simultaneously in the heavens as lightning, in the atmosphere as the fire of the sun, and on earth as the sacrificial flame—reflects the Vedic understanding of cosmic unity and the interconnectedness of all levels of existence. This tripartite manifestation allows Agni to serve as a bridge between the three cosmic realms, facilitating communication and exchange between gods, humans, and the natural world. The hymns often describe Agni as being "kindled" or "awakened" through human ritual activity, suggesting that divine presence can be activated and sustained through proper religious practice.

The domestic and social aspects of Agni's worship cannot be overlooked, as the hearth fire represented the sacred center of Vedic household life. The maintenance of the household fire was considered both a religious duty and a social necessity, with the extinction of the fire representing a serious spiritual and practical crisis. This domestic aspect of Agni worship created a continuous connection between daily life and sacred practice, ensuring that religious consciousness permeated every aspect of human existence. The Rigvedic hymns often describe Agni as the "guest" (atithi) in human homes, emphasizing the hospitality and care required to maintain proper relationship with the divine.

Varuna represents one of the most complex and morally sophisticated deities in the Vedic pantheon, embodying concepts of cosmic order, divine justice, and universal sovereignty that would profoundly influence later Indian religious and philosophical thought. As the guardian of Rita (cosmic order) and the divine king who oversees the moral universe, Varuna occupies a unique position that transcends the more immediate concerns of weather, warfare, and sacrifice that characterize other Vedic deities. His domain encompasses the vast expanses of sky and water, the invisible bonds that hold the universe together, and the moral laws that govern both divine and human behavior.

The Rigvedic hymns consistently portray Varuna as the all-seeing sovereign who observes human actions from his celestial palace, accompanied by his countless spies (spasa) who report on the moral conduct of mortals. This surveillance system reflects a sophisticated understanding of divine justice and moral accountability that distinguishes Varuna from other Vedic deities. While gods like Indra and Agni respond to proper ritual offering and praise, Varuna's favor depends primarily on moral conduct and truthfulness. The hymns often describe the terror and anxiety that accompany the consciousness of being observed by Varuna, reflecting a developed sense of individual moral responsibility that was revolutionary for its time.

Varuna's association with water—both celestial and terrestrial—provides a powerful metaphor for his role as the sustainer of cosmic order. Water, in Vedic thought, represents the primordial substance from which all existence emerges and to which it returns. Varuna's control over the waters of the sky (rainfall) and the waters of the earth (rivers, oceans) symbolizes his power to maintain the natural cycles that sustain life. The hymns often describe Varuna as the deity who "opens the channels" of the sky, allowing rain to fall and rivers to flow, while also having the power to withhold these life-giving waters as punishment for moral transgressions.

The concept of divine bonds (pasha) associated with Varuna represents one of the most sophisticated theological developments in Vedic literature. These invisible bonds are both cosmological and moral: they hold the universe together, maintaining the proper relationships between celestial bodies, natural forces, and living beings, while also binding individuals to moral law and divine justice. The hymns frequently contain prayers for release from Varuna's bonds, not through escape from moral responsibility, but through confession, repentance, and the restoration of proper relationship with cosmic order. This emphasis on confession and moral purification would later influence the development of concepts of karma and spiritual liberation in Indian religious thought.

Soma occupies a unique position in the Vedic pantheon, representing both a sacred substance and a fully personified deity whose worship centered on the preparation, consumption, and spiritual effects of a mysterious plant-based beverage. The entire ninth book of the Rigveda is dedicated to Soma, containing 114 hymns that celebrate the pressing, purification, and consumption of this divine elixir. The identity of the original Soma plant remains one of the great mysteries of Vedic studies, with scholars proposing various candidates including species of ephedra, cannabis, amanita muscaria mushrooms, and other psychoactive plants that might have produced the transcendent experiences described in the hymns.

The preparation of Soma represented one of the most important and elaborate rituals in Vedic religious practice, involving the crushing of the plant stalks between stones, the straining of the juice through woolen filters, and the mixing of the extract with water and milk. This process, described in extraordinary detail in the hymns, was understood as a form of sacrifice in which the plant deity willingly gave himself to be transformed into the divine beverage that would grant immortality and spiritual insight to gods and humans alike. The ritual pressing of Soma was accompanied by elaborate chanting and musical performances, creating a multisensory religious experience that engaged the entire ritual community.

The effects of Soma consumption are described in the hymns as producing profound spiritual experiences, including visions of divine beings, expansion of consciousness, feelings of immortality, and enhanced poetic inspiration. The Rigvedic seers (rishis) who composed the hymns often attribute their inspired utterances to the influence of Soma, suggesting that the beverage played a crucial role in the creation of Vedic literature itself. The hymns describe Soma as granting "immortality" (amrita) to those who consume it, though this appears to refer to temporary transcendence of ordinary consciousness rather than literal eternal life.

The theological significance of Soma extends beyond its use as a psychoactive substance to encompass broader concepts of divine grace, spiritual transformation, and the relationship between material and spiritual realms. As a deity, Soma represents the principle of divine inspiration and the possibility of direct communion with the sacred. The hymns often describe Soma as the "king of plants" and the "lord of speech," emphasizing his power to transform human consciousness and enable direct communication with the divine realm. This association with speech and inspiration would later influence the development of concepts about the sacred power of language and mantra in Indian religious traditions.

The Vedic understanding of the divine was fundamentally rooted in the observation and reverence of natural phenomena, reflecting a worldview that saw the entire cosmos as permeated with sacred power and divine presence. This nature-centered spirituality was not merely primitive animism but rather a sophisticated theological system that recognized the underlying unity and order governing all existence. The Vedic seers developed elaborate cosmological theories that sought to explain the relationship between natural forces, divine beings, and the moral universe, culminating in the concept of Rita—the cosmic order that maintains harmony and balance throughout the universe.

The Sacred in Nature

The Vedic approach to nature worship reflected a profound sensitivity to the divine presence manifest in natural phenomena, from the daily cycle of dawn and dusk to the seasonal rhythms of rain and drought, growth and decay. Every aspect of the natural world was understood to be animated by divine consciousness, with specific deities governing different natural forces and phenomena. The hymns reveal a detailed knowledge of natural processes, astronomical cycles, and ecological relationships that was integrated into a comprehensive spiritual worldview.

The daily worship of Ushas (Dawn) exemplifies this nature-centered spirituality, with numerous hymns celebrating the goddess who brings light to the world each morning. These hymns are not merely poetic descriptions of sunrise but theological statements about the divine power that maintains the cosmic order by ensuring the regular alternation of day and night. The personification of Dawn as a beautiful goddess who awakens the world with her light reflects the Vedic understanding that natural phenomena are not merely mechanical processes but expressions of divine will and consciousness.

Similarly, the worship of Vayu (Wind), Prithvi (Earth), and Dyaus (Sky) reflects the recognition that the basic elements of existence are divine in nature and worthy of reverence and propitiation. The hymns addressed to these deities often emphasize their life-giving properties and their role in maintaining the conditions necessary for human survival and prosperity. This elemental worship provided the foundation for later developments in Indian philosophy and medicine that would emphasize the fundamental importance of maintaining harmony between human beings and the natural world.

Rita: The Cosmic Order

The concept of Rita represents perhaps the most sophisticated and influential theological development in Vedic thought, providing a framework for understanding the moral and physical laws that govern the universe. Rita (from the root "ri" meaning "to move" or "to flow") refers to the cosmic order that maintains the proper relationship between all elements of existence, ensuring that the sun rises and sets, the seasons follow their appointed sequence, and moral actions produce their appropriate consequences. This concept would later evolve into the classical Indian understanding of dharma and karma, but in its original Vedic form, Rita represented a more immediate and naturalistic understanding of cosmic law.

The Rigvedic hymns consistently present Rita as the foundation of all existence, the principle that ensures the regularity of natural phenomena and the efficacy of ritual action. The gods themselves are understood to be subject to Rita, with even the most powerful deities like Indra and Varuna operating within the constraints of cosmic order. This understanding reflects a sophisticated theological development that places law and order above personal divine will, creating a framework for understanding divine justice and moral responsibility that transcends the arbitrary power of individual deities.

The maintenance of Rita requires the active participation of both gods and humans through proper ritual action and moral behavior. The Vedic sacrificial system was understood as a cosmic necessity, with human ritual actions serving to maintain the balance and harmony of the universe. The hymns often describe the sacrifice as "feeding" the gods and maintaining their power to uphold cosmic order, while also suggesting that the gods depend on human cooperation to maintain Rita. This reciprocal relationship between divine and human realms creates a sense of cosmic responsibility that extends beyond individual salvation to encompass the maintenance of universal order.

The concept of Rita also encompasses the moral dimensions of cosmic order, with truthfulness (satya) and righteousness (dharma) understood as fundamental requirements for maintaining harmony between human society and the natural world. The hymns frequently associate Rita with concepts of justice, truth, and proper conduct, suggesting that moral behavior is not merely a matter of social convention but a cosmic necessity. This integration of natural law and moral law would prove profoundly influential in later Indian philosophical and religious traditions.

Seasonal Worship and Agricultural Cycles

The Vedic religious calendar was intimately connected with agricultural cycles and seasonal changes, reflecting the dependence of the ancient Indian pastoral and agricultural economy on natural rhythms. The timing of major rituals and festivals was determined by astronomical observations and seasonal markers, creating a religious system that was synchronized with the natural world. This seasonal worship reinforced the connection between human religious activity and cosmic order, ensuring that ritual practices remained relevant to the practical concerns of daily life.

The spring festivals celebrating the renewal of life and the return of fertility to the earth were particularly important, with elaborate rituals designed to ensure successful crops and the continued prosperity of the community. These ceremonies often involved the recitation of hymns celebrating the earth goddess and the deities associated with growth and fertility, while also including practical elements such as the blessing of seeds and agricultural implements. The integration of religious and agricultural activities reflected the Vedic understanding that spiritual and material prosperity were inseparable aspects of a properly ordered life.

The monsoon season held particular significance in Vedic religious practice, with numerous hymns celebrating Indra's victory over Vritra and the release of the life-giving waters. The arrival of the rains was understood as a divine gift that required proper acknowledgment and gratitude, with special ceremonies designed to ensure the continuation of favorable weather conditions. The hymns often describe the rain as the "seed" of the sky father fertilizing the earth mother, creating a cosmic marriage that produces the abundance necessary for human survival.

Sacrifice (Yajna) and Its Significance

The institution of sacrifice (yajna) stands at the very heart of Vedic religious practice, representing far more than mere ritual offering but constituting a comprehensive system for maintaining cosmic order and facilitating communication between human and divine realms. The Vedic understanding of sacrifice encompassed both the material aspects of offering valuable goods to the gods and the spiritual dimensions of surrendering the ego and aligning human will with cosmic purpose. This sacrificial system created a complex web of reciprocal relationships between gods, humans, and the natural world that would profoundly influence the development of Indian religious thought.

The Cosmic Significance of Sacrifice

The Vedic conception of sacrifice was fundamentally cosmological, understanding ritual offerings as essential activities that maintain the balance and harmony of the universe. The famous Purusha Sukta (Hymn of the Cosmic Person) in the Rigveda describes the creation of the universe itself as a primordial sacrifice, with the gods offering the cosmic being (Purusha) to create the various elements of existence. This foundational myth establishes sacrifice as the creative principle underlying all existence, suggesting that the continued maintenance of the universe requires ongoing sacrificial activity.

The daily performance of sacrificial rituals was understood as a necessary contribution to cosmic maintenance, with human offerings providing the gods with the sustenance and power necessary to uphold natural law and cosmic order. The hymns frequently describe the gods as dependent on human sacrifice for their continued strength and effectiveness, creating a reciprocal relationship in which divine protection and blessing are exchanged for ritual offerings and proper worship. This understanding transforms sacrifice from a mere petition for divine favor into a cosmic responsibility that ensures the continued existence and prosperity of the universe.

The transformative power of sacrifice was understood to operate on multiple levels simultaneously. On the material level, valuable goods such as ghee, grain, and animals were offered to the gods through the medium of fire, with the transformation of these substances into smoke and ethereal essence enabling their transportation to the divine realm. On the spiritual level, the act of sacrifice was understood to transform the participants themselves, purifying them of negative karma and aligning their consciousness with cosmic order. The complex ritual procedures required for proper sacrifice demanded sustained attention, precise knowledge, and coordinated group activity that created profound experiences of unity and transcendence.

The Mechanics of Ritual Offering

The practical aspects of Vedic sacrifice involved elaborate procedures that required extensive knowledge, careful preparation, and precise execution. The establishment of the sacred fire (agni) marked the beginning of sacrificial activity, with specific procedures for kindling, maintaining, and feeding the flames that would consume the offerings and carry them to the gods. The construction of elaborate fire altars (vedi) using specific types of bricks and following precise geometric patterns created sacred spaces that were understood to represent the cosmos in microcosm.

The preparation of offerings required careful attention to purity and quality, with different types of substances appropriate for different deities and purposes. Grain offerings (havishya) were prepared according to specific recipes and cooking methods, while animal sacrifices involved elaborate procedures for the selection, consecration, and ritual slaughter of appropriate victims. The timing of offerings was crucial, with different parts of the ritual cycle requiring offerings at specific moments to ensure their efficacy and proper reception by the intended deities.

The role of sacred substances in Vedic sacrifice extended beyond mere material offerings to encompass the use of purifying and transformative elements that enhanced the spiritual power of the ritual. The use of clarified butter (ghee) as the primary offering substance reflected its symbolic associations with purity, light, and spiritual energy, while the consumption of soma by both priests and participants created altered states of consciousness that facilitated communion with the divine realm. The integration of these sacred substances into complex ritual procedures created multisensory experiences that engaged the entire religious community in transformative spiritual activity.

The performance of Vedic sacrifice was fundamentally a communal activity that required the participation of extended family groups, skilled specialists, and broader social networks. The expense and complexity of major sacrificial ceremonies made them significant social events that demonstrated the wealth and status of the sponsors while also creating opportunities for the redistribution of resources and the strengthening of social bonds. The elaborate feasting that typically accompanied sacrificial ceremonies extended the benefits of the ritual beyond the immediate participants to include the broader community.

The institution of sacrifice also served important educational functions, with the complex procedures and extensive knowledge required for proper performance creating opportunities for the transmission of religious, technical, and cultural knowledge. The training of priests and ritual specialists involved years of study and practice, creating a learned class that preserved and transmitted the sophisticated intellectual traditions of Vedic culture. The performance of sacrifice also provided opportunities for the display and development of artistic skills, including music, poetry, and dance that enhanced the aesthetic and spiritual dimensions of the ritual experience.

The political dimensions of sacrifice cannot be overlooked, as the sponsorship of major ceremonies provided rulers and wealthy individuals with opportunities to demonstrate their power and legitimacy while also fulfilling their obligations to maintain cosmic order. The royal horse sacrifice (ashvamedha) represented the pinnacle of political and religious ceremony, with the successful completion of this elaborate ritual confirming the sovereignty of the king and the divine approval of his rule. The integration of political and religious authority through sacrificial ceremony created a system of legitimate governance that connected earthly power with cosmic order.

The complexity and sophistication of Vedic religious practice required the development of a specialized class of religious professionals who possessed the knowledge, skills, and authority necessary to perform the elaborate rituals that maintained cosmic order and facilitated communication with the divine realm. The Vedic priesthood represented one of the earliest examples of religious specialization in human history, creating institutional structures and educational systems that would profoundly influence the development of Indian civilization and religious thought.

The Vedic sacrificial system required the coordinated activity of four distinct types of priests, each with specialized knowledge and responsibilities that contributed to the successful performance of complex rituals. The hotri priest served as the chief reciter of Rigvedic hymns, possessing extensive knowledge of the traditional verses and their proper application to specific ritual contexts. The udgātri priest specialized in the musical aspects of sacrifice, chanting the elaborate melodies of the Samaveda that accompanied ritual activities and enhanced their spiritual power. The adhvaryu priest functioned as the ritual technician, responsible for the practical aspects of sacrifice including the preparation of offerings, the manipulation of ritual implements, and the precise execution of ceremonial procedures. The brahman priest served as the overall supervisor and coordinator, possessing comprehensive knowledge of all aspects of the ritual and the authority to correct errors and ensure proper performance.

This division of labor reflected the extraordinary complexity of Vedic sacrifice and the impossibility of any single individual mastering all aspects of the ritual system. The coordination required between these different specialists created a highly sophisticated form of religious teamwork that demanded extensive training, precise communication, and shared commitment to ritual excellence. The hierarchical relationships between these priestly roles also reflected broader social structures and the development of specialized knowledge systems that would influence Indian intellectual traditions for millennia.

The training required for each priestly role involved years of intensive study and practice, with students typically beginning their education in childhood and continuing their studies well into adulthood. The memorization of vast quantities of sacred texts, the mastery of complex ritual procedures, and the development of the spiritual qualities necessary for effective religious leadership required sustained commitment and exceptional intellectual ability. The educational systems that developed to train priests represented some of the most sophisticated pedagogical methods in the ancient world, emphasizing not only the acquisition of factual knowledge but also the development of the spiritual insight and moral character necessary for religious leadership.

The emergence of the brahmin class as the hereditary custodians of Vedic religious knowledge represented a crucial development in the institutionalization of religious authority and the preservation of sacred traditions. The brahmins' monopoly on the performance of sacrifice and their exclusive access to the knowledge necessary for proper ritual performance created a powerful religious elite that would play a central role in Indian civilization for thousands of years. This hereditary priesthood developed elaborate systems of education, ordination, and professional regulation that ensured the continuity and integrity of Vedic religious traditions.

The authority of the brahmin class was based not merely on their technical knowledge of ritual procedures but on their understanding of the cosmic principles underlying sacrificial practice. The brahmins were understood to possess special insight into the nature of Rita (cosmic order) and the proper methods for maintaining harmony between human society and the divine realm. This spiritual authority was reinforced by their role as intermediaries between gods and humans, with their ritual activities understood as essential for the continued prosperity and well-being of the entire community.

The development of brahmin identity involved the creation of elaborate codes of conduct and professional ethics that governed both the ritual and daily life of the priestly class. These regulations addressed issues of purity and pollution, dietary restrictions, marriage practices, and social relationships that were understood to affect the spiritual power and ritual efficacy of the priests. The maintenance of these standards required constant vigilance and created a distinctive lifestyle that set the brahmins apart from other members of society while also emphasizing their special responsibilities and obligations.

Regional Variations and Specializations

The spread of Vedic religion across the Indian subcontinent led to the development of regional variations in priestly practices and the emergence of specialized traditions that adapted the basic Vedic framework to local conditions and cultural preferences. Different regions developed distinctive approaches to ritual performance, with variations in the specific procedures, materials, and timing of sacrificial ceremonies that reflected local environmental conditions, available resources, and cultural influences. These regional traditions maintained their connection to the broader Vedic tradition while also developing unique characteristics that enriched the overall diversity of Indian religious practice.

The development of specialized priestly schools (shakhas) created institutional structures for the preservation and transmission of specific textual traditions and ritual practices. Each school maintained its own version of the Vedic texts, with variations in pronunciation, interpretation, and practical application that reflected centuries of regional development and scholarly reflection. The competition and cooperation between these different schools created a dynamic intellectual environment that stimulated innovation and refinement in religious thought and practice.

The emergence of specialized ritual functions led to the development of priestly experts who focused on particular aspects of the sacrificial system, such as the construction of fire altars, the preparation of specific types of offerings, or the performance of particular ceremonies. These specialists possessed detailed knowledge of their areas of expertise and often traveled between different communities to provide their services for important rituals. The network of relationships between these specialists created a pan-Indian system of religious exchange that facilitated the spread of innovations and the maintenance of standards across vast geographical distances.

Hymns and Their Meanings

The Vedic hymns represent one of humanity's earliest and most sophisticated attempts to articulate the relationship between human consciousness and divine reality through the medium of sacred language. These ancient compositions, preserved with extraordinary fidelity through oral transmission for over three millennia, embody a complex integration of religious devotion, philosophical reflection, and poetic artistry that continues to influence spiritual traditions throughout South Asia and beyond. The hymns serve simultaneously as prayers, theological treatises, and repositories of cultural memory, creating a multifaceted literature that rewards multiple levels of interpretation and study.

The Nature of Sacred Language

The Vedic understanding of language was fundamentally different from modern conceptions, viewing words not merely as conventional symbols but as manifestations of divine power that possessed inherent creative and transformative potential. The Sanskrit term "mantra" (from the root "man" meaning "to think" and "tra" meaning "to protect") reflects this understanding of sacred utterances as protective and empowering forces that can influence both the speaker and the cosmic order. The precise pronunciation, rhythm, and intonation of Vedic hymns were understood to be crucial for their effectiveness, with even minor variations potentially altering their spiritual impact.

The concept of vāk (speech) as a goddess in her own right reflects the Vedic recognition of language as a divine force that participates in the creation and maintenance of the universe. The hymns often describe speech as the power through which the gods create and sustain existence, with human use of sacred language understood as participation in this ongoing creative process. This understanding of language as divine activity rather than mere human communication created a profound sense of responsibility for the proper use of words and the maintenance of linguistic purity.

The multilayered nature of Vedic language allowed for simultaneous interpretation on literal, symbolic, and mystical levels, with the same hymns serving as descriptions of natural phenomena, mythological narratives, and metaphysical teachings. This semantic richness reflects the sophisticated hermeneutical traditions that developed around Vedic texts, with different schools of interpretation emphasizing various aspects of meaning while maintaining reverence for the fundamental mystery and inexhaustibility of sacred language.

Poetic Structure and Aesthetic Principles

The Vedic hymns demonstrate extraordinary sophistication in their poetic structure, employing complex metrical patterns, elaborate systems of imagery, and sophisticated rhetorical devices that create profound aesthetic experiences while conveying religious meaning. The various meters used in Vedic poetry, including the gayatri, trishtubh, and jagati, create distinctive rhythmic patterns that enhance the musical quality of the texts and facilitate their memorization and recitation. The careful attention to sound patterns, including alliteration, assonance, and internal rhyme, creates a sonic beauty that reinforces the spiritual power of the words.

The use of extended metaphors and symbolic imagery in Vedic poetry creates multiple layers of meaning that reward careful study and contemplation. The hymns often employ elaborate comparisons drawn from natural phenomena, human activities, and cosmic processes to illuminate the nature of divine reality and the proper relationship between gods and humans. The skilled use of paradox, riddle, and enigmatic statement challenges readers to transcend literal interpretation and engage with the deeper mysteries of existence.

The aesthetic principles underlying Vedic poetry emphasize the integration of beauty, truth, and spiritual power, with the most effective hymns understood to be those that simultaneously please the senses, illuminate the understanding, and transform the consciousness of the participants. This holistic approach to poetic creation reflects the Vedic understanding that aesthetic experience and spiritual realization are intimately connected, with beauty serving as a pathway to divine truth rather than mere decoration or entertainment.

Theological Themes and Philosophical Insights

The Vedic hymns address fundamental theological questions about the nature of divine reality, the origin and structure of the universe, and the proper relationship between human beings and the sacred. The famous "Hymn of Creation" (Nasadiya Sukta) exemplifies the philosophical sophistication of Vedic thought, posing profound questions about the ultimate nature of existence while acknowledging the limitations of human understanding in comprehending cosmic mysteries. This hymn's agnostic conclusion—that even the gods may not know the ultimate truth about creation—reflects a remarkable intellectual humility that would influence later Indian philosophical traditions.

The tension between monotheistic and polytheistic tendencies in Vedic thought creates a complex theological landscape that defies simple categorization. While the hymns address numerous distinct deities with specific attributes and functions, they also contain passages that suggest an underlying unity or supreme principle that encompasses all divine manifestations. The concept of "Ekam sat viprā bahudhā vadanti" (Truth is one, but the wise speak of it in many ways) reflects this sophisticated understanding of divine unity expressed through multiplicity.

The ethical dimensions of Vedic theology emerge particularly clearly in the hymns addressed to Varuna, which emphasize concepts of sin, confession, and moral purification that would profoundly influence later Indian religious thought. These hymns recognize the reality of moral evil and the need for divine forgiveness while also asserting the possibility of spiritual transformation through proper understanding and conduct. The integration of cosmic order and moral law in these compositions creates a framework for understanding individual responsibility within the context of universal harmony.

Ritual Context and Performance

The Vedic hymns were composed for performance within specific ritual contexts, with their meaning and effectiveness intimately connected to their proper recitation during sacrificial ceremonies. The hymns were not intended as literary compositions for private reading but as functional elements of religious practice that derived their power from their integration into the broader sacrificial system. Understanding the ritual context of these hymns is essential for appreciating their original meaning and continued significance in traditional religious practice.

The performance of Vedic hymns required extensive training in proper pronunciation, intonation, and timing, with the effectiveness of the ritual understood to depend on the accurate reproduction of traditional forms. The development of sophisticated systems of textual preservation, including various methods of recitation and cross-checking, ensured the extraordinary fidelity of transmission that has preserved these ancient compositions with remarkable accuracy. The social and spiritual authority of the priests who performed these hymns was closely connected to their mastery of proper recitation and their ability to maintain the traditional forms.

The musical aspects of Vedic recitation created profound aesthetic experiences that enhanced the spiritual impact of the texts while also serving practical functions in terms of memorization and group coordination. The elaborate melodic patterns of Samaveda chanting transformed the hymns into complex musical compositions that engaged multiple senses and created altered states of consciousness in both performers and listeners. The integration of music, poetry, and ritual action in Vedic performance created holistic spiritual experiences that addressed the full range of human capacities for religious expression.

The study and interpretation of Vedic hymns continues to reveal new dimensions of meaning and significance, with contemporary scholars employing linguistic, archaeological, and comparative methods to illuminate aspects of these ancient texts that were previously obscure. The enduring relevance of these compositions reflects their success in articulating fundamental aspects of human spiritual experience in language that transcends cultural and temporal boundaries while remaining rooted in the specific historical context of their creation.

The Vedic religious universe, with its complex pantheon of deities, sophisticated understanding of cosmic order, elaborate sacrificial system, specialized priesthood, and profound hymnological literature, represents one of humanity's most remarkable achievements in the realm of religious thought and practice. This ancient tradition created institutional structures, intellectual frameworks, and spiritual practices that would influence the development of Indian civilization for millennia while also contributing to the broader human understanding of the sacred and its relationship to individual and social life. The continued study and appreciation of this tradition offers valuable insights into the nature of religious consciousness and the human quest for meaning and transcendence.

Conclusion

The Vedic religious universe stands as one of humanity's most profound and enduring spiritual achievements, representing a comprehensive worldview that successfully integrated divine worship, cosmic understanding, moral philosophy, and social organization into a coherent and transformative system of religious practice. The sophisticated theological framework developed by the ancient Indian sages addressed fundamental questions about existence, consciousness, and the relationship between individual souls and universal principles that continue to resonate with spiritual seekers across cultures and centuries.

The pantheon of Vedic deities—from Indra's dynamic warrior energy to Agni's transformative fire, from Varuna's cosmic sovereignty to Soma's transcendent consciousness—created a rich symbolic vocabulary for understanding the multiple dimensions of divine reality and their manifestation in both natural phenomena and human experience. These divine archetypes were not mere mythological constructs but living symbols that encoded profound insights about the nature of power, transformation, justice, and spiritual realization that remain relevant to contemporary spiritual practice.

The concept of Rita, as the underlying cosmic order that governs both physical and moral law, represents perhaps the Vedic tradition's most significant contribution to human religious thought. This understanding of existence as fundamentally ordered and interconnected, with human actions and divine will operating within a framework of universal harmony, provided a foundation for ethical behavior and spiritual development that would influence Indian philosophy for millennia. The recognition that individual welfare is inseparable from cosmic order created a sense of responsibility and purpose that elevated daily life to the level of sacred practice.

The elaborate sacrificial system that formed the heart of Vedic religious practice demonstrated the tradition's understanding that spiritual realization requires not merely belief or devotion but active participation in the maintenance of cosmic harmony. The yajna represented both a practical method for obtaining divine favor and a profound meditation on the nature of sacrifice, surrender, and transformation that continues to inform spiritual practice in various forms. The recognition that human beings bear responsibility for maintaining the balance between material and spiritual realms created a dynamic and participatory approach to religion that engaged the entire community in sacred work.

The sophisticated priesthood that developed to preserve and transmit Vedic knowledge created some of humanity's earliest educational institutions and intellectual traditions. The brahmins' mastery of complex ritual procedures, their preservation of vast oral literatures, and their development of systematic approaches to spiritual instruction established patterns of religious scholarship and practice that would influence Indian civilization for thousands of years. Their integration of practical religious leadership with philosophical inquiry created a model of spiritual authority based on knowledge, moral character, and service to the community.

The hymnological literature of the Vedas, with its integration of poetic beauty, theological sophistication, and spiritual power, demonstrates the tradition's understanding that sacred language serves not merely as a means of communication but as a transformative force that can alter consciousness and facilitate direct experience of divine reality. The multilayered symbolism, complex imagery, and profound philosophical insights contained within these ancient compositions continue to reward careful study and meditation, offering access to dimensions of spiritual understanding that transcend the limitations of purely rational analysis.

The enduring influence of the Vedic religious universe extends far beyond its historical significance as an ancient Indian tradition. The fundamental insights developed by the Vedic sages about the nature of consciousness, the structure of reality, and the methods for achieving spiritual realization have contributed to the development of yoga, meditation, Ayurveda, and other spiritual practices that have gained global recognition for their effectiveness in promoting human welfare and spiritual development. The Vedic understanding of the interconnectedness of all existence has also contributed to contemporary ecological and holistic approaches to health and social organization.

Perhaps most significantly, the Vedic tradition demonstrates that sophisticated religious thought and practice can emerge from careful observation of natural phenomena, profound reflection on the nature of existence, and systematic experimentation with methods for achieving spiritual realization. The ancient Indian sages who developed this tradition showed that human beings possess the capacity for direct spiritual insight and that religious knowledge can be both experiential and systematic, both mystical and practical, both individually transformative and socially beneficial.

The continued relevance of the Vedic religious universe in the modern world reflects not merely historical interest but the recognition that the fundamental questions addressed by this ancient tradition—the nature of consciousness, the meaning of existence, the proper relationship between individual and cosmic welfare, and the methods for achieving lasting happiness and spiritual fulfillment—remain central to human experience across all cultures and historical periods. The sophisticated answers developed by the Vedic tradition continue to offer valuable guidance for contemporary seekers who are willing to engage seriously with this profound spiritual heritage.

In studying the Vedic religious universe, we encounter not merely an ancient historical phenomenon but a living tradition that continues to demonstrate the human capacity for spiritual realization and the possibility of creating social institutions and cultural practices that support the highest potentials of human consciousness. The legacy of this remarkable tradition reminds us that the quest for meaning, transcendence, and harmony with cosmic order represents one of humanity's most noble and enduring aspirations, capable of producing cultural achievements that continue to inspire and guide spiritual seekers across the millennia.

6
The Power of Words

Vedic Sanskrit: Evolution and Characteristics

This chapter explores the remarkable evolution of Vedic Sanskrit, the ingenious techniques used to preserve vast bodies of knowledge through oral transmission, and the profound literary and philosophical concepts that emerged from this unique cultural milieu.

The power of words in Vedic civilization cannot be overstated. Language was not merely a tool for communication but was considered a sacred force capable of connecting the material and spiritual realms. The Vedic seers, known as rishis, believed that properly composed and recited verses could invoke divine powers, maintain cosmic order, and unlock the mysteries of existence. This reverence for language led to the development of sophisticated literary forms, complex philosophical concepts, and preservation techniques that remained virtually unchanged for millennia.

Origins and Historical Development

Vedic Sanskrit represents one of the earliest documented forms of Sanskrit, with its origins being a subject of scholarly debate. The language as preserved in the Rigveda shows distinctive characteristics that set it apart from later Classical Sanskrit.The evolution of Vedic Sanskrit can be traced through several chronological layers within the ancient Indian tradition. The earliest stratum, represented by the Rigveda, contains archaic features that gradually disappeared in later Vedic texts. The language of the Samaveda and Yajurveda shows intermediate characteristics, while the Atharvaveda, though containing some ancient material, displays features that bridge the gap between Vedic and Classical Sanskrit. This linguistic evolution reflects not only natural language change but also the conscious efforts of priestly schools to standardize and refine their sacred texts.

Phonological Characteristics

The phonological system of Vedic Sanskrit was remarkably sophisticated, featuring a complex array of consonants and vowels that allowed for precise articulation and melodic recitation. The language contained thirty-four consonants, including stops, fricatives, nasals, and liquids, organized according to place of articulation from the throat to the lips. This systematic arrangement, later codified in grammatical texts, facilitated the development of intricate metrical patterns and sound symbolism.

Vowel length played a crucial role in Vedic Sanskrit, with distinctions between short and long vowels affecting both meaning and meter. The language also featured complex sandhi rules, which governed the euphonic combination of sounds at word boundaries. These rules, while sometimes making the text appear complex to modern readers, created a flowing, musical quality that was essential for oral recitation and memorization.

The pitch accent system of Vedic Sanskrit was particularly distinctive, with three recognized tones: udatta (high), anudatta (low), and svarita (falling). This tonal system was not merely decorative but carried semantic and ritual significance. Proper pronunciation with correct pitch was considered essential for the effectiveness of mantras and sacrificial formulas, leading to the development of sophisticated techniques for teaching and preserving these tonal patterns.

Morphological Features

Vedic Sanskrit exhibited a rich morphological system that allowed for great flexibility in word formation and sentence structure. The language featured eight cases for nouns, three numbers (singular, dual, and plural), and three genders (masculine, feminine, and neuter). This inflectional complexity enabled speakers to express subtle relationships between concepts and to create elaborate compounds that could convey complex ideas in concise forms.

The verbal system was equally sophisticated, with multiple tenses, moods, and aspects. Vedic Sanskrit distinguished between present, perfect, and aorist stems, each with its own set of endings and semantic implications. The language also featured a complex system of verbal prefixes and suffixes that could modify meaning in various ways, creating a rich vocabulary of verbal expressions suitable for describing both concrete actions and abstract concepts.

Nominal composition was a particularly productive feature of Vedic Sanskrit, allowing for the creation of lengthy compounds that could express complex relationships between ideas. These compounds, ranging from simple determinative types to elaborate descriptive formations, became a hallmark of Sanskrit literary style and contributed to the language's capacity for precise philosophical expression.

Syntactic Characteristics

The syntax of Vedic Sanskrit was characterized by considerable freedom in word order, with the arrangement of words often determined by metrical requirements, emphasis, or stylistic preferences rather than rigid grammatical rules. This flexibility allowed poets and ritualists to create verses that were both metrically correct and semantically powerful, adapting their language to the specific demands of different literary and ritual contexts.

The language made extensive use of participial constructions, absolute constructions, and other nonfinite verbal forms that could express complex temporal and causal relationships. These features, combined with the rich case system, enabled the creation of dense, interconnected texts that could convey multiple layers of meaning simultaneously.

Vedic Sanskrit also displayed distinctive patterns of pronoun usage, verb placement, and clause structure that reflected the oral nature of the tradition. Sentences were often constructed with built-in mnemonic devices, such as alliteration, assonance, and rhythmic patterns, that facilitated memorization and accurate transmission.

Oral Composition and Memorization Techniques

The Oral Tradition

The Vedic tradition was fundamentally oral, with texts being composed, transmitted, and preserved through spoken recitation rather than written records. This oral character was not merely a practical necessity due to the absence of writing systems but represented a conscious choice reflecting deepseated beliefs about the nature of sacred knowledge. The spoken word was considered more immediate, more powerful, and more sacred than any written representation could be.

The oral tradition required the development of sophisticated techniques for composition, memorization, and transmission.

Poets and ritualists had to create verses that were not only meaningful and beautiful but also easy to remember and difficult to corrupt through repeated recitation. This led to the development of distinctive features such as regular meter, formulaic expressions, and structural patterns that served both aesthetic and mnemonic functions.

The success of the oral tradition is evidenced by the remarkable consistency of Vedic texts across different regions and centuries. Modern scholars have found that manuscripts from widely separated geographical areas and time periods show minimal variation, suggesting that the oral transmission techniques were extraordinarily effective in preserving textual integrity.

The preservation of vast bodies of Vedic literature required the development of sophisticated mnemonic techniques that could ensure accurate transmission across generations. These techniques were not merely mechanical aids but were integrated into the very structure of the texts themselves, creating a symbiotic relationship between content and preservation method.

One of the most important mnemonic devices was the use of regular meter and rhythm. Vedic poetry was composed in a variety of metrical patterns, each with its own specific syllable count, stress patterns, and rhythmic flow. These metrical constraints served not only aesthetic purposes but also created natural breaking points and organizational structures that facilitated memorization. The rhythm of the verse became a guide for recitation, helping reciters maintain accuracy and detect errors.

Formulaic composition was another crucial mnemonic technique. Vedic poets developed a repertoire of standard phrases, epithets, and metrical formulae that could be adapted to different contexts while maintaining their essential form. These formulae served as building blocks for composition and provided reliable reference points for memorization. The repetition of these formulaic elements across different hymns created a web of interconnections that reinforced memory and provided multiple pathways for recall.

The use of sound symbolism and wordplay also served mnemonic functions. Vedic poets exploited the relationships between sound and meaning, creating verses where the phonetic structure reinforced the semantic content. Alliteration, assonance, and other sound patterns created memorable combinations that were difficult to forget or alter without detection.

The recitation of Vedic texts was governed by elaborate rules and practices that ensured both accuracy and proper ritual effect. Different schools developed their own traditions of recitation, each with distinctive melodic patterns, pronunciations, and interpretative approaches. These schools, known as shakhas, maintained their specific versions of the texts while preserving the overall integrity of the tradition.

The training of reciters began in childhood and continued for many years, with students learning not only the words of the texts but also the proper pronunciation, intonation, and ritual context. This intensive training created a class of specialist reciters who could perform the texts with extraordinary accuracy and understanding.

Group recitation was also employed as both a training method and a preservation technique. When multiple reciters performed the same text simultaneously, errors became immediately apparent, and the collective memory of the group provided a check against individual lapses. This practice also created a sense of communal participation in the preservation of sacred knowledge.

Memory Aids and Structural Devices

Vedic texts incorporated numerous structural devices that aided memorization and prevented corruption. These included numerical sequences, alphabetical arrangements, and systematic repetitions that created predictable patterns within the texts. Such organizational principles helped reciters navigate through long compositions and provided checkpoints for verifying accuracy.

The use of dialogue and narrative structures also served mnemonic functions. Many Vedic hymns are structured as conversations between gods and mortals, or as stories that unfold through multiple verses. These narrative elements created a logical sequence that was easier to remember than abstract philosophical discourse, while still conveying complex theological and philosophical concepts.

Cross-referencing and internal consistency were maintained through elaborate systems of correspondences and associations. Hymns were often grouped according to theme, deity, or ritual function, creating networks of related material that reinforced memory and provided multiple contexts for understanding individual verses.

Literary Forms: Hymns, Prayers, and Incantations

Hymns (Suktas)

The hymn, or sukta, represents the most elaborate and sophisticated literary form in Vedic literature. These compositions typically consist of multiple verses dedicated to specific deities, natural phenomena, or abstract concepts, and they demonstrate the highest achievements of Vedic poetic art. The hymns served multiple functions simultaneously: they were vehicles for religious expression, artistic creation, and philosophical speculation.

The structure of Vedic hymns reveals careful attention to both content and form. Most hymns begin with an invocation that establishes the identity of the deity and the purpose of the composition. The body of the hymn typically develops themes through a series of verses that may describe the deity's attributes, recount mythological narratives, or express the poet's requests and aspirations. The conclusion often includes a prayer for divine favor or a statement of the hoped-for results of the ritual performance.

The language of the hymns is characterized by rich imagery, complex metaphors, and sophisticated wordplay. Vedic poets employed a vast vocabulary of epithets and descriptive phrases that could evoke the power and majesty of the gods while creating memorable poetic effects. The use of nature imagery was particularly prominent, with deities often described through metaphors drawn from natural phenomena such as lightning, fire, water, and the movements of celestial bodies.

Many hymns display a remarkable unity of theme and development, suggesting careful composition and revision. The progression of ideas within a hymn often follows logical or emotional patterns that enhance both the aesthetic impact and the ritual effectiveness of the composition. This sophisticated structure indicates that Vedic poets were not merely preserving traditional material but were actively engaged in creative literary activity.

Prayers (Prarthanas)

Prayers in Vedic literature range from simple requests for material benefits to elaborate theological meditations on the nature of divinity and cosmic order. These compositions reveal the practical concerns of ancient peoples while demonstrating sophisticated understanding of the relationship between human needs and divine power.

The language of Vedic prayers is typically more direct and personal than that of the elaborate hymns, though it maintains the same attention to poetic form and metrical structure. Prayers often employ firstperson pronouns and conversational tone, creating a sense of intimate communication between the worshipper and the deity. This personal quality makes the prayers particularly revealing of ancient attitudes toward divinity and religious practice.

The content of Vedic prayers covers a wide range of concerns, from requests for material prosperity and protection from enemies to appeals for spiritual insight and liberation from suffering. Some prayers focus on specific life circumstances, such as marriage, childbirth, or death, while others address universal human concerns such as the search for meaning and the fear of mortality.

The formulaic nature of many prayers suggests that they were composed for repeated use in various ritual contexts. Standard phrases and conventional requests appear across different compositions, indicating that certain forms of expression were considered particularly effective or appropriate for communication with specific deities.

Incantations (Mantras)

Incantations represent perhaps the most mysterious and powerful category of Vedic literature. These compositions were believed to possess inherent spiritual power that could be activated through proper pronunciation and ritual use. The effectiveness of mantras was thought to depend not only on their semantic content but also on their sound patterns, syllable structure, and the circumstances of their recitation.

The language of incantations is often more compressed and enigmatic than that of hymns or prayers. Many mantras employ cryptic symbolism, esoteric terminology, and complex sound patterns that may have been meaningful primarily to initiated specialists. This esoteric quality suggests that incantations were part of a specialized tradition of ritual knowledge that was carefully guarded and transmitted only to qualified practitioners.

The most famous of all Vedic incantations is the Gayatri mantra, which exemplifies the sophisticated integration of sound, meaning, and spiritual purpose that characterizes this literary form. The mantra's structure creates a perfect balance between phonetic beauty and semantic depth, while its traditional associations with solar worship and spiritual enlightenment demonstrate the complex symbolic systems that underlay Vedic religious practice.

The use of seed syllables (bija mantras) and sacred sounds represents another distinctive feature of Vedic incantations. These short, often untranslatable syllables were believed to contain concentrated spiritual power that could be released through proper recitation. The most famous of these is the sacred syllable "Om," which appears at the beginning of many mantras and is considered to represent the fundamental sound of the universe.

Liturgical Forms

Beyond the major categories of hymns, prayers, and incantations, Vedic literature includes numerous specialized liturgical forms designed for specific ritual contexts. These include offerings formulae, benedictions, curses, and protective charms that demonstrate the practical applications of sacred language in daily life.

The Brahmana texts, which provide detailed instructions for ritual performance, preserve numerous examples of these liturgical forms along with explanations of their proper use and significance. These texts reveal the elaborate ceremonial contexts in which Vedic literature was employed and provide insight into the sophisticated ritual systems that gave meaning to the sacred compositions.

The diversity of liturgical forms reflects the comprehensive nature of Vedic religious practice, which addressed all aspects of human experience from birth to death. This inclusiveness contributed to the preservation of the texts by ensuring that they remained relevant to successive generations of practitioners.

Philosophical Concepts in the Rigveda

Cosmological Speculation

The Rigveda contains some of the earliest and most profound cosmological speculation in human literature. The famous Nasadiya Sukta (Hymn of Creation) presents a remarkably sophisticated meditation on the origins of the universe that anticipates many later philosophical developments. This hymn begins with the striking assertion that "there was neither existence nor non-existence" before creation, immediately establishing a level of abstract thinking that challenges conventional categories of understanding.

The cosmological hymns of the Rigveda reveal a worldview that sees the universe as an ordered, interconnected whole governed by fundamental principles of law and harmony. The concept of rita, often translated as "cosmic order" or "natural law," represents one of the most important philosophical contributions of Vedic thought. Rita is conceived as the principle that maintains regularity in natural phenomena, ensures the effectiveness of ritual actions, and provides the foundation for moral behavior.

The Vedic understanding of time is particularly sophisticated, incorporating both cyclical and linear elements. The hymns speak of recurring natural cycles, such as the daily journey of the sun and the seasonal return of the rains, while also acknowledging processes of development and change. This temporal framework provides the context for understanding both cosmic processes and human destiny.

The relationship between the microcosm and macrocosm is another fundamental theme in Vedic cosmology. The hymns frequently draw correspondences between human experience and cosmic processes, suggesting that the individual person is a reflection of the universal order. This principle of correspondence became central to later Hindu philosophy and ritual practice.

Theological Concepts

The theological concepts expressed in the Rigveda reveal a complex and evolving understanding of divinity that cannot be reduced to simple polytheism or monotheism. The hymns present a pantheon of distinct deities, each with specific attributes and functions, while simultaneously suggesting underlying unity and interconnection among the divine powers.

The concept of divine hierarchy is fluid and contextual in the Rigveda, with different deities being praised as supreme in different hymns. This apparent inconsistency reflects a sophisticated understanding of the multifaceted nature of divine reality rather than confusion or primitive thinking. The Vedic seers recognized that ultimate reality might be too complex to be fully comprehended through any single theological formulation.

The famous verse "Ekam sat vipra bahudha vadanti" ("Truth is one, but the wise call it by many names") encapsulates this inclusive approach to divine truth. This perspective allows for the coexistence of multiple divine manifestations while maintaining the underlying unity of spiritual reality.

The concept of divine grace and human agency is explored through the complex relationship between gods and mortals portrayed in the hymns. While the deities are clearly superior to humans in power and knowledge, they are also shown to be responsive to human prayers and dependent on human ritual offerings. This reciprocal relationship suggests a sophisticated understanding of the dynamics of religious experience.

Ethical and Moral Concepts

The Rigveda presents ethical and moral concepts that are closely integrated with cosmic order and divine will. The principle of rita extends beyond physical laws to encompass moral and social obligations, suggesting that ethical behavior is not merely conventional but is rooted in the fundamental structure of reality.

The concept of dharma, though not fully developed in the Rigveda, appears in embryonic form as the principle of righteous action that supports both individual welfare and cosmic harmony. The hymns suggest that moral behavior is rewarded not only by divine favor but also by natural consequences that flow from the cosmic order itself.

The treatment of social relationships in the Rigveda reveals sophisticated understanding of the tension between individual desires and collective obligations. The hymns acknowledge the legitimacy of personal ambitions while emphasizing the importance of maintaining social harmony and fulfilling one's duties to family, community, and the gods.

The concept of karma, though not explicitly articulated, is implicit in many Rigvedic passages that suggest a connection between actions and consequences. The hymns frequently emphasize the importance of proper behavior and warn against the dangers of moral transgression, suggesting a worldview in which ethical choices have lasting significance.

Psychological and Spiritual Concepts

The Rigveda contains remarkable insights into human psychology and spiritual experience that anticipate later developments in Indian philosophy and psychology. The hymns recognize the complexity of human consciousness and the multiple factors that influence thoughts, emotions, and behavior.

The concept of the mind (manas) is explored through various hymns that describe its functions, limitations, and potential for development. The Vedic understanding of consciousness includes recognition of both rational and intuitive modes of knowing, with particular emphasis on the importance of inspiration and direct spiritual experience.

The practice of meditation and contemplation is implicit in many hymns that describe states of expanded awareness and direct contact with divine reality. These passages suggest that the Vedic seers had direct experience of altered states of consciousness and understood their significance for spiritual development.

The concept of liberation or spiritual freedom appears in various forms throughout the Rigveda, though it is not systematically developed. The hymns speak of release from suffering, transcendence of limitations, and attainment of divine knowledge, suggesting that spiritual development was understood as a process of gradual transformation rather than sudden enlightenment.

Philosophical Methodology

The Rigveda demonstrates sophisticated philosophical methodology that combines rational analysis with intuitive insight. The hymns employ logical argumentation, systematic questioning, and careful observation of natural phenomena, while also acknowledging the limitations of purely rational approaches to ultimate questions.

The use of paradox and contradiction as philosophical tools is evident in many hymns that present seemingly incompatible statements as complementary perspectives on complex truths. This approach reflects understanding that reality may be too complex to be fully captured by any single conceptual framework.

The integration of myth and philosophy is another distinctive feature of Rigvedic thought. Mythological narratives are employed not merely as entertainment or primitive explanation but as vehicles for conveying sophisticated philosophical insights that might be difficult to express in abstract terms.

The dialogical structure of many hymns suggests that philosophical understanding was seen as emerging from conversation and debate rather than from solitary reflection.

This interactive approach to truthseeking became characteristic of later Indian philosophical traditions.

Preservation of Knowledge

The Oral Tradition System

The preservation of Vedic knowledge through oral transmission represents one of the most remarkable achievements in human cultural history. For over three millennia, vast bodies of sacred texts were maintained with extraordinary accuracy through sophisticated systems of oral preservation that ensured both textual integrity and interpretive continuity.

The oral tradition was not merely a practical expedient but reflected fundamental beliefs about the nature of sacred knowledge. The spoken word was considered more immediate and powerful than written text, and the act of recitation was believed to activate the spiritual power inherent in the sacred verses. This understanding created strong motivation for maintaining the tradition with absolute fidelity.

The preservation system was based on multiple redundancies and cross-checks that made corruption virtually impossible. Different families and schools maintained their own versions of the texts, creating a network of parallel traditions that could be compared and verified. Any deviation from the accepted version would be immediately detected and corrected through this system of mutual verification.

The training of students in the oral tradition was intensive and comprehensive, involving not only memorization of the texts but also understanding of their proper pronunciation, interpretation, and ritual application. This thorough education ensured that each generation of practitioners could maintain the tradition with full competence and authority.

Specialized Preservation Techniques

Beyond the basic methods of memorization and recitation, Vedic schools developed highly specialized techniques for ensuring textual preservation. These included various patterns of recitation that created additional checkpoints for verification and made corruption more difficult.

The ghana patha (bell recitation) was one of the most sophisticated of these techniques, involving the recitation of words in complex patterns that created multiple opportunities for error detection. In this method, words were recited in forward and backward sequences that created a distinctive rhythmic pattern. Any mistake would immediately disrupt the pattern and alert the reciter to the error.

The jata patha (braid recitation) was even more complex, involving the weaving of words into intricate patterns that resembled braided hair. These techniques required extraordinary skill and concentration, but they created virtually foolproof methods for detecting and preventing textual corruption.

The use of numerical and alphabetical arrangements provided additional security for the preservation of textual integrity. Words and verses were often arranged according to systematic principles that created predictable patterns. Any deviation from these patterns would be immediately apparent to trained practitioners.

Schools and Lineages

The preservation of Vedic knowledge was organized through a system of schools (shakhas) that maintained specific traditions of interpretation and recitation. Each school preserved its own version of the texts along with distinctive practices of performance and explanation. This diversity within unity ensured that the tradition remained vital and adaptable while maintaining essential consistency.

The relationship between teacher and student was central to the preservation system. Students lived with their teachers for extended periods, receiving not only instruction in the texts but also training in the proper attitude and conduct required for handling sacred knowledge. This intensive personal relationship ensured that subtle aspects of the tradition were transmitted along with the explicit textual content.

The geographical distribution of different schools created a network of preservation that extended across the Indian subcontinent. Even if one school or region faced difficulties, the tradition could be reconstructed from other sources. This distributed system proved remarkably resilient and contributed to the survival of the texts through periods of political upheaval and cultural change.

The development of specialist roles within the preservation system allowed for efficient division of labor while maintaining overall coherence. Different individuals and families specialized in particular aspects of the tradition, such as specific texts, ritual procedures, or interpretive approaches. This specialization created deep expertise while ensuring that all aspects of the tradition were properly maintained.

Transition to Written Form

The eventual transition from oral to written preservation occurred gradually over many centuries and was motivated by various practical and cultural factors. The development of writing systems, the expansion of the tradition beyond its original cultural context, and the need to ensure preservation in changing circumstances all contributed to this transition.

The early manuscripts were not intended to replace the oral tradition but to supplement it. Written texts served as aids to memory and as references for verification, while the oral tradition continued to be the primary means of transmission and teaching. This dual system combined the advantages of both approaches and provided additional security for preservation.

The process of reducing the oral tradition to writing revealed many features that had been implicit in the oral system. The detailed attention to pronunciation, meter, and ritual context that characterized oral transmission had to be made explicit in written form, leading to the development of sophisticated systems of notation and commentary.

The written tradition also facilitated new forms of scholarship and interpretation that were difficult to pursue within the constraints of oral transmission. Scholars could now compare texts, trace developments, and develop systematic commentaries that enhanced understanding of the tradition while maintaining its essential character.

Modern Preservation Efforts

Contemporary efforts to preserve Vedic knowledge combine traditional methods with modern technology to ensure the continued vitality of the tradition. Digital recordings, computer databases, and international scholarly networks have created new opportunities for preservation and study while maintaining respect for traditional approaches.

The training of traditional reciters continues in various institutions throughout India and other countries, ensuring that the oral tradition remains alive and functional. These contemporary practitioners maintain the same high standards of accuracy and dedication that characterized their predecessors, while adapting to modern circumstances and opportunities.

Scholarly research has enhanced understanding of the preservation techniques and their effectiveness, providing new appreciation for the sophistication of traditional methods. Modern linguistic analysis has confirmed the remarkable accuracy of oral transmission and has revealed features of the texts that were not apparent to earlier scholars.

The global spread of interest in Vedic knowledge has created new contexts for preservation and study, while also raising questions about the appropriate methods for maintaining the tradition in diverse cultural settings. The challenge of preserving the essential character of the tradition while making it accessible to contemporary audiences continues to generate creative solutions and innovative approaches.

Conclusion

The study of Vedic language and literature reveals an extraordinary achievement in human cultural development that continues to influence civilization to this day. The sophistication of Vedic Sanskrit, the ingenuity of oral composition and preservation techniques, the beauty and depth of literary forms, and the profundity of philosophical concepts all testify to the remarkable intellectual and spiritual achievements of ancient Indian civilization.

The power of words in Vedic culture extended far beyond mere communication to encompass the fundamental forces that shape reality itself. This understanding led to the development of literary and linguistic practices that combined practical effectiveness with aesthetic beauty and spiritual significance. The result was a tradition that could preserve vast amounts of knowledge while maintaining its relevance and power across millennia.

The preservation of Vedic knowledge through oral transmission demonstrates the extraordinary capacity of human memory and the effectiveness of well-designed cultural institutions. The techniques developed for this purpose represent sophisticated solutions to complex problems of information storage and transmission that remained unmatched until the development of modern technology.

The philosophical concepts explored in Vedic literature continue to influence contemporary thought and provide insight into fundamental questions about the nature of reality, consciousness, and human purpose. The integration of rational analysis with intuitive insight, the recognition of multiple perspectives on truth, and the emphasis on practical application of knowledge all remain relevant to contemporary philosophical inquiry.

The transition from oral to written preservation marked a significant development in the history of human culture, but it did not diminish the essential character of the Vedic tradition. Instead, it created new opportunities for study and appreciation while maintaining the living connection between past and present that gives the tradition its continuing vitality.

The legacy of Vedic language and literature extends far beyond its historical importance to encompass ongoing influence on literature, philosophy, religion, and culture throughout the world. The principles of composition, preservation, and interpretation developed in the Vedic tradition continue to provide models for understanding the relationship between language, knowledge, and spiritual insight.

As we face contemporary challenges in preserving and transmitting knowledge in an increasingly complex world, the Vedic tradition offers valuable lessons about the importance of maintaining high standards of accuracy, the value of diverse approaches to truth, and the essential role of dedicated practitioners in keeping traditions alive. The power of words, so clearly recognized in Vedic culture, remains as relevant today as it was three millennia ago, reminding us that language is not merely a tool but a sacred trust that connects us to our deepest sources of wisdom and understanding.

7
The Gurukul

The Foundation of Vedic Education

The word "gurukul" itself reveals the profound nature of this system. Derived from "guru" (teacher, literally meaning "one who brings light to darkness") and "kul" (family or home), it signified that education was not a separate, institutional activity but an integral part of familial and spiritual life. Unlike modern educational systems that compartmentalize learning into subjects and grades, the gurukul represented a holistic approach where knowledge, wisdom, character, and spiritual development were woven together in an indivisible tapestry.

This system emerged from the fundamental Vedic understanding that knowledge was divine, that learning was a sacred act, and that the relationship between teacher and student was one of the most sacred bonds in human society. The Mundaka Upanishad beautifully captures this essence: "Tad vijnanartham sa gurum evabhigacchet samitpanih srotriyam brahmanistham" (To know that truth, one must approach a guru with reverence, one who is learned in scriptures and established in Brahman).

The Historical Context and Origins

The gurukul system did not emerge in isolation but was deeply rooted in the socio-religious framework of Vedic society. During the early Vedic period, society was primarily pastoral and agricultural, organized around the principles of dharma (righteousness), artha (material prosperity), kama (pleasure), and moksha (liberation). Knowledge was considered sacred property that needed to be preserved, transmitted, and protected from corruption.

The absence of a written script during the early Vedic period made oral transmission not just preferable but essential. The Vedas, considered eternal truths (sanatana dharma), had to be preserved with absolute accuracy. This requirement gave birth to sophisticated methods of memorization, recitation, and oral preservation that became hallmarks of the gurukul system. The precision with which these texts were preserved—so accurate that even today's written versions match the oral traditions maintained over three millennia—testifies to the remarkable effectiveness of this educational approach.

The gurukul system also reflected the Vedic understanding of human development as occurring in distinct stages (ashramas). The student phase (brahmacharya ashrama) was considered foundational, where young minds were shaped not just intellectually but morally and spiritually. This period was seen as crucial for developing the discipline, character, and knowledge base that would serve individuals throughout their lives.

Archaeological evidence from Indus Valley sites and later Vedic settlements suggests that even pre-Vedic civilizations valued learning and had sophisticated educational practices. However, it was during the Vedic period that these practices crystallized into the systematic gurukul model that would profoundly influence Indian education for centuries.

The Physical and Spiritual Architecture of the Gurukul

A typical gurukul was far from the imposing institutional buildings we associate with education today. Instead, it was usually a simple ashram (hermitage) located in serene natural surroundings—often near rivers, in forest clearings, or on the outskirts of villages. This location was deliberately chosen to provide an environment conducive to learning and spiritual development, away from the distractions and materialism of urban life.

The physical structure of a gurukul was modest yet functional. The guru's residence formed the central building, typically constructed of wood, bamboo, and other natural materials. Around this central structure were arranged student quarters—simple huts or dormitories where brahmacharis (studentdisciples) lived. A crucial component was the yajna-shala (fire altar area) where daily prayers and sacrificial rituals were conducted, emphasizing the integration of learning with spiritual practice.

The ashram also included practical facilities: storage areas for grain and other necessities, spaces for cattle (goshala), gardens where medicinal herbs and food crops were grown, and open areas for physical exercises and outdoor classes. Some larger gurukulam had libraries (though these were primarily collections of palm leaf manuscripts in later periods), workshops for various crafts, and guest houses for visiting scholars.

But the true architecture of the gurukul was not physical but spiritual. The entire environment was designed to create what we might call a "learning ecosystem"—a space where every element contributed to the educational process. The natural surroundings taught lessons about the interconnectedness of life, the daily routines developed discipline and character, and the communal living fostered values of cooperation and service.

The absence of luxury was deliberate. Students slept on simple mats, ate basic vegetarian food, and wore simple clothes. This austerity served multiple purposes: it developed resilience and adaptability, prevented the distractions that material comforts might bring, and emphasized that true wealth lay in knowledge and character rather than material possessions.

The Guru- Embodiment of Knowledge and Wisdom

In the Gurukul system, the guru occupied a position of unparalleled reverence and authority. The Sanskrit term "guru" is often translated simply as "teacher," but this translation fails to capture the profound significance of the role. The guru was simultaneously teacher, guide, father figure, spiritual mentor, and moral exemplar. The Advaya Taraka Upanishad defines the guru as one who is "gurur brahma gurur vishnuh gurur devo maheshwarah, guru sakshaat parabrahma tasmai shree gurave namah" (The guru is Brahma, the guru is Vishnu, the guru is Shiva, the guru is verily the Supreme Absolute, salutations to that guru).

The selection and preparation of a guru was a matter of utmost importance in Vedic society. A true guru was expected to have mastered not just the texts and subjects he would teach but to have integrated that knowledge into his very being. He was required to be "srotriya" (learned in scriptures) and "brahmanishtha" (established in the highest truth). This meant that theoretical knowledge alone was insufficient; the guru had to embody the wisdom he taught.

The guru's qualifications were comprehensive and demanding. He needed to have complete mastery over the Vedas and their auxiliary sciences (vedangas), including phonetics (shiksha), grammar (vyakarana), prosody (chhanda), etymology (nirukta), astronomy (jyotisha), and ritual science (kalpa). Beyond these, many gurus were also experts in specialized fields such as medicine (ayurveda), mathematics (ganita), logic (tarka), philosophy (darshana), and various practical arts.

But intellectual qualifications, however impressive, were considered secondary to character and spiritual attainment. A guru was expected to exemplify the highest moral and ethical standards. He needed to be truthful, compassionate, patient, and completely free from ego and material desires. The teaching role was viewed as a sacred duty (dharma) rather than a profession, and taking payment for imparting knowledge, especially spiritual knowledge, was generally discouraged.

The guru's teaching methods were as important as his knowledge. He needed to be an astute observer of human nature, capable of understanding each student's unique temperament, capabilities, and learning style. The Vedic educational philosophy recognized that students were not uniform recipients of standardized knowledge but unique individuals requiring personalized guidance. The guru was expected to adapt his teaching methods accordingly, being strict with some students while being gentle with others, pushing some toward greater challenges while providing additional support to those who struggled.

The relationship between guru and student extended far beyond the formal educational period. The guru maintained lifelong interest in his students' welfare and development. Many texts describe gurus continuing to advise and guide their former students throughout their lives, and students regularly returning to seek their guru's blessing and guidance at important life junctures.

Perhaps most significantly, the guru served as a living link in the chain of knowledge transmission (gurushishya parampara). He was not just teaching subjects but preserving and transmitting an entire civilization's wisdom. This sacred responsibility meant that the guru was custodian not just of information but of cultural values, spiritual insights, and traditional knowledge that had been refined over generations.

The Student- The Seeker's Journey

The life of a student (brahmachari) in the gurukul system was one of complete dedication to learning and self-development. The term "brahmachari" literally means "one who moves in Brahman" or "one whose conduct is divine," indicating that studentship was viewed as a spiritual discipline rather than merely an academic pursuit.

The formal beginning of a student's education was marked by the upanayana ceremony, one of the most important samskaras (sacraments) in Hindu tradition. This sacred thread ceremony, typically performed between the ages of 8 and 12 for boys of the three upper varnas (castes), symbolized the student's second birth—this time into the world of knowledge and spirituality. During this ceremony, the student received the sacred thread (yajnopavita) and was taught the Gayatri mantra, marking his formal initiation into the brahmacharya ashrama.

The selection of students was not purely based on social status, though caste considerations did play a role, particularly in later periods. More importantly, students were chosen based on their demonstrated capacity for learning, moral character, and sincere desire for knowledge. The Chandogya Upanishad tells the story of Satyakama Jabala, who despite not knowing his father's identity (usually a barrier to higher learning), was accepted by the sage Haridrumata Gautama because of his commitment to truth.

Once accepted into a gurukul, students underwent a complete transformation of lifestyle. They left behind the comforts and protections of home to embrace a life of discipline, service, and intensive learning. This separation from family was considered essential for several reasons: it prevented the distractions that emotional attachments might cause, it fostered independence and self-reliance, and it created an environment where the guru-student relationship could develop without competing loyalties.

The daily routine of a brahmachari was rigorous and carefully structured. The day began before dawn with personal hygiene and prayers, followed by the morning sandhya vandana (twilight prayers) and meditation. After these spiritual practices, students participated in collective prayers and the lighting of the sacred fire, reinforcing the connection between learning and spiritual practice.

The morning hours were typically devoted to the study of sacred texts, as the mind was considered most receptive during this time. Students would sit in the traditional posture, often on deer skins or simple mats, and engage in various forms of learning: recitation, memorization, discussion, and contemplation. The guru might teach through direct instruction, storytelling, questioning, or guided discovery, depending on the subject matter and the students' needs.

After the morning study session, students participated in various service activities (seva). This might include collecting firewood, fetching water, tending cattle, maintaining the ashram grounds, or assisting in food preparation. These activities were not mere chores but integral parts of the educational process, designed to develop practical skills, humility, and a service mentality.

The midday period often involved meals prepared collectively, followed by rest and informal discussions. Afternoons might be devoted to specialized subjects, practical skills, or physical training. Many gurukulam included training in martial arts, as the kshatriya students needed to develop warrior skills alongside their academic education.

Evenings were particularly important in the gurukul routine. After the evening prayers and rituals, students gathered around their guru for satsang (spiritual discourse) and informal teaching. These sessions often took the form of storytelling, where moral and philosophical principles were conveyed through engaging narratives from the Puranas, Itihasas, and other traditional sources.

The discipline required of students was comprehensive but not harsh. They were expected to observe celibacy (brahmacharya) strictly, consume only vegetarian food, avoid luxury and comfort, speak truthfully, show respect to all beings, and maintain absolute obedience to their guru. This discipline was understood not as restriction but as training that would develop the strength of character and spiritual foundation necessary for a meaningful life.

Students typically remained in the gurukul for twelve to sixteen years, though this varied depending on their area of specialization and capacity for learning. Some exceptional students might remain longer, eventually becoming assistant teachers or even establishing their own gurukulam.

The Sacred Curriculum- Knowledge as Divine Inheritance

The curriculum in Vedic gurukulam was both comprehensive and sophisticated, encompassing what we might today call the humanities, sciences, practical arts, and spiritual studies. However, unlike modern educational systems that compartmentalize knowledge into separate disciplines, Vedic education viewed all knowledge as interconnected aspects of a single, unified truth.

At the foundation of all learning were the Vedas—the Rigveda, Samaveda, Yajurveda, and Atharvaveda. These texts were not merely studied but lived, with students spending years memorizing entire portions and understanding their deeper meanings. The method of Vedic study was extraordinarily sophisticated, involving eleven different ways of recitation (vikritis) designed to preserve textual accuracy and develop mental discipline.

Alongside the Vedas, students studied the Vedangas (literally "limbs of the Vedas"), six auxiliary sciences that were considered essential for proper understanding of the sacred texts. Shiksha (phonetics) ensured proper pronunciation and intonation of Sanskrit mantras. Vyakarana (grammar) provided the linguistic foundation necessary for understanding complex Sanskrit texts. Chhanda (prosody) dealt with poetic meters and rhythms. Nirukta (etymology) explored the origins and meanings of words. Jyotisha (astronomy/astrology) covered mathematical calculations, calendar systems, and celestial observations necessary for determining proper timing of rituals. Kalpa (ritual science) detailed the procedures for various ceremonies and sacrifices.

Mathematics (ganita) held a particularly important place in the curriculum. Vedic mathematics was remarkably advanced, including sophisticated understanding of algebra, geometry, and even early concepts that would later develop into calculus. The mathematical precision required for constructing fire altars (agnichayana) according to specific geometric principles demonstrates the high level of mathematical knowledge possessed by Vedic scholars.

Astronomy and astrology (jyotisha) formed another crucial component of Vedic education. Students learned to calculate planetary positions, predict eclipses, and understand the relationship between celestial movements and earthly events. This knowledge was considered essential not just for ritual purposes but for agriculture, navigation, and understanding the cosmic order that governed all existence.

Medicine (ayurveda) was taught as both theoretical knowledge and practical skill. Students learned about the three doshas (vata, pitta, kapha), the properties of various herbs and minerals, surgical techniques, and the holistic approach to health that characterizes Ayurvedic medicine. Many gurukulam had their own medicinal gardens where students could study plants directly and prepare medicines under their guru's guidance.

Philosophy (darshana) formed the crown of Vedic education. Students were introduced to different schools of philosophical thought and encouraged to engage in rigorous logical analysis and debate. The ability to argue effectively, understand different viewpoints, and arrive at truth through reasoned discussion was highly valued. The famous debates (shastrartha) between scholars of different schools were considered important educational events.

Literature and poetry (kavya) were integral to the curriculum, not merely for aesthetic appreciation but as vehicles for moral and spiritual instruction. Students studied great works like the Ramayana and Mahabharata not just as stories but as complex explorations of dharma, human nature, and spiritual truth.

Practical subjects were not neglected. Students learned various crafts and skills relevant to their future roles in society. This might include agriculture, animal husbandry, metallurgy, architecture, music, dance, painting, or martial arts. The principle was that education should prepare individuals not just intellectually and spiritually but practically for their life's work.

The teaching methodology employed in gurukulam was remarkably sophisticated and varied. Memorization formed the foundation but was accompanied by explanation, discussion, and practical application. The guru employed various techniques including storytelling (kathakalakshepa), questioning (prashna-uttara), debate (vada-vivada), and guided reflection (manana-nididhyasana).

The use of sutras (literally "threads")—brief, condensed statements that captured essential principles— was particularly ingenious. These served as memory aids while requiring students to engage in deep thinking to understand their full implications. The guru's role was often to help students "unpack" these condensed teachings and understand their broader significance.

Daily Life and Spiritual Discipline in the Gurukul

The rhythm of life in a gurukul was carefully designed to create an environment conducive to both learning and character development. Every aspect of daily routine served educational purposes, from the early morning prayers that cultivated spiritual awareness to the evening discussions that integrated the day's learning.

The day began in the brahma muhurta (approximately 4:00-6:00 AM), considered the most auspicious time for spiritual practices when the mind is naturally peaceful and receptive. Students would rise before dawn, perform their morning ablutions in nearby rivers or ponds, and engage in personal prayers and meditation. This early morning period was crucial for developing self-discipline and connecting with the spiritual dimension of existence.

The morning sandhya vandana (twilight worship) was a collective activity that reinforced the sense of community within the gurukul while connecting students to the cosmic rhythms that governed Vedic spiritual practice. The lighting of the sacred fire (agnihotra) served both practical and symbolic purposes —providing light and warmth while representing the divine presence that blessed all learning activities.

Meals in the gurukul were simple but nutritionally complete, consisting primarily of rice, lentils, vegetables, milk, and fruits. The food was prepared collectively and consumed together, fostering a sense of equality and community among students from different backgrounds. The practice of eating together also served as an opportunity for informal teaching, as conversations during meals often touched on philosophical or practical topics.

The concept of anna brahma (food as divine) meant that meals were approached with reverence and gratitude. Students learned to see the interconnectedness of all life through their food—understanding how their sustenance depended on farmers, cattle, rain, and ultimately the divine grace that made all life possible.

Physical cleanliness and hygiene were emphasized not just for health reasons but as expressions of inner purity. Regular bathing, clean clothes, and orderly living spaces were seen as external manifestations of the disciplined mind that students were developing through their studies.

The practice of seva (service) was central to gurukul life and served multiple educational purposes. By participating in the maintenance of the ashram, students developed practical skills, learned the value of honest work, and cultivated humility. Whether collecting firewood, tending cattle, or cleaning the study areas, every task was approached as an opportunity for spiritual growth and character development.

The evening satsang sessions were perhaps the most cherished part of gurukul life. As the day's formal studies concluded and the sacred fire cast dancing shadows around the gathering place, students would sit with their guru for informal teaching, storytelling, and discussion. These sessions often featured tales from the Puranas or Itihasas, through which moral principles and spiritual insights were conveyed in memorable, engaging forms.

Seasonal festivals and celebrations were important aspects of gurukul life, connecting students to the broader cultural and spiritual traditions of their society. These occasions provided opportunities for artistic expression, community service, and the practical application of knowledge gained through study.

The gurukul also maintained connections with the broader community through various means. Traveling scholars would visit to share knowledge and engage in philosophical discussions. Local rulers and wealthy merchants might seek the guru's advice or blessing. These interactions helped students understand their future roles as educated members of society while exposing them to diverse perspectives and experiences.

The Art of Teaching- Pedagogical Methods and Approaches

The teaching methods employed in Vedic gurukulam were remarkably sophisticated and demonstrate deep understanding of human psychology and learning processes. Unlike modern educational systems that often employ standardized approaches, the gurukul system was inherently personalized, with gurus adapting their methods to the unique needs, temperament, and capabilities of individual students.

The foundation of all teaching was the oral tradition (shruti), which developed extraordinary methods for preserving and transmitting knowledge with perfect accuracy. The technique of svara (proper intonation) ensured that mantras were pronounced with precisely the right pitch, tone, and rhythm. Students learned not just the words of sacred texts but their proper musical expression, understanding that the sound itself carried spiritual power.

The method of repetitive recitation (abhyasa) served multiple purposes beyond mere memorization. Constant repetition created deep neural pathways that made knowledge instantly accessible while also inducing meditative states that facilitated spiritual development. The rhythm and musicality of Sanskrit verse made memorization easier while creating aesthetic pleasure that motivated continued learning.

Question and answer sessions (prashnottar) formed a crucial component of the teaching process. Gurus would pose challenging questions that required students to think deeply about what they had learned and apply it to new situations. The Upanishads themselves are largely structured as dialogues between teachers and students, demonstrating the importance placed on interactive learning.

The use of analogies and metaphors (upamana) was particularly sophisticated in Vedic teaching. Complex philosophical concepts were often explained through comparison with familiar objects or experiences, making abstract ideas concrete and understandable. The famous analogy of the two birds sitting on a tree branch (from the Mundaka Upanishad) brilliantly illustrates the relationship between the individual soul and universal consciousness.

Storytelling (kathakalakshepa) was perhaps the most engaging teaching method, especially effective for conveying moral and spiritual principles. The great epics—Ramayana and Mahabharata—served as vast repositories of stories that illustrated every conceivable human situation and the dharmic response to it. Students learned not just facts but wisdom through these narratives.

The practice of debate (vada-vivada) developed critical thinking skills and the ability to examine issues from multiple perspectives. Students were encouraged to question and challenge ideas, but always with respect and the genuine desire to arrive at truth. The formal rules of debate (tarka-shastra) ensured that discussions remained constructive and logical.

Meditation and contemplation (dhyana and manana) were integral to the learning process. Students were taught to move beyond mere intellectual understanding to direct, experiential knowledge. The guru would guide students through various meditation techniques appropriate to their temperament and level of development.

The principle of gradual progression (krama) ensured that students built knowledge systematically, with each new learning building upon previous understanding. Like constructing a building, the educational process began with strong foundations and gradually built toward more complex and subtle knowledge.

The guru employed different approaches for different types of students. The Mundaka Upanishad describes two categories of knowledge: para vidya (higher, spiritual knowledge) and apara vidya (lower, worldly knowledge). Depending on a student's capacity and inclination, the guru would emphasize different aspects of the curriculum while ensuring that all students received comprehensive education.

Assessment in the gurukul system was continuous and holistic rather than based on periodic examinations. Gurus observed students constantly, noting not just their intellectual progress but their character development, practical skills, and spiritual growth. The ability to recite texts perfectly, engage in meaningful discussions, and demonstrate moral integrity were all considered equally important measures of educational success.

Student-Teacher Relationships- The Sacred Bond

The relationship between guru and student (guru-shishya sambandha) in the Vedic educational system transcended the simple transmission of information to become one of the most sacred and transformative bonds recognized in human society. This relationship was understood to be divinely ordained, with both parties having specific duties and responsibilities that extended far beyond the formal educational period.

The Sanskrit verse "Matru devo bhava, Pitru devo bhava, Acharya devo bhava" (Treat your mother as divine, father as divine, and teacher as divine) places the guru in the exalted company of parents, reflecting the belief that while parents gave physical birth, the guru granted spiritual birth through the gift of knowledge and wisdom.

For the student, the relationship began with complete surrender and devotion (shraddha). This was not blind submission but rather the recognition that genuine learning required humility and openness. The ego, which often blocks receptivity to new ideas, had to be surrendered for true education to occur. The traditional gesture of touching the guru's feet (sashtanga pranam) symbolized this humility and the student's readiness to receive knowledge.

The guru, in accepting a student, undertook enormous responsibility. He became not just a teacher but a spiritual parent, responsible for the student's physical welfare, intellectual development, moral character, and spiritual evolution. This comprehensive responsibility meant that gurus were extremely selective in choosing students, as they were committing to a relationship that would last a lifetime.

The daily interactions between guru and student were characterized by profound respect, affection, and mutual care. The guru observed each student closely, understanding his strengths, weaknesses, fears, and aspirations. This intimate knowledge allowed for personalized guidance that addressed not just academic needs but the total development of the individual.

The tradition of guru seva (service to the teacher) was central to this relationship. Students performed various services for their guru—from simple household tasks to more complex responsibilities like assisting in teaching younger students. This service was not exploitation but rather a means of expressing gratitude while developing humility, practical skills, and the understanding that knowledge comes through dedicated effort and sacrifice.

The guru's teaching often extended beyond formal instruction to include guidance on every aspect of life. Students learned not just from what their guru taught but from observing how he lived, how he handled challenges, how he interacted with others, and how he embodied the principles he taught. This modeling of ideal behavior was perhaps the most powerful teaching method of all.

The relationship was also characterized by intense emotional bonds. Many ancient texts describe the deep affection between gurus and students, with gurus often treating students like their own children and students regarding their guru with filial love and respect. This emotional connection created motivation for learning and made the educational experience deeply meaningful and memorable.

Discipline within this relationship was maintained through moral authority rather than external force. Students obeyed their guru not from fear but from respect and recognition of his wisdom and benevolence. When correction was necessary, it was administered with love and explanation, helping students understand why certain behaviors were inappropriate rather than simply punishing them.

The guru-student relationship also included an element of testing and challenge. Gurus often put their students through various trials to assess their commitment, character, and readiness for advanced knowledge. These tests were designed not to humiliate but to strengthen and prepare students for the responsibilities that would come with their education.

The tradition of guru-dakshina (offering to the teacher) at the completion of education symbolized the culmination of this sacred relationship while marking its transformation into a different phase.

Interestingly, gurus often requested not material wealth but something that would benefit society or test the student's character—demonstrating that the true purpose of education was service to the larger good.

Even after formal education ended, the guru-student relationship continued. Students were expected to honor their guru throughout their lives, seek his blessings on important occasions, and support him in old age if necessary. Many successful students established their own gurukulam, continuing the lineage of knowledge transmission (guru parampara) and ensuring that their guru's teachings reached future generations.

Graduation and the Sacred Gift- Guru Dakshina

The completion of education in the gurukul system was marked by one of the most significant and symbolic traditions in Vedic culture—the offering of guru dakshina. This practice, far from being a simple payment for services rendered, represented the culmination of the sacred guru-student relationship and the student's transformation from receiver to giver of knowledge.

The term "dakshina" derives from the Sanskrit root meaning "right" or "skilled," indicating that this offering should be appropriate, thoughtful, and demonstrate the student's understanding of what he had received. Unlike modern tuition fees paid at the beginning of education, guru dakshina came at the end, after the student had fully experienced the value of his education and could offer something meaningful in return.

The timing of this offering was significant. It typically occurred during the samavartana ceremony, which marked the student's formal graduation and return to worldly life. This ritual transformation from brahmachari (student) to grihastha (householder) was accompanied by various ceremonies including ritual baths, new clothing, and the guru's final blessings and instructions for life.

What makes the tradition of guru dakshina particularly fascinating is that the amount and nature of the offering was entirely at the guru's discretion. Students would approach their guru and ask, "Guravo, kim dakshina?" (O teacher, what is my dakshina?). The guru's response often revealed his deep understanding of the student's character, capabilities, and the lessons that still needed to be learned.

Historical and mythological accounts provide remarkable examples of guru dakshina that illuminate the spiritual and moral dimensions of this practice. The story of Ekalavya, who offered his thumb to Dronacharya, illustrates how dakshina could involve profound personal sacrifice. While this particular story raises complex questions about social justice, it demonstrates the principle that guru dakshina should represent the student's most valued possession or capability.

In the Chandogya Upanishad, we find the story of Aruni, whose guru asked him to repair a breach in a field's embankment. When conventional methods failed, Aruni lay down in the breach himself, using his body to stop the water flow. This act of complete dedication and creative problem-solving pleased his guru so much that he blessed Aruni with supreme knowledge. Here, the dakshina was not a formal offering but the demonstration of total commitment to the guru's instruction.

Sometimes guru dakshina took the form of a challenging task that would benefit society. A guru might ask his student to establish a school in a remote area, serve a particular community, or undertake a difficult mission that would utilize and further develop the student's education. Such requests ensured that the knowledge received would be shared with others rather than hoarded for personal benefit.

The tradition also included instances where gurus asked for something that would complete the student's character development. A proud student might be asked to serve humbly in a menial capacity, while a timid student might be challenged to undertake something requiring courage and initiative. These requests served as final examinations that tested not just knowledge but character and wisdom.

Interestingly, many great gurus refused material wealth as dakshina, recognizing that knowledge was priceless and could not be repaid with money. Some gurus specifically asked that their students pass on their knowledge freely to others, ensuring the continuation of the guru-shishya parampara. This practice reflected the understanding that knowledge belonged not to individuals but to humanity as a whole.

The psychological and spiritual impact of guru dakshina was profound. It marked the student's transition from receiver to giver, from dependent to contributor. The act of offering something significant in return for their education helped students internalize the value of what they had received while preparing them for their roles as responsible members of society.

For gurus, the dakshina served as validation of their teaching effectiveness and provided resources for continuing their educational mission. However, the most valued dakshina was often not material but the success and character of the students themselves. A guru's greatest satisfaction came from seeing his students become exemplary individuals who embodied and transmitted the values and knowledge they had received.

The tradition of guru dakshina also reinforced the cyclical nature of knowledge transmission. Students who received freely were expected to give freely in return, ensuring that knowledge continued to flow through society. This created a sustainable system where education was supported not by external funding but by the gratitude and contribution of those who had benefited from it.

In contemporary times, while the formal practice of guru dakshina has largely disappeared, its underlying principles remain relevant. The idea that education creates obligations, that knowledge should be shared rather than hoarded, and that students should give back to their educational institutions and teachers continues to influence Indian educational culture.

The Decline and Transformation of the Gurukul System

The gurukul system, which had flourished for over two millennia, began experiencing significant challenges and transformations during the later Vedic period and especially during the medieval era. Understanding this decline requires examining the complex interplay of social, political, economic, and cultural factors that gradually undermined the foundations upon which this educational system had been built.

One of the earliest challenges came from within Vedic society itself through the increasing rigidification of the caste system. While early Vedic education had shown some flexibility in admitting students based on merit and inclination, later periods witnessed growing restrictions based on birth. The principle of varnaashrama dharma, which originally emphasized duty and function, gradually became hereditary and exclusionary. This transformation limited access to higher education and reduced the diversity of perspectives and talents within gurukulam.

The rise of urbanization and commercial activity during the later Vedic period created new demands for education that the traditional gurukul system struggled to meet. As society became more complex and specialized, there was growing need for practical, technical, and commercial education that the classical curriculum, focused primarily on religious and philosophical studies, did not adequately address. This gap led to the emergence of alternative educational institutions and approaches.

The advent of Buddhism and Jainism in the 6th century BCE represented both a challenge to and an evolution of the gurukul tradition. These new religious movements established their own educational institutions—Buddhist viharas and Jain upashayas—which, while borrowing many features from the gurukul system, offered more egalitarian access to education and emphasized different philosophical perspectives. The success of these institutions demonstrated both the limitations of the traditional system and the continuing demand for spiritual and intellectual education.

The establishment of great universities like Nalanda, Takshashila, and Vikramashila marked a significant evolution in Indian education. These institutions, while maintaining many gurukul principles, introduced new elements: larger scale operations, more diverse faculty, structured curricula, formal degrees, and international exchange. While these developments enriched Indian education, they also began the process of institutionalizing learning in ways that differed from the intimate, personalized gurukul model.

Foreign invasions, beginning with the Greeks under Alexander and continuing through various Central Asian rulers, disrupted the traditional social and cultural order that supported the gurukul system. Many ancient seats of learning were destroyed, learned families were displaced, and the patronage system that supported gurus was undermined. While Indian culture showed remarkable resilience and adaptability, these disruptions had cumulative effects on traditional educational institutions.

The medieval Islamic period brought both challenges and opportunities. While some rulers were hostile to traditional Indian learning, others were remarkably supportive, leading to interesting syntheses of different educational traditions. The translation movement, where Sanskrit texts were translated into Arabic and Persian, helped preserve some aspects of Indian knowledge while transforming others. However, the overall effect was to marginalize traditional Sanskrit education and reduce its social relevance.

The arrival of European colonial powers marked the beginning of the most dramatic transformation in Indian education. The British, in particular, introduced a completely different educational philosophy based on Macaulay's famous minute of 1835, which explicitly aimed to create "a class of persons Indian in blood and color, but English in taste, in opinions, words and intellect." This approach directly challenged the foundations of traditional Indian education.

The colonial educational system emphasized English language, Western knowledge systems, and preparation for administrative and commercial roles within the colonial framework. Government support and recognition shifted decisively toward these new institutions, while traditional gurukulam found themselves increasingly marginalized and unsupported. The introduction of formal examination systems, standardized curricula, and institutional degrees created a new paradigm that made traditional education seem outdated and irrelevant.

Economic factors also played a crucial role in the decline. The colonial economic system disrupted traditional patronage networks that had supported gurus and their ashrams. Land revenue policies often impoverished the rural communities and wealthy families who had historically supported traditional education. Simultaneously, new economic opportunities in the colonial administration and modern commerce required different skills and knowledge than what traditional gurukulam provided.

The introduction of the printing press, while revolutionary in making knowledge more accessible, also undermined one of the key strengths of the gurukul system—the oral tradition. As books became available, the need for human repositories of knowledge decreased, and the intimate relationship between teacher and student that had characterized the gurukul system became less essential for knowledge transmission.

Social reform movements of the 19th and early 20th centuries, while progressive in many ways, often viewed traditional educational systems as obstacles to modernization and social progress. Reformers like Ram Mohan Roy, while deeply appreciative of Indian philosophical traditions, advocated for Westernstyle education as necessary for India's advancement. This perspective, though well-intentioned, contributed to the marginalization of traditional learning systems.

However, it's important to note that the gurukul system didn't simply disappear but rather transformed and adapted. Many of its principles and methods found new expression in modern Indian educational institutions. The emphasis on character development, the importance of the teacher-student relationship, and the integration of moral and spiritual values with academic learning continued to influence Indian educational philosophy.

Legacy and Contemporary Relevance

Despite its historical decline as a dominant educational system, the gurukul tradition has left an indelible mark on Indian civilization and continues to offer valuable insights for contemporary education. The fundamental principles underlying this ancient system remain remarkably relevant to modern educational challenges and have begun attracting renewed attention from educators and policymakers worldwide.

The holistic approach of gurukul education, which viewed human development as encompassing intellectual, moral, spiritual, and practical dimensions, offers a compelling alternative to the often fragmented nature of modern education. Contemporary educational theorists increasingly recognize the limitations of purely academic or technical education that neglects character development and spiritual growth. The gurukul model's integration of these various aspects of human development provides a framework for creating more complete and meaningful educational experiences.

The personalized nature of gurukul education, where teaching was adapted to individual students' needs, temperaments, and capabilities, anticipates many principles of contemporary educational psychology. Modern concepts like multiple intelligences, differentiated instruction, and personalized learning paths echo the ancient understanding that students are unique individuals requiring customized approaches to education.

The emphasis on experiential learning in the gurukul system, where students learned through direct participation in various activities rather than passive reception of information, aligns with contemporary educational research emphasizing active learning, project-based education, and hands-on experience.

The integration of theoretical knowledge with practical application remains a key challenge in modern education.

The community-based nature of gurukul education, where students lived and learned together in a supportive environment, offers insights for addressing contemporary concerns about social isolation and lack of community in modern educational settings. The emphasis on service (seva) and social responsibility built into the gurukul system provides models for developing civic engagement and social consciousness among students.

The environmental setting of traditional gurukulam, located in natural surroundings and emphasizing harmony with nature, resonates strongly with contemporary environmental consciousness and the growing recognition that connection with nature is essential for human well-being and learning.

Several modern educational initiatives have explicitly drawn inspiration from the gurukul model while adapting it to contemporary needs and contexts. In India, institutions like the Gurukul Kangri University, various schools run by the Arya Samaj, and numerous ashram schools attempt to revive gurukul principles within modern educational frameworks. These institutions typically emphasize value-based education, close teacher-student relationships, residential learning communities, and the integration of traditional wisdom with contemporary knowledge.

Internationally, educational approaches like Waldorf/Steiner education, Montessori methods, and various alternative education movements share many principles with the gurukul system, including respect for individual development, integration of academic and practical learning, and emphasis on moral and spiritual development alongside intellectual growth.

The growing interest in mindfulness and contemplative practices in education reflects another area where gurukul wisdom remains relevant. The traditional emphasis on meditation, self-reflection, and inner development as integral parts of education is being rediscovered by educators seeking to address stress, attention issues, and the need for deeper meaning in learning.

However, any attempt to revive or adapt gurukul principles must also honestly confront the limitations and problems of the historical system. The exclusionary aspects based on caste and gender, the potential for abuse of authority in highly hierarchical relationships, and the challenges of scaling intimate, personalized education to serve large populations are serious concerns that require careful attention.

Modern adaptations of gurukul principles must also address contemporary realities including technological advancement, global interconnectedness, democratic values, and the need for education that prepares students for rapidly changing economic and social conditions. The challenge is to preserve the valuable insights of the ancient system while adapting them to serve contemporary needs and values.

Conclusion- The Eternal Teacher-Student Journey

The gurukul system of ancient India represents one of humanity's most comprehensive and sophisticated approaches to education, embodying a vision of learning that encompassed not merely the transmission of information but the complete transformation of human beings. Through its emphasis on the sacred relationship between teacher and student, its integration of intellectual, moral, and spiritual development, and its understanding of education as a lifelong journey rather than a temporary preparation for life, the gurukul tradition offers timeless insights into the nature of authentic learning and human growth.

The genius of the gurukul system lay not in any single innovation but in its holistic integration of numerous elements: the carefully designed environment that supported learning; the profound relationship between guru and student that went far beyond mere instruction; the curriculum that balanced sacred and practical knowledge; the methods that engaged multiple dimensions of human intelligence; the community life that fostered character development; and the understanding that true education must serve not only individual fulfillment but the welfare of society as a whole.

Perhaps most significantly, the gurukul system recognized that education is fundamentally a spiritual endeavor—not in the narrow sense of religious doctrine, but in the deeper understanding that learning involves the awakening and development of human consciousness itself. The transformation of students from ignorance to knowledge, from selfishness to service, from bondage to freedom was seen as a sacred process worthy of the highest respect and care.

While the classical gurukul system was a product of its time and reflected the limitations as well as the wisdom of ancient Indian society, its core insights remain profoundly relevant. In an era when education is increasingly commodified, standardized, and divorced from deeper human values, the gurukul tradition reminds us that authentic learning requires relationship, reverence, and recognition of the sacred dimension of human development.

The challenges facing contemporary education—from the crisis of meaning and purpose among students to the difficulties of developing character and wisdom alongside intellectual capabilities—are remarkably similar to those addressed by the gurukul system thousands of years ago. While we cannot and should not attempt to recreate the ancient system in its historical form, we can learn from its insights and adapt its wisdom to contemporary needs.

The relationship between teacher and student, characterized by mutual respect, love, and commitment to truth, remains as relevant today as it was in ancient times. The understanding that education should serve the development of complete human beings rather than merely skilled workers continues to challenge educational systems worldwide. The integration of contemplative practices, moral development, and service to society with academic learning offers a path toward more meaningful and effective education.

As we face unprecedented global challenges requiring both technical expertise and deep wisdom, the gurukul vision of education as transformation rather than mere information transfer becomes increasingly compelling. The ancient recognition that those who receive the gift of knowledge have a responsibility to serve and teach others remains essential for creating sustainable and just educational systems.

The story of the gurukul system is ultimately the story of humanity's eternal quest for wisdom, meaning, and authentic human development. While the specific forms may change, the underlying principles—the sacred nature of learning, the importance of transformative relationships, the integration of knowledge with character, and the understanding that education serves both individual fulfillment and collective welfare—remain as relevant today as they were in the forest ashrams of ancient India.

In honoring the legacy of the gurukul tradition, we honor the countless gurus and students who dedicated their lives to the preservation and transmission of knowledge, wisdom, and culture. Their commitment to learning as a sacred endeavor continues to inspire all who recognize that education, at its best, is not merely about preparing for a career but about awakening the full potential of human consciousness and contributing to the welfare of all beings.

The eternal conversation between teacher and student, seeker and guide, continues in every genuine educational encounter. The gurukul system reminds us that this conversation is sacred, that it requires our highest attention and care, and that through it, the light of knowledge continues to illuminate the path toward wisdom, compassion, and freedom for all humanity.

8
Education in the Vedic Period

The Gurukula System and Its Comprehensive Curriculum

The Vedic period (approximately 1500-600 BCE) stands as one of the most formative epochs in Indian civilization, laying the foundational stones for education, philosophy, religion, and social organization that would influence the subcontinent for millennia to come. During this era, education was not merely the transmission of information but a comprehensive system of human development that sought to create individuals capable of understanding the cosmos, society, and their place within both. The gurukula system, which emerged during this period, represented one of humanity's earliest and most sophisticated educational frameworks, combining intellectual rigor with spiritual development, practical skills with philosophical inquiry.

The term "gurukula" derives from two Sanskrit words: "guru" (teacher) and "kula" (family or home), literally meaning the teacher's family or household. This system was far more than an educational institution in the modern sense; it was a complete way of life where students lived with their teacher for extended periods, typically ranging from twelve to sixteen years, absorbing not only knowledge but also values, ethics, and the subtle aspects of character formation that could only be transmitted through intimate daily interaction.

The curriculum of these ancient centers of learning was remarkably comprehensive, encompassing what we might today call the humanities, sciences, arts, and professional training. Students studied the Vedas as the core texts, but their education extended far beyond religious instruction to include Itihasas (historical narratives), Upasanas (worship and spiritual practices), and a vast array of subjects that prepared them for various roles in society. This holistic approach to education created individuals who were not merely specialists in one field but were equipped with the broad knowledge and wisdom necessary to contribute meaningfully to their communities.

The significance of Vedic education extends far beyond its historical importance. Many of its principles and methods continue to influence educational thought today, offering insights into the nature of learning, the teacher-student relationship, and the ultimate purposes of education that remain relevant in our contemporary world.

The Philosophical Foundation of Vedic Education

The Vedic educational system was built upon profound philosophical foundations that viewed education as a sacred duty and a transformative process. The fundamental principle underlying this system was the concept of "vidya" - knowledge that liberates. This was distinguished from mere "avidya" or ignorance, but more importantly, from superficial information that might inform the mind without transforming the individual.

The sages who developed this system believed that true education must address the whole human being - body, mind, and spirit. They recognized that knowledge without wisdom could be dangerous, that intellectual development without moral development could lead to societal harm, and that learning without practical application remained incomplete. This holistic vision shaped every aspect of the gurukula system, from its daily routines to its ultimate objectives.

Central to Vedic educational philosophy was the concept of "dharma" - righteous duty or the natural order. Education was seen as the means by which individuals discovered their dharma and developed the capacity to fulfill it. This was not a rigid predetermination but rather a process of discovering one's natural talents, inclinations, and the role one was best suited to play in the cosmic and social order.

The relationship between teacher and student was viewed as sacred, governed by the principle of "gurushishya parampara" - the continuous tradition of knowledge transmission from teacher to student. The guru was not merely an instructor but a spiritual guide who took responsibility for the student's complete development. The student, in turn, was expected to approach learning with humility, dedication, and complete trust in the teacher's guidance.

This philosophical framework created an educational environment that was both demanding and nurturing, challenging students to reach their highest potential while providing the support and guidance necessary for their development. The ultimate goal was not merely the accumulation of knowledge but the transformation of the individual into a wise, capable, and virtuous member of society.

The Structure and Organization of Gurukulas

The physical and organizational structure of gurukulas reflected the educational philosophy that guided them. These institutions were typically located in natural settings, away from the distractions of urban life, often in forest clearings near rivers or in mountainous regions where the beauty and tranquility of nature could contribute to the learning environment. The ashram, as these educational communities were called, consisted of simple dwellings for the guru and students, spaces for study and discussion, areas for practical activities, and often facilities for various crafts and occupations.

The daily routine in a gurukula was carefully structured to maximize learning while maintaining physical and mental health. Students typically rose before dawn, beginning their day with prayers and meditation. This was followed by physical exercises and personal hygiene, after which the formal study period began. The morning hours, when the mind was fresh and alert, were devoted to the most challenging subjects typically the memorization and recitation of Vedic texts.

The afternoon might be spent in discussion and interpretation of the texts studied in the morning, practical activities such as agriculture or crafts, or instruction in specialized subjects according to the student's aptitude and intended vocation. Evenings were often devoted to storytelling, music, or other cultural activities that reinforced the lessons learned during the day while providing recreation and community bonding.

The organizational structure of gurukulas was hierarchical but not rigid. The guru held ultimate authority, but senior students often assisted in teaching junior ones, creating a system of peer learning and mentorship. Students were grouped not necessarily by age but by their level of advancement in particular subjects, allowing for more personalized instruction and enabling advanced students to progress at their own pace.

The economic model of gurukulas was based on the principle of "gurudakshina" - the offering made to the teacher at the completion of studies. During their time at the ashram, students contributed to their maintenance through various forms of work, making the community largely self-sufficient. This system ensured that education was available to all qualified students regardless of their family's economic status, while also teaching them the value of work and contribution to community welfare.

The Core Curriculum- Vedas as the Foundation

At the heart of Vedic education lay the study of the Vedas themselves - the Rigveda, Samaveda, Yajurveda, and Atharveda. These ancient texts, composed over several centuries, contained not only hymns and ritual instructions but also profound philosophical insights, astronomical observations, mathematical concepts, and practical knowledge about medicine, agriculture, and governance.

The study of the Vedas began with memorization, a process that might seem mechanical to modern educators but served multiple purposes in the Vedic system. First, it preserved the texts with remarkable accuracy across generations, as the oral tradition was considered more reliable than written records, which could be corrupted or destroyed. Second, the process of memorization itself was viewed as a form of mental discipline that developed concentration, memory, and precision. Third, having the texts committed to memory allowed for deeper contemplation and understanding, as students could reflect on the verses during any quiet moment.

The Rigveda, the oldest of the Vedas, contained over a thousand hymns addressed to various deities, but students learned to see beyond the surface religious content to the deeper philosophical and scientific insights contained within. They studied the cosmological hymns that described the creation of the universe, the philosophical speculation about the nature of reality, and the social and political ideals embedded in the prayers for righteous rulers and just society.

The Samaveda focused on the musical aspects of Vedic recitation, teaching students not only the melodies but also the theory of music, the relationship between sound and consciousness, and the practical applications of music in ritual and healing. This study developed aesthetic sensibilities and understanding of the power of sound and vibration.

The Yajurveda provided instruction in ritual procedures, but students learned to understand these not as mere ceremonies but as sophisticated technologies for focusing the mind, creating community cohesion, and maintaining cosmic harmony. The study included detailed knowledge of altar construction, which involved advanced geometric principles, and the timing of rituals, which required astronomical knowledge.

The Atharvaveda, often considered the most practical of the Vedas, contained hymns related to daily life, medicine, magic, and popular religion. Through its study, students gained knowledge of herbalism, psychology, and the practical application of spiritual principles to everyday problems.

Itihasas- Learning Through Historical Narratives

The study of Itihasas - historical narratives and epic literature - formed a crucial component of Vedic education, serving multiple pedagogical purposes that extended far beyond mere entertainment or cultural preservation. These stories, which included early versions of what would later become the great epics Ramayana and Mahabharata, as well as numerous Puranic tales and genealogical accounts, were sophisticated educational tools that conveyed complex moral, philosophical, and practical lessons through engaging narratives.

The pedagogical approach used in teaching Itihasas was remarkably sophisticated. Rather than simply narrating stories, teachers used them as case studies for ethical analysis, encouraging students to examine the motivations of characters, the consequences of their actions, and the underlying principles that governed success and failure, happiness and suffering. Students learned to identify with noble characters while understanding the flaws that led to the downfall of others, developing moral imagination and ethical reasoning skills.

These narratives served as repositories of practical wisdom about governance, leadership, interpersonal relationships, and crisis management. The stories of kings and queens, sages and warriors, merchants and farmers provided students with vicarious experience in dealing with a wide range of human situations they might encounter in their own lives. The detailed descriptions of how wise rulers managed their kingdoms, how conflicts were resolved, and how communities dealt with challenges provided practical education in statecraft, diplomacy, and social organization.

The Itihasas also served an important function in developing students' understanding of dharma righteous duty - in all its complexity. Through stories that presented moral dilemmas without easy answers, students learned that ethical behavior often required careful consideration of context, competing obligations, and long-term consequences. They developed the capacity for moral reasoning that would serve them throughout their lives.

Furthermore, these narratives were vehicles for transmitting cultural memory and collective identity. They connected students to their ancestral heritage while providing models of exemplary behavior and cautionary tales of moral failure. The genealogical portions helped students understand their place in the ongoing stream of history and their responsibilities to past and future generations.

Upasanas- The Science of Spiritual Practice

Upasanas - worship and spiritual practices - constituted a vital dimension of Vedic education, representing not merely religious observance but a systematic science of consciousness development and inner transformation. The term "upasana" literally means "sitting near" or "approaching closely," indicating the intimate, experiential nature of these practices that brought students into direct contact with deeper dimensions of reality.

The study of Upasanas began with understanding the theoretical foundations of spiritual practice. Students learned about the nature of consciousness, the relationship between individual and universal awareness, and the principles governing inner development. They studied the symbolism of various deities not as external beings to be worshipped but as representations of different aspects of cosmic consciousness and inner psychological states.

Practical instruction in Upasanas included various forms of meditation, from simple concentration practices to sophisticated techniques for exploring different states of consciousness. Students learned pranayama - breath control practices that were understood to influence not only physical health but also mental states and spiritual awareness. They practiced mantra recitation, understanding how specific sound combinations could focus the mind and invoke particular qualities of consciousness.

The study of yajna - sacrificial rituals - formed an important component of Upasana education, but students learned to understand these practices on multiple levels. While they mastered the external procedures for conducting various rituals, they also understood the inner significance of each element, seeing the external ritual as a map for inner transformation. The lighting of the sacred fire represented the awakening of inner wisdom, the offering of ghee symbolized the surrender of ego, and the recitation of mantras created specific states of consciousness.

Students also learned about the relationship between Upasana and daily life, understanding how spiritual principles could be applied to ordinary activities. They learned to see work as worship, relationships as opportunities for spiritual growth, and challenges as chances to develop inner strength and wisdom. This integration of spiritual practice with daily life was considered essential for authentic spiritual development.

The ultimate goal of Upasana education was not otherworldly escape but the development of individuals who could function effectively in the world while maintaining connection to deeper sources of wisdom and compassion. Students learned to cultivate qualities such as equanimity, compassion, courage, and wisdom that would serve them in all aspects of life.

The Vedangas: Auxiliary Sciences

The Vedangas - literally "limbs of the Vedas" - represented six auxiliary sciences that were considered essential for the proper understanding and application of Vedic knowledge. These subjects - Shiksha (phonetics), Vyakarana (grammar), Chhanda (prosody), Nirukta (etymology), Jyotisha (astronomy), and Kalpa (ritual procedures) - provided students with the technical skills necessary for mastering the Vedic tradition while also developing their analytical and scientific thinking abilities.

Shiksha, the science of phonetics and pronunciation, was fundamental to Vedic education because the tradition emphasized the precise recitation of sacred texts. Students learned not only correct pronunciation but also the subtle effects of different sounds on consciousness and the environment. They studied the anatomy of speech production, the classification of sounds, and the rules governing sound combination and modification. This training developed extraordinary precision in language use and sensitivity to the power of spoken words.

Vyakarana, or grammar, provided students with sophisticated tools for language analysis and clear expression. The study of Sanskrit grammar, as systematized by Panini and other ancient grammarians, was considered one of the highest intellectual achievements of the time. Students learned to analyze the structure of language, understand the relationships between words and meanings, and express complex ideas with precision and elegance. This training developed logical thinking skills and attention to detail that served them well in all areas of study.

Chhanda, the study of prosody or poetic meter, taught students about rhythm, balance, and aesthetic principles that applied not only to poetry but to all aspects of life. They learned to recognize different metrical patterns, understand their emotional and spiritual effects, and compose their own verses. This study developed aesthetic sensitivity and understanding of the relationship between form and content, beauty and meaning.

Nirukta, or etymology, involved the scientific study of word origins and semantic development. Students learned to trace words back to their roots, understand how meanings evolved over time, and recognize the deep connections between apparently different concepts. This study developed historical consciousness and understanding of the evolution of human thought and culture.

Jyotisha, astronomy and astrology, provided students with scientific knowledge about celestial movements and their correlation with earthly events. They learned mathematical techniques for calculating planetary positions, understanding seasonal changes, and determining auspicious times for various activities. This study developed mathematical skills and understanding of natural cycles and cosmic relationships.

Kalpa, the science of ritual procedures, taught students the precise methods for conducting various ceremonies and observances. They learned not only the external procedures but also their inner significance and the principles governing their effectiveness. This study developed organizational skills, attention to detail, and understanding of the relationship between individual actions and cosmic harmony.

The Upavedas: Applied Sciences and Arts

The Upavedas represented applied branches of Vedic knowledge that prepared students for various professional and practical aspects of life. These four major divisions - Ayurveda (medicine and health sciences), Dhanurveda (military science and archery), Gandharvaveda (music and performing arts), and Sthapatyaveda (architecture and engineering) - demonstrated the practical orientation of Vedic education and its concern with preparing students for effective participation in all aspects of civilized life.

Ayurveda, the science of life and longevity, provided students with comprehensive understanding of health, disease, and healing. They studied human anatomy and physiology, the properties of medicinal plants and minerals, diagnostic techniques, and therapeutic procedures. The Ayurvedic approach was holistic, considering physical, mental, and spiritual dimensions of health and emphasizing prevention rather than merely treatment of disease. Students learned to understand the human body as a microcosm of the universe, governed by the same principles that operated in the cosmos.

The study of Ayurveda included practical training in pulse diagnosis, herbal medicine preparation, surgical procedures, and therapeutic practices such as massage, yoga, and meditation. Students also learned about nutrition, lifestyle practices that promoted health, and the relationship between mental states and physical well-being. This comprehensive medical education produced practitioners who could address the full range of human health needs.

Dhanurveda, the martial sciences, prepared students for the responsibilities of protection and defense that were essential in ancient society. They learned not only archery and weapons handling but also strategy, tactics, and the ethics of warfare. The training emphasized that martial skills should be used only for protection of the innocent and maintenance of dharmic order, never for aggression or personal gain.

Students practiced with various weapons, learned hand-to-hand combat techniques, studied military organization and logistics, and developed the physical fitness and mental discipline necessary for effective warriors. They also learned about diplomacy and conflict resolution, understanding that the highest skill lay in preventing conflicts rather than winning them.

Gandharvaveda encompassed music, dance, drama, and other performing arts that were considered essential for cultural refinement and spiritual development. Students learned to play various instruments, understood the theory of music including scales, rhythms, and their emotional and spiritual effects, and practiced vocal techniques. They also studied dance, which was seen as a form of moving meditation and prayer, and dramatic arts that could convey profound truths through entertainment.

The study of performing arts was not merely aesthetic but was understood to have therapeutic and spiritual dimensions. Different musical modes were believed to have specific effects on consciousness and could be used for healing or spiritual awakening. Dance and drama provided ways of embodying spiritual truths and sharing them with the community.

Sthapatyaveda, architecture and engineering, taught students the principles of design, construction, and urban planning that created environments supportive of human flourishing. They learned about the properties of different building materials, structural engineering principles, aesthetic guidelines, and the subtle influences of architectural forms on human consciousness and behavior.

Students studied temple architecture, understanding how sacred buildings could facilitate spiritual experience through their proportions, orientations, and decorative elements. They also learned about residential and civic architecture, city planning principles that promoted health and harmony, and engineering techniques for water management, agriculture, and transportation.

Teaching Methods and Pedagogical Approaches

The pedagogical methods employed in Vedic gurukulas were sophisticated and varied, adapted to the different subjects being taught and the individual needs of students. The primary method was oral instruction, which took several forms depending on the nature of the material and the stage of the student's development.

For the basic memorization of Vedic texts, teachers used repetitive recitation techniques that helped students commit vast amounts of material to memory. These sessions were conducted in groups, with students reciting together in various patterns - sometimes in unison, sometimes in overlapping sequences, and sometimes in question-and-answer formats that reinforced the material through multiple repetitions.

Once students had mastered the basic texts, instruction moved to interpretation and analysis. Teachers used dialogue and questioning techniques that encouraged students to think deeply about the material, explore its implications, and connect it to other areas of knowledge. The Socratic method, though not known by that name, was widely used to help students discover insights for themselves rather than merely receiving information passively.

Practical subjects were taught through direct experience and apprenticeship. Students learning medicine accompanied their teachers on visits to patients, observed diagnostic and treatment procedures, and gradually took on increasing responsibility under supervision. Those studying crafts or arts worked alongside master craftsmen, learning through imitation, practice, and gradual mastery of increasingly complex techniques.

Storytelling was used as a powerful pedagogical tool, not only for transmitting cultural values but also for developing imagination, memory, and moral reasoning. Teachers were skilled narrators who could adapt stories to their audience, emphasize different themes, and encourage students to extract various levels of meaning from the same narrative.

Debate and discussion were encouraged as means of developing critical thinking and communication skills. Students learned to present arguments clearly, respond to challenges thoughtfully, and modify their positions when presented with better evidence or reasoning. These intellectual exercises developed both analytical abilities and intellectual humility.

Field trips and pilgrimages provided opportunities for experiential learning that complemented classroom instruction.

Students might travel to different regions to observe various customs and practices, visit sacred sites to deepen their spiritual understanding, or journey to centers of learning to engage with other teachers and students.

The teacher-student relationship was characterized by personal attention and individualized instruction. Teachers observed their students carefully, identifying their particular talents, interests, and learning styles, and adapted their instruction accordingly. This personal approach ensured that each student could develop their full potential while receiving the support they needed for their particular challenges.

Assessment and Evaluation

The evaluation of student progress in Vedic gurukulas was comprehensive and multifaceted, focusing not merely on intellectual achievement but on the complete development of the student as a human being. Assessment was ongoing rather than concentrated in formal examinations, and it emphasized practical demonstration of knowledge and skills rather than abstract testing.

The memorization of Vedic texts was evaluated through regular recitation sessions where students demonstrated their mastery of assigned portions. Teachers listened not only for accuracy of recall but also for proper pronunciation, appropriate rhythm and intonation, and evidence of understanding through the student's expression and emphasis.

Understanding and interpretation were assessed through questioning and discussion sessions where students demonstrated their ability to explain the meaning of texts, connect different passages, and apply the principles they had learned to new situations. Teachers looked for evidence of genuine comprehension rather than mere repetition of explanations they had heard.

Practical skills were evaluated through direct observation of student performance in real-world situations. Medical students were assessed by their ability to diagnose and treat actual patients, architecture students by their success in designing and supervising construction projects, and students of statecraft by their performance in handling administrative responsibilities.

Character development and moral growth were evaluated through observation of student behavior in various situations, particularly those involving challenges, temptations, or conflicts. Teachers looked for evidence of the virtues that Vedic education was meant to cultivate - truthfulness, compassion, courage, self-discipline, and wisdom.

The final assessment came at the completion of studies in the form of a comprehensive demonstration of the student's knowledge and abilities. This might involve public recitation of major texts, demonstration of practical skills, or presentation of original work that showed the student's mastery and creative application of what they had learned.

The ultimate validation of a student's education, however, came not from any formal assessment but from their subsequent contributions to society. The true test of Vedic education was whether it produced individuals who could fulfill their dharmic responsibilities effectively, contribute to the welfare of their communities, and continue the tradition of learning by passing their knowledge on to the next generation.

Impact and Legacy

The impact of the Vedic educational system extended far beyond the period of its initial development, influencing educational thought and practice throughout Indian history and continuing to offer insights relevant to contemporary educational challenges. The principles and methods developed in the gurukulas provided a foundation for later educational developments while establishing ideals that have continued to inspire educators across cultures and centuries.

The emphasis on holistic development - addressing intellectual, physical, emotional, and spiritual dimensions of human growth - established a model of comprehensive education that contrasted sharply with more narrowly focused systems. This holistic approach recognized that true education must develop the complete human being, not merely train specialists or impart information.

The integration of theoretical knowledge with practical application, exemplified in the study of both Vedas and Upavedas, demonstrated the importance of connecting learning to real-world needs and applications. Students were prepared not only to understand their world but to contribute effectively to its improvement and maintenance.

The personalized approach to instruction, with its emphasis on individual mentorship and adaptation to student needs, established principles of differentiated instruction that remain relevant today. The recognition that different students have different learning styles, interests, and potentials, and that effective education must accommodate these differences, continues to influence progressive educational theory.

The emphasis on character development and ethical formation as integral parts of education established a tradition that viewed moral and spiritual growth as essential outcomes of the learning process. This understanding that education should produce not merely knowledgeable individuals but wise and virtuous ones remains a challenge and aspiration for contemporary educators.

The oral tradition and emphasis on memorization, while sometimes criticized in modern contexts, demonstrated the importance of developing mental discipline and creating internalized knowledge that could be accessed and applied readily. The balance between memorization and understanding, between preservation of tradition and creative innovation, offers insights for contemporary debates about educational methods.

The community-based nature of gurukulas, where learning took place within supportive communities of teachers and fellow students, highlighted the social dimensions of education and the importance of creating environments conducive to learning and growth. The model of learning communities continues to influence educational design today.

Conclusion

The educational system that emerged during the Vedic period represents one of humanity's most remarkable achievements in the organization and transmission of knowledge. Through the gurukula system, ancient Indian civilization created a comprehensive approach to education that addressed the full range of human needs and potentials, producing individuals equipped not merely with information but with wisdom, not merely with skills but with character.

The study of Vedas, Itihasas, Upasanas, and the various auxiliary and applied sciences provided students with a broad foundation of knowledge that prepared them for the diverse challenges and opportunities they would encounter in life. The pedagogical methods employed - from memorization and recitation to dialogue and practical application - engaged different aspects of human learning capacity and ensured that knowledge was not merely acquired but deeply integrated into the student's understanding and character.

The philosophical foundations of this system - its emphasis on dharma, its understanding of the teacherstudent relationship as sacred, its commitment to the complete development of human potential established principles that continue to offer guidance for educational practice today. While the specific content and methods of Vedic education may need adaptation for contemporary contexts, its fundamental insights about the nature and purposes of education remain profoundly relevant.

As we face the challenges of educating young people for an increasingly complex and rapidly changing world, the Vedic educational tradition offers valuable perspectives on the integration of knowledge, the importance of character development, the need for personalized instruction, and the ultimate goals of the educational enterprise. The ancient sages who developed this system understood that education is ultimately about human transformation - the development of individuals who can contribute wisely and compassionately to the world they inherit and the future they will create.

The legacy of Vedic education reminds us that learning is not merely the acquisition of information but the cultivation of wisdom, that teaching is not merely the transmission of knowledge but the facilitation of human development, and that education is not merely preparation for livelihood but preparation for life in its fullest sense. These insights, preserved and transmitted through millennia, continue to illuminate our understanding of what education can be and should aspire to become.

9
The Warrior's Path

The Sacred Art of Combat

In the golden age of Vedic civilization, education was not merely an intellectual pursuit confined to sacred texts and philosophical discourse. The ancient seers understood that true learning must encompass the complete development of human potential—mind, body, and spirit working in harmonious unity. Nowhere was this holistic approach more evident than in the teaching of martial and weapon arts, which formed an integral cornerstone of the traditional gurukul system.

The Vedic period, spanning roughly from 1500 to 500 BCE, witnessed the flourishing of a sophisticated educational framework that produced not only learned scholars and spiritual masters but also skilled warriors capable of defending dharma and protecting society. The concept of the warrior-scholar, embodied in figures like Arjuna and Rama, emerged from this comprehensive educational philosophy that viewed combat training as both a practical necessity and a spiritual discipline.

Unlike modern military training focused primarily on physical prowess and tactical efficiency, Vedic martial education was deeply rooted in ethical principles, cosmic understanding, and spiritual development. The ancient texts reveal that weapon mastery was considered a divine art, with deities themselves serving as the ultimate teachers and weapons possessing sacred significance that transcended their material form.

The Gurukul System and Martial Training

Structure of Vedic Education

The gurukul system formed the backbone of Vedic education, where students lived in forest hermitages under the direct guidance of accomplished gurus. These ashrams were not merely academic institutions but comprehensive centers of learning where knowledge was transmitted through lived experience and practical application. Within this system, martial training occupied a position of paramount importance, particularly for students of the Kshatriya varna, though elements of combat education were available to all deserving students regardless of their birth.

The typical gurukul day began before dawn with meditation and prayers, followed by physical exercises and weapon practice. The integration of spiritual discipline with martial training was deliberate—ancient educators understood that true strength came not from physical power alone but from the alignment of body, mind, and spirit. Students would spend hours each day perfecting their stance, breathing techniques, and weapon handling under the watchful eyes of masters who had themselves spent decades perfecting these arts.

The Guru-Shishya Tradition in Combat Arts

The relationship between guru and student in martial education was particularly sacred and intense. Unlike other subjects where knowledge could be transmitted through books or lectures, combat skills required direct, personal transmission from master to disciple. The guru would carefully observe each student's temperament, physical capabilities, and spiritual inclinations before determining the appropriate martial path for their development.

This personalized approach meant that no two students received identical training. Some might excel in archery and receive advanced instruction in the subtle arts of long-range combat, while others might show aptitude for close-quarters combat and be guided toward mastery of swords and maces. The guru's responsibility extended far beyond technical instruction—they were also moral guides who ensured that deadly skills were wielded only in service of dharma.

The process of learning was gradual and methodical. Students began with basic physical conditioning, flexibility training, and meditation practices designed to develop the mental clarity essential for combat effectiveness. Only after demonstrating proficiency in these fundamentals would they be permitted to handle actual weapons, and even then, training progressed through carefully structured stages that emphasized safety, respect for the weapons, and understanding of their proper use.

The Sacred Science of Dhanurvidya

Archery as the Supreme Martial Art

Among all martial disciplines taught in the Vedic period, archery (dhanurvidya) held the position of supreme importance. The bow and arrow were not merely weapons but sacred instruments that connected the warrior to cosmic principles. The tension of the bowstring represented the balance between opposing forces in the universe, while the arrow's flight symbolized the focused mind piercing through illusion to reach its target of truth.

The Dhanurveda, the ancient treatise on archery, describes elaborate training methods that began with meditation and breath control. Students learned to still their minds completely, for even the slightest mental disturbance would affect their accuracy. They practiced shooting at increasingly difficult targets— from large stationary objects to small moving targets, and eventually to shooting arrows in complete darkness using only sound as guidance.

Advanced practitioners were taught the mysterious techniques of shooting multiple arrows simultaneously, curving arrows around obstacles, and even the legendary art of stopping incoming arrows with their own shots. These skills required not only exceptional physical coordination but also deep understanding of physics, geometry, and timing that bordered on the supernatural.

The Mystical Dimensions of Archery

The highest levels of archery training delved into mystical territories that modern minds might find difficult to comprehend. Ancient texts describe techniques where master archers could imbue their arrows with specific intentions or energies, creating effects that went far beyond mere physical impact. The Mahabharata speaks of divine arrows that could summon fire, water, or wind, suggesting that advanced practitioners understood subtle energies and their manipulation through concentrated will.

Students were taught that the true target was not the external object but their own inner limitations and mental fluctuations. The moment of release—when the archer let go of the arrow—was seen as a meditation on surrender and non-attachment. This philosophical dimension transformed archery from a mere combat skill into a powerful tool for spiritual development and self-realization.

The training included various specialized techniques such as shooting while mounted on horses or chariots, rapid-fire shooting methods, and the ability to maintain accuracy while in motion or under extreme stress. Master archers were expected to demonstrate their skills in elaborate competitions that tested not only their technical proficiency but also their mental composure and ethical understanding.

Sword Arts and Close Combat Training

The Philosophy of Blade Mastery

While archery represented the principle of focused intention manifesting at a distance, swordsmanship embodied the warrior's direct engagement with immediate challenges. The sword in Vedic tradition was more than a cutting tool—it was an extension of the warrior's will, a manifestation of discriminating wisdom that could separate truth from falsehood, just from unjust.

Training in sword arts began with extensive conditioning of the hands, wrists, and forearms, as the ability to wield a sword effectively required exceptional strength and flexibility in these areas. Students spent months perfecting basic cuts, thrusts, and parries before being allowed to engage in any form of sparring. The emphasis was on developing fluid, natural movements that conserved energy while maximizing effectiveness.

The ancient masters distinguished between various types of swords and their appropriate uses. The long straight sword (asi) required different techniques than the curved blade (krpana), and students were expected to achieve proficiency with multiple weapon types. Each sword was treated with reverence and maintained with meticulous care, as the condition of the weapon was seen as reflecting the spiritual state of its wielder.

Advanced Techniques and Combat Applications

Advanced sword training included complex forms and combinations that resembled elaborate dances. These kata-like sequences served multiple purposes—they developed muscle memory for combat situations, provided a method for solo practice, and preserved advanced techniques through structured movements that could be passed down through generations.

Students learned to fight with sword and shield combinations, dual-wielding techniques for those with exceptional coordination, and the integration of sword work with unarmed combat methods. The training emphasized adaptability and creativity, as real combat situations rarely conformed to predetermined patterns.

The psychological aspects of sword fighting received equal attention with the physical techniques. Students learned to read their opponents' intentions through subtle body language cues, to maintain mental clarity under extreme pressure, and to distinguish between necessary force and excessive violence. The ethical dimension of sword work was continually emphasized—the blade was to be drawn only in defense of dharma and never in anger or for personal gain.

The Arsenal of Vedic Warriors

Diverse Weapon Systems

The Vedic warrior's education encompassed proficiency with a vast array of weapons, each serving specific tactical purposes and requiring distinct skill sets. Beyond the primary weapons of bow and sword, students learned to wield spears (sula), maces (gada), battle-axes (parashu), and various throwing weapons with deadly effectiveness.

The spear represented the principle of extension and reach, allowing warriors to maintain distance from opponents while still delivering powerful strikes. Training with spears emphasized footwork and positioning, as the weapon's length made it both advantageous and potentially cumbersome in different situations. Students practiced formations where groups of spear-wielders could create nearly impenetrable defensive walls or devastating charging formations.

Mace fighting required exceptional physical strength and endurance, as these heavy weapons could deliver crushing blows but demanded careful timing and positioning. The training for mace work included extensive physical conditioning and the development of devastating striking techniques that could shatter armor and bones with equal efficiency.

Specialized and Exotic Weapons

Advanced students might be introduced to more specialized weapons such as the chakra (discus), various types of daggers and short swords optimized for close-quarters combat, and even exotic weapons like the urumi (flexible sword) that required years of dedicated practice to master safely.

Each weapon carried its own philosophical significance and training methodology. The chakra, for instance, represented the wheel of time and cosmic order, and its use required perfect timing and understanding of rotational forces. Students who showed aptitude for such specialized weapons would receive individualized instruction from masters who had dedicated their lives to these particular arts.

The training also included the use of improvised weapons and the ability to adapt common objects into effective fighting tools. This flexibility was considered essential, as warriors might find themselves in situations where their primary weapons were unavailable or inappropriate for the circumstances.

Physical Conditioning and Athletic Development

The Foundation of Warrior Fitness

The physical preparation required for effective martial arts training was comprehensive and demanding. Students began each day with elaborate exercise routines that developed strength, flexibility, balance, and endurance simultaneously. These exercises were often disguised as games or competitions, making the rigorous training more engaging for young learners.

Running was emphasized not just for cardiovascular fitness but for developing the specific type of endurance required in combat situations. Students learned to maintain their breath control and mental clarity even during intense physical exertion, as the ability to think clearly under pressure could mean the difference between victory and defeat.

Wrestling (malla-yuddha) formed a crucial component of physical training, as it developed the closequarters combat skills, body awareness, and strength needed for situations where weapons were unavailable or inappropriate. The training included various grappling techniques, throws, and submission holds, but always with the underlying emphasis on control and restraint rather than brutality.

Specialized Physical Training Methods

Advanced students engaged in increasingly challenging physical conditioning exercises designed to push their bodies to extraordinary levels of performance. These might include practicing forms while balancing on narrow beams, training in difficult weather conditions, or maintaining their skills while fasting or under other forms of controlled stress.

The development of ambidextrous fighting ability was considered essential, as a truly skilled warrior should be equally dangerous with either hand. Students spent considerable time developing their non-dominant side until the distinction between left and right became meaningless in combat situations.

Breath control (pranayama) techniques formed an integral part of physical training, as proper breathing could enhance strength, improve focus, and maintain endurance during extended combat. Students learned specific breathing patterns for different types of combat situations and practiced maintaining these patterns even under extreme physical stress.

Mental Discipline and Psychological Training

Developing the Warrior Mind

The mental aspects of martial training received as much attention as physical skills, for the ancient masters understood that the mind was the true battlefield where victory or defeat was determined. Students learned meditation techniques specifically designed to develop the qualities essential for effective combat—unwavering focus, emotional equilibrium, rapid decision-making, and the ability to remain calm under extreme pressure.

Visualization exercises played a crucial role in mental training. Students would spend hours mentally rehearsing combat scenarios, visualizing themselves successfully executing techniques and overcoming various challenges. This mental practice was considered as valuable as physical training, as it programmed successful responses into the subconscious mind and built confidence for actual combat situations.

The development of situational awareness was cultivated through various exercises and games. Students learned to observe their environment constantly, noting potential threats, escape routes, and advantageous positions without appearing to do so. This heightened awareness became second nature through consistent practice and was considered one of the hallmarks of a truly trained warrior.

Overcoming Fear and Developing Courage

One of the most challenging aspects of martial training was helping students overcome their natural fear responses and develop genuine courage. The ancient masters distinguished between reckless bravado and true courage—the latter being a calm, centered state of mind that could function effectively even in the face of mortal danger.

Students were gradually exposed to increasingly stressful situations, always under controlled conditions with proper supervision. This might include sparring with more experienced opponents, training in simulated life-or-death scenarios, or facing various forms of psychological pressure designed to test their mental resilience.

The ethical dimensions of combat were continuously reinforced through stories, discussions, and practical examples. Students learned that true warriors fought not from anger or hatred but from a sense of duty and protection of the innocent. This moral foundation provided the psychological stability necessary for wielding deadly skills responsibly.

Strategic Training and Battlefield Tactics

The Art of War Planning

Beyond individual combat skills, advanced students received comprehensive training in military strategy and battlefield tactics. This education included the study of historical battles, analysis of successful and unsuccessful strategies, and the development of strategic thinking capabilities that could be applied to both military and civilian leadership situations.

The ancient texts describe elaborate war games and simulated battles where students could practice coordinating large groups, implementing complex strategies, and adapting to changing battlefield conditions. These exercises developed leadership skills and strategic thinking while providing practical experience in the chaos and confusion of large-scale combat.

Students learned to read terrain for tactical advantages, understand the strengths and weaknesses of different military formations, and coordinate various types of units (infantry, cavalry, chariots, elephants) for maximum effectiveness. The emphasis was on achieving victory through superior strategy and coordination rather than mere brute force.

Intelligence and Information Warfare

The importance of intelligence gathering and information warfare was well understood in Vedic times. Students learned techniques for gathering information about enemy capabilities and intentions, methods for protecting sensitive information, and ways to mislead opponents through various forms of deception and misdirection.

Training included the development of observation skills, memory techniques for retaining large amounts of detailed information, and methods for communicating sensitive information securely. Students also learned to recognize and counter enemy intelligence operations directed against their own forces.

The ethical aspects of intelligence work received careful attention, as the methods involved could easily cross the boundaries of honorable conduct. Students were taught to distinguish between legitimate military intelligence and dishonorable spying, maintaining their moral integrity even while engaging in the necessarily secretive aspects of warfare.

The Role of Women in Martial Education

Female Warriors and Combat Training

Contrary to many later historical periods, the Vedic age recognized the potential for women to achieve excellence in martial arts and acknowledged their right to defend themselves and their communities. While the majority of intensive martial training was directed toward male students destined for warrior roles, exceptional women could and did receive comprehensive combat education.

The training for female students was often modified to take advantage of their typically superior flexibility and agility while addressing differences in average physical strength through technique and strategy. Women warriors were particularly noted for their skill with ranged weapons such as bows and throwing weapons, where technique and accuracy were more important than raw physical power.

The stories of legendary female warriors like Chitrangada and various Rani (queen) figures who led armies into battle indicate that women's martial training could reach the highest levels when circumstances demanded it. These examples served as inspiration for female students and demonstrated that martial excellence was not limited by gender when combined with proper training and determination.

Specialized Training for Women

Female students often received specialized training in areas particularly suited to their social roles and physical capabilities. This might include defensive techniques for protecting children and noncombatants, stealth and escape methods, and the use of improvised weapons that could be concealed or disguised as ordinary household items.

The training emphasized techniques that relied on speed, timing, and precision rather than brute strength, allowing smaller practitioners to effectively defend against larger, stronger opponents. These methods required more intensive mental training and strategic thinking, developing intellectual capabilities alongside physical skills.

Integration with Spiritual Practice

Combat as Spiritual Discipline

One of the most distinctive features of Vedic martial education was its integration with spiritual practice and philosophical understanding. Combat training was viewed not merely as preparation for warfare but as a powerful method for spiritual development and self-realization.

The physical disciplines required for martial excellence—strength, flexibility, endurance, and coordination —were seen as necessary foundations for advanced spiritual practices. The mental qualities developed through combat training—focus, courage, determination, and emotional equilibrium—were equally valuable for those seeking spiritual liberation.

Students learned to approach their martial practice as a form of moving meditation, maintaining awareness of their breath, body position, and mental state throughout their training. This mindful approach transformed routine exercises into opportunities for deepening self-understanding and developing greater consciousness.

The Warrior's Path to Enlightenment

Advanced practitioners understood that the ultimate victory was not over external enemies but over their own inner limitations and negative tendencies. The discipline, sacrifice, and dedication required for martial mastery served as preparation for the even greater challenges of spiritual awakening.

The concept of dharmic warfare—fighting only in defense of righteousness and cosmic order—provided a spiritual context for martial skills that elevated them beyond mere violence. Students learned to see themselves as instruments of divine will, responsible for maintaining balance and protecting the innocent from harm.

The integration of martial and spiritual training produced individuals who were simultaneously fierce warriors and compassionate spiritual practitioners, capable of devastating effectiveness in combat while maintaining their ethical principles and inner peace.

Assessment and Graduation in Martial Arts

Testing Methods and Standards

The evaluation of martial arts progress in the Vedic system was comprehensive and demanding, encompassing not only technical skill but also mental discipline, ethical understanding, and spiritual development. Students could not advance to higher levels of training based solely on physical prowess—they had to demonstrate maturity, wisdom, and unwavering commitment to dharmic principles.

Practical testing involved demonstrations of skill with various weapons, sparring matches with students of equal and superior skill levels, and the ability to perform techniques under various forms of stress and distraction. Students were also tested on their knowledge of strategy, tactics, and the historical and philosophical foundations of their arts.

The final examinations were elaborate affairs that might last several days and include challenges designed to test every aspect of the student's development. Only those who demonstrated complete integration of physical skill, mental discipline, and spiritual understanding would be certified as masters worthy of teaching others.

The Transition to Mastery

Graduation from martial training marked not an end but a beginning—the start of a lifelong journey of continued learning and service. New masters were expected to continue their own development while beginning to transmit their knowledge to the next generation of students.

The responsibilities of mastership were considerable, as teachers were held accountable not only for their students' technical development but also for their moral and spiritual growth. A master whose students brought dishonor to their arts through misuse of their skills would himself face serious consequences.

The tradition emphasized that true mastery was demonstrated not through prowess in combat but through the ability to avoid unnecessary conflict while being prepared to act decisively when dharma was threatened. The highest masters were often those who rarely needed to use their deadly skills, as their presence and wisdom were sufficient to resolve conflicts peacefully.

Legacy and Historical Impact

Influence on Later Military Traditions

The comprehensive martial education system developed during the Vedic period provided the foundation for all subsequent military and martial traditions in the Indian subcontinent. The principles of integrated training, ethical conduct, and spiritual development continued to influence warrior training throughout various historical periods, even as specific techniques and weapons evolved.

The concept of the warrior-scholar, fully developed in Vedic times, became a cultural ideal that persisted through centuries of political change. This integration of intellectual and martial excellence contributed to the development of leaders who could govern wisely in peace and fight effectively in war.

The systematic approach to martial education, with its emphasis on gradual progression, comprehensive development, and ethical foundation, served as a model for educational systems in other fields. The gurukula method's success in producing exceptional martial artists demonstrated the effectiveness of personalized, holistic education that addressed all aspects of human development.

Cultural and Spiritual Contributions

Beyond their immediate military applications, the martial arts of the Vedic period made significant contributions to spiritual practice, physical culture, and philosophical understanding. The integration of combat training with meditation and spiritual discipline created powerful methods for personal transformation that influenced religious and philosophical traditions for millennia.

The emphasis on dharmic conduct and ethical restraint in the use of force provided important moral foundations for later legal and political systems. The concept that might must be guided by right, and that true strength comes from inner development rather than external power, became central to Indian cultural values.

The sophisticated understanding of human psychology, physical development, and strategic thinking that emerged from martial training contributed to advances in medicine, education, and governance that extended far beyond military applications.

Conclusion- The Eternal Relevance of Vedic Martial Education

The martial and weapon arts education of the Vedic period represents far more than an interesting historical curiosity—it embodies timeless principles of human development that remain relevant in our contemporary world. The integration of physical training with mental discipline, ethical development, and spiritual growth offers a holistic approach to education that addresses the complete human being rather than fragmenting learning into isolated subjects.

The emphasis on personal responsibility, ethical conduct, and service to higher principles provides essential guidance for any individual seeking to develop their capabilities while maintaining their moral integrity. The recognition that true strength comes from inner development rather than external force offers wisdom that transcends cultural and temporal boundaries.

Perhaps most importantly, the Vedic approach to martial education demonstrates that the development of potentially dangerous capabilities must always be balanced with the cultivation of wisdom, compassion, and ethical restraint. In our current age, where technology has provided humanity with unprecedented power to create and destroy, the ancient understanding of the relationship between capability and responsibility becomes more crucial than ever.

The warrior-scholars produced by the Vedic educational system exemplified the possibility of combining strength with gentleness, effectiveness with compassion, and skill with wisdom. Their example continues to inspire those who seek to develop their full potential while remaining committed to the highest human values and aspirations.

The legacy of Vedic martial education reminds us that true education must address not only what we can do, but why we should do it, and how we can act in harmony with the deepest principles of existence. In this integration of power and principle, capability and conscience, lies the eternal relevance of these ancient teachings for our modern world.

10
Warfare in the Vedic Age

The Nature of Vedic Warfare

Warfare during the Vedic period was not merely a matter of brute force or spontaneous conflict. It was a highly organized, ritualized, and technologically sophisticated enterprise that reflected the broader cultural values and religious beliefs of Vedic society. The conduct of war involved elaborate preparations, the deployment of advanced weaponry for its time, and the strategic use of various animals, particularly horses and elephants, which gave Vedic armies their distinctive character and tactical advantages.

The sources for understanding Vedic warfare are primarily literary, drawn from the hymns of the Rig Veda, the ritual texts of the Brahmanas, archaeological evidence, while limited, provides additional insights into the material culture of warfare, including weapons, chariots, and fortifications. These sources reveal a complex military tradition that combined practical battlefield tactics with deeply held religious and social beliefs about the nature of conflict, honor, and victory.

Political Context and Motivations

Warfare in the Vedic age was fundamentally shaped by the political structure of the period, which was characterized by numerous small kingdoms and tribal confederations competing for resources, territory, and prestige. The Rig Veda mentions various tribes such as the Bharatas, Purus, Yadus, Turvasas, and Druhyus, who were frequently engaged in conflicts with each other and with non-Aryan peoples referred to as Dasyus or Dasas.

The motivations for warfare were diverse and interconnected. Cattle raids (*gavishti*) were among the most common forms of conflict, as cattle represented both economic wealth and social status. The famous "Battle of the Ten Kings" (*Dasarajna Yuddha*) described in the Rig Veda illustrates how territorial disputes could escalate into major military confrontations involving multiple tribal alliances. Religious motivations also played a significant role, as wars were often justified as struggles between the forces of cosmic order (*rita*) and chaos, with Vedic peoples positioning themselves as champions of divine law.

Economic factors underlying warfare included competition for fertile agricultural land, control over trade routes, and access to mineral resources. The expansion of Vedic civilization eastward from the Punjab into the Gangetic plains was driven partly by the search for new lands to support growing populations and the desire to control the wealth generated by river valley agriculture.

Social Dimensions of War

The social organization of Vedic society was deeply influenced by its military culture. The *Kshatriya* class, comprising warriors and rulers, occupied a position of high status second only to the Brahmins in the emerging varna system. This warrior aristocracy was defined by its military prowess, its ownership of horses and chariots, and its role in protecting the community from external threats.

Military service was not limited to professional warriors, however. The concept of *vishti*, or obligatory military service, required able-bodied men from various social groups to participate in warfare when called upon by their rulers. This system ensured that Vedic armies could mobilize substantial forces when needed, while also reinforcing social hierarchies and political loyalties.

The relationship between warfare and social mobility was complex. While birth into the warrior class provided certain advantages, exceptional military skill could elevate individuals from lower social positions. The Vedic texts celebrate heroes who distinguished themselves in battle, suggesting that martial prowess was a recognized path to social advancement and royal favor.

Preparations for War

Ritual and Religious Preparations

The preparation for warfare in Vedic times was as much a religious undertaking as a military one. Before any major military campaign, elaborate rituals were performed to secure divine favor and ensure victory. The most important of these was the *Rajasuya* sacrifice, which legitimized a king's authority and prepared him for conquest. This complex ceremony involved multiple priests, extensive offerings, and symbolic acts that transformed the ruler into a divine agent capable of righteous warfare.

The *Ashvamedha* or horse sacrifice represented the pinnacle of royal military ritual. In this ceremony, a specially consecrated horse was allowed to roam freely for a year, with the king's army following to claim any territory the horse entered. This ritual not only demonstrated a ruler's military power but also established his sovereignty over vast territories through divine sanction.

Individual warriors also engaged in personal rituals before battle. These included prayers to Indra, the god of war and storms, offerings to Agni for protection, and the recitation of specific mantras believed to grant courage and strength. The *Atharva Veda* contains numerous spells and charms designed to protect warriors in battle, disable enemies, and ensure victory.

The timing of military campaigns was carefully calculated according to religious and astronomical considerations. Certain months were considered auspicious for warfare, while others were avoided. The lunar calendar played a crucial role in determining when battles should be fought, with new moon and full moon periods having particular significance.

Strategic Planning and Intelligence

Vedic warfare involved sophisticated strategic planning that went far beyond simple raids or spontaneous conflicts. Military leaders, often kings themselves, engaged in careful analysis of enemy strengths and weaknesses, terrain considerations, and seasonal factors that might affect campaign outcomes.

Intelligence gathering was a crucial component of military preparation. Spies (*spasa*) were employed to infiltrate enemy territories, assess military capabilities, and identify potential allies or defectors. The Rig Veda contains references to these intelligence operatives, suggesting that information warfare was already well-developed during this period.

The concept of *mandala* theory, later formalized in texts like the *Arthashastra*, had its origins in Vedic strategic thinking. This approach viewed the political landscape as a series of concentric circles, with natural allies and enemies determined by geographical proximity and political interests. Kings were advised to maintain friendly relations with distant rulers while remaining vigilant against neighboring powers.

Logistical planning for extended campaigns required careful coordination of supplies, transportation, and communication.

Vedic armies needed to secure adequate provisions for both human and animal participants, establish supply lines, and maintain contact with home territories during lengthy expeditions.

Military Organization and Training

The organization of Vedic armies reflected the hierarchical nature of society while also accommodating the practical requirements of battlefield effectiveness. At the apex stood the king or war chief (*raja* or *senani*), who held supreme command and was responsible for overall strategy and major tactical decisions.

Below the supreme commander were various grades of officers, including chariot commanders (*rathika*), cavalry leaders (*asvapati*), and infantry captains (*pattika*). These positions were typically filled by members of the warrior class, though exceptional individuals from other backgrounds could sometimes achieve military leadership through demonstrated skill and loyalty.

Training for warfare began early in life for members of the warrior class. Young men underwent rigorous physical conditioning, weapons training, and instruction in military tactics. The use of various weapons required specialized skills that took years to master, particularly in the case of archery and chariot warfare.

The formation and deployment of troops followed established patterns that were believed to have divine sanction. The *Vyuha* formations, geometric arrangements of military units, were not merely tactical expedients but sacred patterns that reflected cosmic order. Training in these formations required extensive practice and coordination among units.

Weapons and Military Technology

Projectile Weapons

The bow and arrow system formed the technological foundation of Vedic warfare, representing both the most prestigious and most effective weapons of the period. Vedic bows were composite constructions, typically made from horn, wood, and sinew, which provided superior power and range compared to simple wooden bows. The *Rig Veda* describes bows that could shoot arrows over considerable distances with sufficient force to penetrate armor and inflict fatal wounds.

Arrows were crafted with meticulous attention to balance, weight, and aerodynamic properties. Arrow shafts were made from reed (*nala*) or specific types of wood chosen for their straightness and durability. Arrowheads varied according to their intended purpose, with different designs for penetrating armor, causing maximum tissue damage, or creating psychological terror through distinctive sounds in flight.

The *Rig Veda* mentions specialized arrow types including the *kshurapra* (razor-edged arrows), *naracha* (iron-tipped arrows), and *bhalla* (broad-headed arrows). Some arrows were designed with barbed tips that made removal difficult, while others featured hollow heads that produced whistling sounds to frighten enemies and horses.

Slings (*asmahana*) provided an alternative projectile system that was particularly effective against unarmored opponents. Vedic slingers could hurl stones with considerable accuracy and force, making them valuable auxiliaries in siege warfare and skirmishing actions.

Close Combat Weapons

The sword (*asi*) held special significance in Vedic warfare, often being treated as a sacred object with its own spiritual power. Early Vedic swords were typically made of bronze or iron, with straight, doubleedged blades designed for both cutting and thrusting. The quality of metalworking during this period was sufficiently advanced to produce weapons of considerable effectiveness and durability.

Spears and lances (*rishti* and *prasa*) served as the primary weapons for infantry combat and chariot warfare. These weapons varied in length and design according to their specific tactical applications. Long spears were used by foot soldiers in formation fighting, while shorter spears were preferred by chariot warriors who needed weapons manageable in the confined space of a war chariot.

Axes (*paraśu*) and maces (*gada*) provided heavy shock weapons capable of penetrating armor and inflicting devastating wounds. The battle-axe was particularly associated with certain deities and carried both practical and religious significance. Maces were often elaborately decorated and served as symbols of royal authority as well as effective weapons.

The *vajra*, frequently mentioned in Vedic texts, remains somewhat enigmatic in terms of its exact physical form. Described as the weapon of Indra, it may have been a type of club, mace, or even an early form of military hammer. Its mythological associations suggest that it was considered an extremely powerful and prestigious weapon.

Defensive Equipment

Shields (*carman*) were essential defensive equipment for Vedic warriors, typically constructed from layers of hide stretched over wooden frames. The size and design of shields varied according to the tactical role of their users, with larger shields providing better protection for infantry and smaller, more maneuverable shields preferred by chariot crews.

Body armor (*varman*) during the early Vedic period was primarily made from leather, though metal armor became increasingly common in later periods. Leather armor was often reinforced with metal studs or plates, providing a compromise between protection and mobility. The development of metalworking techniques allowed for the production of mail armor and scale armor that offered superior protection against both projectile and close combat weapons.

Helmets (*shirmastra*) protected the head, which was particularly vulnerable to sword cuts and arrow wounds. Early helmets were made from leather or bronze, often decorated with crests or plumes that served both practical and psychological purposes. The visibility of distinctive helmet designs helped in battlefield identification and contributed to the psychological warfare that was an important component of Vedic military tactics.

Siege Technology and Fortifications

While Vedic warfare was primarily characterized by open field battles and mobile operations, siege warfare was not unknown. The *Rig Veda* contains references to fortified settlements (*pur*) and the techniques used to capture them. These fortifications were typically earthwork constructions reinforced with wooden palisades, though some may have incorporated stone elements.

Siege techniques included the construction of earthworks to overtop defensive walls, the use of fire arrows to ignite wooden fortifications, and direct assault using scaling ladders and siege towers. The undermining of walls through tunneling was also practiced, requiring considerable engineering skill and coordination.

The defense of fortified positions involved the use of projectile weapons from elevated positions, the deployment of obstacles such as sharpened stakes (*shulakas*), and the maintenance of adequate supplies to withstand prolonged sieges. Counter-siege operations could include sorties by defending forces and attempts to relieve besieged positions through external military intervention.

Animals in Warfare

The Horse and Chariot System

The introduction of the horse and chariot to the Indian subcontinent during the Vedic period represented a revolutionary development in military technology and tactics. The horse (*ashva*) was not merely a military tool but a sacred animal associated with the sun, speed, and divine power. The veneration of horses in Vedic religion reflected their crucial importance in both warfare and social organization.

Vedic war chariots (*ratha*) were typically two-wheeled vehicles drawn by two or more horses, though some references suggest that four-horse teams were used by the most prestigious warriors. The chariot provided a stable platform for archers while offering superior mobility on the battlefield. The combination of speed, firepower, and prestige made chariot warfare the dominant military system of the Vedic age.

The construction of war chariots required sophisticated carpentry and metalworking skills. The wheels were reinforced with metal fittings, the body was designed for optimal weight distribution, and the entire vehicle was built to withstand the stresses of high-speed maneuvering and combat. Archaeological evidence suggests that Vedic chariots were comparable in quality to those used in other contemporary civilizations such as Egypt and Mesopotamia.

Chariot crews typically consisted of two individuals: a charioteer (*suta*) who managed the horses and maneuvered the vehicle, and a warrior (*rathin*) who fought with bow and arrow or other weapons. This division of labor allowed for specialized skills development and more effective tactical coordination. The relationship between charioteer and warrior was often close and personal, reflected in numerous Vedic hymns that celebrate these partnerships.

The training of war horses required considerable time and expertise. Horses needed to be conditioned for the noise and chaos of battle, trained to respond to subtle commands, and maintained in peak physical condition. The breeding and care of military horses became a specialized occupation, with horse trainers (*ashvapa*) holding positions of considerable importance in Vedic society.

Cavalry Development

While chariot warfare dominated early Vedic military practices, the development of cavalry represents an important evolution in military technology during the later Vedic period. The transition from chariotbased to horse-based warfare was gradual and reflected changing tactical requirements and technological capabilities.

Early Vedic cavalry was likely limited to scouting, messaging, and pursuit operations rather than direct combat roles. The lack of stirrups and advanced saddle technology made mounted combat more difficult, though not impossible. Cavalry units provided valuable mobility for reconnaissance missions and could exploit battlefield opportunities that were not accessible to heavier chariot forces.

The development of mounted archery required new training methods and equipment adaptations. Cavalry archers needed to master the complex skill of shooting accurately while controlling a moving horse, a capability that took years to develop. The shorter composite bows used by mounted warriors were specifically designed for use on horseback and represented a significant technological adaptation.

Cavalry organization followed patterns similar to other military units, with commanders (*ashvapati*) responsible for training, equipment, and tactical deployment. The social status of cavalry warriors was generally lower than that of chariot fighters but higher than infantry, reflecting the prestige associated with horse ownership and mounted combat skills.

Elephants in Early Warfare

The role of elephants in Vedic warfare is less clearly documented than that of horses, but evidence suggests that these animals were known and occasionally used for military purposes. The *Rig Veda* contains references to elephants (*hastin*), though their military application may have been limited during the early Vedic period.

Elephants provided several military advantages including their psychological impact on enemy forces, their ability to carry heavy equipment and supplies, and their effectiveness in breaking through enemy formations. However, the training and maintenance of war elephants required considerable resources and expertise that may not have been widely available during the early Vedic period.

The capture and training of wild elephants was a specialized skill that developed gradually over time. Elephant catchers (*hastyaroha*) used various techniques including pit traps, noose snares, and the use of trained elephants to capture wild animals. The training process was lengthy and required experienced handlers who understood elephant behavior and psychology.

War elephants were typically equipped with protective armor and carried crews of two to four men, including a driver (*mahout*), archers, and spearmen. The platform (*howdah*) mounted on the elephant's back provided an elevated fighting position that offered tactical advantages in both offensive and defensive operations.

Supporting Animals and Logistics

Beyond the primary war animals, Vedic military operations depended on various other animals for logistical support and specialized functions. Cattle (*go*) were essential for providing food supplies during extended campaigns, both through direct consumption and dairy products. The protection and capture of cattle herds were often primary objectives of military operations.

Dogs (*shvan*) served as sentries, trackers, and companions for military forces. Vedic texts describe war dogs that were trained to attack enemies and protect their handlers. The loyalty and acute senses of dogs made them valuable assets for reconnaissance and camp security.

Camels (*ushtra*) were used for transportation in desert and semi-arid regions, though their role in Vedic warfare was probably limited given the geographical focus of early Vedic civilization. However, as Vedic culture expanded into diverse geographical regions, the use of camels for military logistics became more important.

The care and feeding of military animals required specialized knowledge and considerable resources. Veterinary practices (*ashvavaidya*) developed to maintain animal health and treat battlefield injuries. The loss of valuable war animals could significantly impact military effectiveness, making their protection a high priority during combat operations.

Tactical Formations and Battle Strategies

Classical Battle Formations

The *vyuha* system of battle formations represented one of the most sophisticated aspects of Vedic military science. These formations were not merely practical arrangements of troops but sacred geometric patterns believed to channel divine power and ensure victory. The most important formations included the *makara* (crocodile), *garuda* (eagle), *varaha* (boar), and *padma* (lotus), each designed for specific tactical situations.

The *chakravyuha* or circular formation was perhaps the most famous and complex of these

arrangements. This formation required exceptional coordination and training, as units needed to maintain their positions while rotating around a central core. The psychological impact of well-executed formations was as important as their tactical effectiveness, as disciplined troop movements could demoralize enemy forces before actual combat began.

Formation fighting required extensive training and discipline among troops. Soldiers needed to understand not only their own role within the formation but also how their actions affected the overall tactical plan. The breakdown of formation integrity could lead to rapid defeat, making training in formation discipline a crucial component of military preparation.

The adaptation of formations to terrain and enemy capabilities demonstrated the tactical flexibility of Vedic military leaders. Different formations were appropriate for different types of ground, enemy compositions, and strategic objectives. The ability to transition between formations during battle was a mark of superior military skill and training.

Combined Arms Tactics

Vedic warfare employed sophisticated combined arms tactics that integrated chariots, cavalry, infantry, and elephants into coordinated military operations. The effective coordination of these different military arms required careful planning and extensive training to ensure that each component supported the others rather than interfering with their effectiveness.

Chariots typically formed the elite striking force, providing mobile firepower and serving as the primary means of engaging enemy chariots. Infantry supported chariot operations by providing protection against enemy foot soldiers and securing key terrain features. Cavalry performed reconnaissance, pursuit, and flank protection missions that complemented the heavier combat units.

The timing of attacks by different military arms was crucial to tactical success. Coordinated assaults that combined chariot charges, infantry advances, and cavalry flanking movements could overwhelm enemy forces that were unprepared for multi-directional attacks. The failure to coordinate these elements properly often resulted in military disaster.

Communication systems during battle employed various methods including horn signals, flag movements, and mounted messengers. The maintenance of communication between dispersed units was essential for executing complex tactical maneuvers and adapting to changing battlefield conditions.

Social and Cultural Impact of Warfare

Warrior Culture and Values

The pervasive influence of warfare on Vedic society extended far beyond the battlefield itself, shaping social values, religious beliefs, and cultural practices. The warrior ideal (*kshatriya dharma*) emphasized courage, honor, loyalty, and skill in arms as the highest virtues for members of the military class. These values were celebrated in hymns, stories, and ritual practices that reinforced the importance of martial excellence.

The concept of heroic death in battle was central to Vedic warrior culture. Warriors who died fighting courageously were promised eternal glory and favorable treatment in the afterlife. This belief system encouraged aggressive fighting and reduced the fear of death that might otherwise compromise military effectiveness.

Military competitions and displays of martial skill were important social events that reinforced warrior values and provided opportunities for young men to demonstrate their capabilities. These events included chariot racing, archery contests, wrestling matches, and exhibitions of weapons handling that served both entertainment and military training purposes.

The relationship between warfare and poetry was particularly strong during the Vedic period. Military victories were commemorated in elaborate hymns that praised the heroic deeds of warriors and rulers. These poetic celebrations served both historical and propaganda purposes, preserving the memory of important battles while inspiring future generations of warriors.

Economic Consequences of Military Activity

The economic impact of warfare during the Vedic period was substantial and multifaceted. Military campaigns required significant resource investments for equipment, supplies, and personnel, but successful operations could yield enormous returns through plunder, tribute, and territorial acquisition.

The cattle raids that were common during this period had both economic and social dimensions. Cattle represented wealth, status, and economic security, making their capture a primary objective of many military operations. The redistribution of captured cattle strengthened the bonds between rulers and their followers while providing material rewards for military service.

The development of military technology stimulated advances in metallurgy, carpentry, and other crafts that had broader economic implications. The demand for high-quality weapons, chariots, and armor encouraged specialization and innovation among artisans, contributing to overall technological progress.

Trade relationships were often disrupted or redirected by military conflicts, but successful military powers could also establish new commercial networks through conquest and alliance formation. The control of trade routes became an increasingly important strategic objective as Vedic civilization expanded and economic complexity increased.

Archaeological Evidence and Material Culture

Weapons and Equipment Discoveries

Archaeological excavations at Vedic period sites have provided valuable material evidence that supplements the literary sources for understanding warfare during this period. Weapon finds include iron and bronze spearheads, arrowheads, sword blades, and axe heads that demonstrate the technological sophistication of Vedic military equipment.

The analysis of metallurgical techniques used in weapon production reveals considerable skill in working with both bronze and iron. The transition from bronze to iron weaponry during the Vedic period represented a significant technological advance that provided military advantages to those who mastered the new metallurgy.

Chariot remains and horse harness equipment found at archaeological sites confirm the importance of these military technologies in Vedic warfare. The construction techniques and materials used in chariot production demonstrate the high level of craftsmanship required to produce effective military vehicles.

Fortification remains at various sites provide evidence for defensive architecture and siege warfare capabilities during the Vedic period. These archaeological features help to confirm and expand the information available from literary sources about military engineering and siege tactics.

Conclusion

The study of warfare during the Vedic age reveals a complex and sophisticated military tradition that played a crucial role in shaping early Indian civilization. The integration of advanced weaponry, strategic animal use, and elaborate ritual preparations created a distinctive form of warfare that reflected broader cultural values while effectively serving political and economic objectives.

The technological innovations of the Vedic period, particularly the development of chariot warfare and advanced metallurgy, had lasting impacts that extended well beyond the military sphere. These advances contributed to broader patterns of technological and social development that influenced the subsequent course of Indian history.

The social and cultural dimensions of Vedic warfare were equally important in establishing patterns of political organization, social stratification, and religious belief that continued to influence Indian society for centuries. The warrior ideal developed during this period became a foundational element of classical Indian civilization.

The legacy of Vedic military traditions can be traced through later periods of Indian history,

with many tactical innovations, organizational principles, and cultural values maintaining their relevance in subsequent military systems. Understanding these early developments provides crucial insights into the foundations of Indian military thought and practice.

The study of Vedic warfare also contributes to broader comparative studies of ancient military systems, demonstrating both the universal principles of military organization and the specific cultural adaptations that characterized different civilizations. The Vedic military tradition represents a unique synthesis of practical military needs with religious and social values that created an enduring and influential military culture

11
Political

The Tribal Foundation

To understand the political evolution toward kingdoms, we must first examine the tribal origins from which these states emerged. The early Vedic period (1500-500 BCE) was characterized by pastoral and semi-nomadic communities organized around kinship ties and tribal affiliations. These early societies were led by chiefs (raja) whose authority was largely ceremonial and dependent on the consent of tribal assemblies such as the Sabha and Samiti.

The Rigvedic society was fundamentally egalitarian, with the raja serving more as a war leader and protector than an absolute ruler. The concept of divine kingship was minimal, and the chief's power was constrained by tribal councils and customary law. However, as these communities settled into agricultural life and territorial boundaries became more defined, the need for more sophisticated political organization became apparent.

The transition period witnessed the gradual transformation of tribal leadership into more institutionalized forms of governance. The increasing complexity of agricultural society, the need for irrigation management, territorial defense, and trade regulation demanded more centralized authority. This shift was further accelerated by population growth, technological advances in iron working, and the expansion of trade networks.

Formation of Janapadas: The Birth of Territorial States

The term "Janapada" literally means "foothold of the people" and represents the first significant departure from tribal organization toward territorial statehood. These early states emerged around 800-600 BCE across the Indo-Gangetic plain, marking the beginning of India's historical period proper. The Janapadas were characterized by defined territorial boundaries, sedentary populations, and increasingly centralized political authority.

The geographical distribution of Janapadas was heavily influenced by the fertility of river valleys, particularly the Ganga and its tributaries. The alluvial soil of these regions supported dense agricultural populations, which in turn provided the economic foundation for state formation. The sixteen principal Janapadas (Mahajanapadas) mentioned in Buddhist and Jaina texts included Kashi, Kosala, Anga, Magadha, Vajji, Malla, Chedi, Vatsa, Kuru, Panchala, Machcha, Surasena, Assaka, Avanti, Gandhara, and Kamboja.

The process of state formation in the Janapadas was gradual and varied across different regions. In some areas, powerful tribal chiefs extended their authority over neighboring territories through conquest and alliance. In others, merchant communities and agricultural elites collaborated to establish more sophisticated governance structures. The emergence of urban centers played a crucial role in this process, as cities became focal points for political, economic, and cultural activity.

The political structure of early Janapadas combined elements of tribal tradition with innovations necessitated by territorial administration. The raja remained the central figure, but his authority was now supported by a nascent bureaucracy, a regular army, and institutionalized revenue collection. The transformation from tribal chief to territorial king represented a fundamental shift in the nature of political authority, moving from personal leadership based on kinship and charisma to institutional power based on territory and resources.

Monarchical Institutions: The Evolution of Kingship

The development of monarchical institutions in ancient India was a complex process that involved the gradual centralization of power, the creation of supporting ideologies, and the establishment of formal court structures. The king (raja) evolved from a tribal leader into a sovereign ruler with extensive powers over his subjects and territory.

The ideological foundation of monarchical power underwent significant transformation during this period. The concept of divine kingship, while never as absolute as in some other ancient civilizations, began to take shape. The king was increasingly seen as the protector of dharma (righteous order) and the maintainer of cosmic balance. This ideological shift was supported by Brahmanical texts that emphasized the king's role as the earthly representative of divine authority.

The royal court became the center of political power and cultural patronage. The king was surrounded by various officials, advisors, and courtiers who formed the core of the administrative apparatus. The purohita (royal priest) held a position of particular importance, serving as the king's spiritual advisor and legitimizing his authority through religious ceremonies. The senani (military commander) and the gramani (village headman) represented the military and administrative arms of royal power.

The institution of succession became increasingly formalized as monarchical power consolidated. While early tribal leadership often involved some form of election or acclamation, the Janapadas moved toward hereditary succession as the primary means of transferring power. This shift had profound implications for political stability and the development of dynastic traditions.

The king's judicial role expanded significantly during this period. While tribal chiefs had always mediated disputes, the territorial kings of the Janapadas developed more sophisticated legal systems. The king became the ultimate source of justice, supported by a hierarchy of judges and legal officials. The concept of royal law (rajadharma) emerged as a complement to traditional customary law, providing rulers with greater flexibility in governance.

The ceremonial aspects of kingship also evolved considerably. The rajasuya (royal consecration) and ashvamedha (horse sacrifice) became elaborate rituals that demonstrated the king's power and legitimacy. These ceremonies not only reinforced the king's authority among his subjects but also served as diplomatic tools in relations with neighboring states.

Administrative Systems: The Machinery of Governance

The transition from tribal organization to territorial statehood necessitated the development of sophisticated administrative systems. The Janapadas created the first systematic approaches to governance in Indian history, establishing precedents that would influence administrative practices for centuries to come.

The central administration was organized around the royal court, with the king serving as the ultimate authority. Below the king, a council of ministers (mantriparishad) provided advice and supervised various departments of government. The chief minister (mahamantri) often served as the king's principal advisor and coordinator of administrative activities. Other important officials included the treasurer (koshadhyaksha), the chief judge (dharmadhyaksha), and the commander-in-chief (senapati).

Provincial administration was developed to manage territories that extended beyond the immediate vicinity of the capital. The kingdom was divided into provinces (rashtra) governed by appointed officials who reported directly to the central authority. These provincial governors were responsible for maintaining order, collecting taxes, and implementing royal policies within their jurisdictions.

Local administration remained largely based on traditional village structures, but with increasing integration into the state system. Village headmen (gramani) served as intermediaries between the central administration and local communities. They were responsible for tax collection, maintaining records, and ensuring compliance with royal decrees. The village council (gramapanchayat) continued to handle local disputes and administrative matters, but under the oversight of state officials.

The revenue system underwent significant development during this period. The state's increasing need for resources to support the army, bureaucracy, and public works led to the systematization of taxation. The primary source of revenue was the land tax (bhaga), typically set at one-sixth of the agricultural produce. Other taxes included customs duties, market fees, and various professional taxes. The development of a money economy facilitated more efficient tax collection and resource allocation.

Record-keeping became increasingly important as administrative complexity grew. The Janapadas developed systems for maintaining records of land ownership, tax payments, and legal decisions. These records were typically kept on palm leaves or birch bark and stored in administrative centers. The emergence of a literate bureaucratic class was essential for the functioning of these administrative systems.

Public works and infrastructure development became important functions of the state. The construction of roads, bridges, irrigation systems, and fortifications required coordinated planning and execution. The state also took responsibility for maintaining law and order, protecting trade routes, and ensuring the smooth functioning of markets.

Warfare and Military Organization

The political evolution of the Janapadas was closely linked to military developments. The need for territorial defense, expansion, and maintaining internal order drove significant innovations in military organization, tactics, and technology. The emergence of professional armies marked a crucial departure from the tribal militia system of the Vedic period.

The military structure of the Janapadas was typically organized around four main components: infantry (padati), cavalry (ashva), chariots (ratha), and elephants (gaja). This four-fold division (chaturanga) became the standard military organization in ancient India. The infantry formed the backbone of most armies, recruited from various social groups and trained in the use of bows, spears, swords, and shields.

Cavalry played an increasingly important role as horse-breeding and training techniques improved. The superior mobility of mounted warriors made them particularly valuable for reconnaissance, rapid strikes, and pursuit operations. However, the availability of suitable horses remained a limiting factor, as the subcontinent was not naturally suited for horse breeding.

War chariots, while important in the earlier Vedic period, gradually declined in significance as infantry and cavalry tactics evolved. Nevertheless, they retained ceremonial importance and continued to be used in certain tactical situations. The chariot represented elite status and was often associated with royal and aristocratic warriors.

The use of war elephants became a distinctive feature of military organization in ancient Bharatavarsha. These massive animals provided both psychological and tactical advantages on the battlefield. Elephants could break enemy formations, carry archers and spear-throwers, and serve as mobile command posts. The training and maintenance of war elephants required significant resources and expertise, making them symbols of royal power and military prestige.

Fortification technology advanced considerably during this period. The Janapadas built increasingly sophisticated defensive structures around their capital cities and strategic locations. These fortifications typically included multiple walls, moats, gates, and towers designed to withstand prolonged sieges. The construction of these defensive works required significant labor and resources, demonstrating the organizational capacity of the emerging states.

Military recruitment evolved from the tribal system of voluntary service to more systematic approaches. Professional soldiers formed the core of most armies, supplemented by militia forces during times of crisis. The state provided training, equipment, and regular pay to professional soldiers, creating a dedicated military class. Military service became an important avenue for social mobility, allowing individuals to rise in status through martial prowess.

Siege warfare became increasingly sophisticated as states sought to capture fortified cities. The development of siege engines, including catapults and battering rams, allowed armies to breach enemy fortifications. The art of siege warfare required specialized knowledge and equipment, leading to the emergence of military engineers and specialists.

Naval warfare, while less prominent than land-based conflicts, played a role in regions with significant water bodies. River fleets were used for transportation, supply, and combat along major waterways. Coastal states developed maritime capabilities for trade protection and territorial expansion.

Inter-state Relations: Diplomacy and Conflict

The emergence of multiple Janapadas led to a complex system of inter-state relations characterized by both cooperation and conflict. The political landscape of ancient Bharatavarsha became increasingly sophisticated as states developed formal diplomatic practices, alliance systems, and codes of conduct for warfare.

Diplomatic relations among the Janapadas were conducted through various means. Royal envoys (duta) served as the primary channel for communication between states. These diplomats were typically skilled in negotiation, well-versed in protocol, and granted special protection under customary law. The institution of diplomatic immunity, while not as formalized as in modern times, was generally respected among the Janapadas.

Alliance systems played a crucial role in maintaining the balance of power among the states. Rulers formed temporary and permanent alliances based on mutual interests, shared threats, or dynastic connections. Marriage alliances were particularly important, as they created lasting bonds between ruling families and provided mechanisms for peaceful conflict resolution.

The concept of mandala (circle of states) began to emerge as a framework for understanding inter-state relations. According to this theory, a king's immediate neighbors were natural enemies, while the neighbors of neighbors were potential allies. This strategic thinking influenced diplomatic and military policies, encouraging rulers to maintain complex networks of relationships.

Trade relations formed an important aspect of inter-state contact. The Janapadas developed commercial agreements, standardized weights and measures, and established safe passage for merchants. Trade routes became important diplomatic channels, and their protection was often a subject of inter-state negotiation.

Conflict resolution mechanisms evolved to manage disputes between states. While warfare remained a common means of settling disagreements, diplomatic alternatives were increasingly employed. Arbitration by neutral rulers, compensation payments, and negotiated settlements became accepted practices for resolving conflicts without resorting to arms.

The rules of warfare underwent gradual codification during this period. While ancient warfare in Bharatavarsha was often brutal by modern standards, certain conventions emerged regarding the treatment of prisoners, the protection of non-combatants, and the conduct of sieges. These rules were not always observed, but they represented an attempt to limit the destructive impact of conflict.

Territorial expansion became a driving force in inter-state relations. The stronger Janapadas gradually absorbed weaker neighbors through conquest, alliance, or intimidation. This process of political consolidation led to the emergence of larger, more powerful states that would eventually dominate the political landscape.

The role of geography in shaping inter-state relations cannot be understated. River valleys, mountain passes, and trade routes became strategic assets that influenced diplomatic and military policies. Control of key geographical features often determined the balance of power between neighboring states.

Economic Foundations of Political Power

The political evolution of the Janapadas was closely linked to economic developments that provided the material foundation for state formation. The transition from subsistence agriculture to surplus production, the growth of trade and commerce, and the development of specialized crafts created the wealth necessary to support professional armies, administrative bureaucracies, and elaborate court systems.

Agriculture remained the primary economic activity and the main source of state revenue. The fertile river valleys of the Ganga-Yamuna plain supported intensive cultivation of rice, wheat, barley, and other crops. Technological innovations, including iron plowshares and improved irrigation techniques, increased agricultural productivity and enabled the support of larger populations.

The development of urban centers created new economic opportunities and challenges. Cities became focal points for trade, craft production, and administration. The concentration of population in urban areas required sophisticated systems for food distribution, public health, and law enforcement. The growth of cities also created new sources of tax revenue through market fees, professional taxes, and property assessments.

Trade networks expanded significantly during this period, connecting the Janapadas with distant regions. Long-distance trade in luxury goods, raw materials, and specialized products generated substantial wealth for merchants and rulers. The state's role in protecting trade routes and regulating commerce became increasingly important as commercial activity grew.

The development of coinage revolutionized economic transactions and state finance. The earliest Bharatavarsha coins appeared around 600 BCE and were typically made of silver or copper. Standardized coinage facilitated trade, simplified tax collection, and enhanced the state's ability to pay soldiers and officials. The right to mint coins became an important symbol of sovereign authority.

Craft specialization increased dramatically as society became more complex. Skilled artisans produced goods for local consumption and long-distance trade. The organization of crafts into guilds (shreni) provided a framework for professional regulation and collective bargaining. These guilds often played important roles in urban politics and economics.

Social Transformation and Political Change

The political evolution of the Janapadas was accompanied by significant social transformations that both influenced and were influenced by changing governance structures. The emergence of territorial states accelerated social stratification, altered traditional kinship patterns, and created new opportunities for social mobility.

The varna system, which had begun to develop during the later Vedic period, became more rigid and elaborate in the Janapadas. The four main varnas - Brahmins (priests), Kshatriyas (warriors), Vaishyas (merchants and farmers), and Shudras (servants) - acquired more defined roles and restrictions. The political system reinforced these social divisions while also creating new categories of status based on administrative and military service.

The relationship between rulers and the priestly class became increasingly complex. While Brahmins provided ideological legitimacy for royal authority, they also competed with kings for social influence and economic resources. The tension between temporal and spiritual authority would remain a recurring theme in the political thought of ancient Bharatavarsha.

Urban growth created new social classes and altered traditional rural hierarchies. Merchants, artisans, and skilled workers gained economic importance that translated into political influence. The emergence of a wealthy merchant class challenged traditional notions of social status and provided rulers with new sources of support and revenue.

Women's roles in society and politics evolved during this period. While the general trend was toward greater restrictions on women's freedom, some royal women continued to wield significant influence. Queens and princesses played important roles in diplomacy, succession disputes, and court politics. The institution of royal marriage alliances elevated the political importance of certain women.

The rise of new religious movements, particularly Buddhism and Jainism, challenged traditional social and political structures. These religions questioned the authority of the Brahmanical priesthood and offered alternative models of social organization. The patronage of these movements by some rulers created new dynamics in the relationship between religion and politics.

Cultural and Intellectual Developments

The political evolution of the Janapadas coincided with remarkable cultural and intellectual developments that both supported and were supported by the emerging state systems. The growth of literature, philosophy, and artistic expression created a rich cultural foundation for political legitimacy and social cohesion.

The development of writing systems revolutionized administration, law, and cultural transmission. The Brahmi script, which emerged around 500 BCE, enabled the recording of laws, administrative records, and literary works. Literacy became increasingly important for administrative and commercial functions, leading to the emergence of a educated class that served the state.

Legal literature began to emerge as states required more sophisticated approaches to justice and governance. Early legal texts, while not yet as elaborate as later works like the Arthashastra, provided frameworks for understanding royal duties, legal procedures, and administrative practices. The concept of dharma (righteous duty) became central to political legitimacy.

Philosophical developments influenced political thought and practice. The Upanishads and early Buddhist texts explored questions of authority, justice, and the proper relationship between rulers and subjects. These intellectual traditions provided conceptual frameworks for understanding political power and its limitations.

Artistic patronage became an important function of the state. Rulers commissioned architectural projects, sculptures, and other artistic works that demonstrated their power and piety. The development of distinctive artistic styles associated with particular kingdoms helped create cultural identities that supported political cohesion.

The emergence of historical consciousness marked an important intellectual development. While full historical writing would not emerge until later periods, the Janapadas began to maintain genealogies, record important events, and develop narratives about their origins and achievements. This historical awareness contributed to the development of political legitimacy and cultural identity.

Technological Innovations and Political Power

Technological developments played a crucial role in the political evolution of the Janapadas. Innovations in metallurgy, agriculture, transportation, and communication enhanced the capacity of states to exercise control over their territories and populations.

Iron technology was perhaps the most significant technological development of this period. The widespread adoption of iron tools and weapons revolutionized agriculture, warfare, and craft production. Iron plowshares increased agricultural productivity, while iron weapons provided military advantages. The control of iron production and distribution became an important source of political power.

Improvements in transportation infrastructure facilitated political control and economic development. The construction of roads, bridges, and waterways enabled more efficient movement of armies, officials, and goods. The development of standardized weights and measures simplified trade and taxation across diverse regions.

Communication technologies, while still rudimentary, improved the ability of rulers to maintain contact with distant parts of their territories. The development of efficient messenger systems and the use of written communications enhanced administrative efficiency and political control.

Agricultural innovations, including improved irrigation techniques and crop rotation practices, increased food production and supported larger populations. The ability to generate agricultural surpluses provided the economic foundation for professional armies, administrative bureaucracies, and urban centers.

Decline and Transformation

The political system of the Janapadas was not static but underwent continuous evolution and transformation. Some states declined due to internal conflicts, external pressures, or economic difficulties, while others grew stronger and eventually dominated their neighbors.

The process of political consolidation led to the emergence of larger, more powerful states that gradually absorbed smaller neighbors. This trend toward centralization created the conditions for the eventual rise of major empires like the Mauryans. The Mahajanapadas represented an intermediate stage in this process of political evolution.

Environmental factors also played a role in the transformation of the Janapadas. Changes in river courses, climate variations, and natural disasters could significantly impact agricultural production and political stability. States that were able to adapt to these challenges survived and prospered, while others declined.

The rise of new religious and philosophical movements challenged traditional political structures and created new sources of legitimacy. Rulers who successfully adapted to these changes and incorporated new ideas into their governance systems were more likely to maintain power and influence.

Conclusion: The Legacy of the Janapadas

The political evolution from tribes to kingdoms during the Janapada period represents a fundamental transformation in the history of ancient Bharatavarsha. This transition established many of the institutional, ideological, and cultural foundations that would characterize political systems for centuries to come.

The development of territorial states created the framework for more sophisticated forms of governance, including professional bureaucracies, standing armies, and systematic revenue collection. The concept of kingship evolved from tribal leadership to a complex institution supported by religious ideology, legal theory, and administrative machinery.

The inter-state system that emerged among the Janapadas established precedents for diplomacy, alliance formation, and conflict resolution that would influence political practice throughout the ancient period. The balance between cooperation and competition among states created a dynamic political environment that encouraged innovation and adaptation.

The social and cultural developments that accompanied political evolution enriched the civilization of ancient Bharatavarsha and provided the foundation for later intellectual and artistic achievements. The tension between traditional and innovative elements in political thought created a rich tradition of political philosophy that continued to evolve throughout ancient history.

The economic foundations established during this period, including agricultural surplus production, urban commerce, and craft specialization, provided the material basis for the great empires that would follow. The integration of diverse regions into coherent political units created the conditions for cultural exchange and synthesis that would characterize classical civilization.

The legacy of the Janapadas extends far beyond the ancient period. The institutional innovations, political concepts, and cultural developments of this era influenced the later evolution of political systems and continue to resonate in modern political thought and practice. The transition from tribes to kingdoms represents not just a change in political organization but a fundamental transformation in human social organization that had lasting implications for civilization.

The study of this political evolution provides valuable insights into the processes of state formation, the relationship between political power and social organization, and the factors that contribute to the success or failure of political institutions. The Janapadas represent a crucial chapter in the long story of human political development, offering lessons that remain relevant for understanding political change and continuity in all societies.

12
Religious - Rituals and Philosophy

Elaborate Sacrificial Ceremonies

The foundation of Vedic religious practice rested upon an intricate system of sacrificial ceremonies that grew increasingly complex over time. These rituals, known as yajna, evolved from relatively simple offerings into elaborate performances requiring extensive preparation, precise execution, and substantial resources. The transformation of sacrificial practice reflects broader changes in society, economy, and religious understanding during the Vedic period.

The Nature and Purpose of Vedic Sacrifice

Vedic sacrifice operated on multiple levels of meaning and function. At its most fundamental level, sacrifice represented a transaction between the human and divine realms, maintaining the cosmic order known as rita. The sacrificial fire served as a messenger, carrying offerings to the gods and ensuring their continued favor. This reciprocal relationship between mortals and deities formed the cornerstone of Vedic religious thought, establishing patterns of devotion, obligation, and cosmic responsibility that would influence Indian religious consciousness for centuries.

The cosmological significance of sacrifice extended beyond mere petition or appeasement. Vedic texts suggest that sacrifice was understood as a creative act that participated in the ongoing maintenance and renewal of the universe. The ritual recreation of cosmic processes through carefully orchestrated ceremonies reflected a sophisticated understanding of the interconnectedness of human action and universal order. This concept would later develop into more complex philosophical formulations about the relationship between individual action (karma) and cosmic consequence.

Development of Sacrificial Complexity

The evolution of sacrificial ceremonies from simple domestic offerings to elaborate public rituals reflects significant changes in Vedic society. Early Vedic sacrifices, as described in the Rigveda, were relatively straightforward affairs involving offerings of soma, milk, clarified butter, and grain to various deities. These ceremonies could be performed by householders with minimal priestly assistance, emphasizing the direct relationship between devotees and divine powers.

As Vedic society became more stratified and specialized, sacrificial practice correspondingly increased in complexity. The development of the Brahmana texts, ritual manuals that provided detailed instructions for sacrificial performance, marks a crucial phase in this evolution. These texts reveal an extraordinary attention to procedural detail, specifying precise gestures, vocal intonations, timing, and materials required for effective ritual performance. The elaboration of these procedures served multiple purposes: ensuring ritual efficacy, demonstrating religious knowledge, and establishing the indispensable role of trained priests.

The most elaborate of these ceremonies, such as the Ashvamedha (horse sacrifice) and Rajasuya (royal consecration), required months of preparation and the coordination of numerous specialists. These grand sacrifices involved complex architectural constructions, the preparation of specific ritual implements, the training of participants in their roles, and the gathering of enormous quantities of offerings. The scale and complexity of these ceremonies reflected not only religious devotion but also political ambition, economic prosperity, and social hierarchy.

The Soma Sacrifice and Its Significance

Among the various sacrificial ceremonies, the soma sacrifice held particular importance in Vedic religion. Soma, identified with both a plant and a deity, represented the paradigmatic sacrificial offering, embodying the transformation of earthly substance into divine essence. The elaborate rituals surrounding soma preparation, offering, and consumption reveal fundamental Vedic concepts about the nature of sacrifice and its effects on both cosmic and individual levels.

The soma sacrifice required extensive preparation, including the gathering of specific plants, the construction of elaborate altars, and the performance of preliminary ceremonies. The actual pressing of soma involved precise techniques passed down through generations of priests, with each step accompanied by specific hymns and gestures. The resulting liquid was offered to various deities while portions were consumed by the priests and patrons, creating a communion between human and divine participants.

The psychological and spiritual dimensions of soma sacrifice have generated extensive scholarly debate. The euphoric effects described in Vedic hymns suggest that soma consumption produced altered states of consciousness that were interpreted as divine inspiration or communion with the gods. These experiences provided direct validation of religious beliefs and reinforced the authority of those who controlled access to such transformative rituals.

Sacrificial Symbolism and Cosmology

The development of sacrificial ceremonies was accompanied by increasingly sophisticated symbolic interpretations. The altar came to represent the universe in miniature, with its construction paralleling cosmic creation. The arrangement of bricks, the orientation of structures, and the placement of offerings all carried specific cosmological significance. This symbolic elaboration transformed sacrifice from a practical transaction into a complex theological statement about the nature of reality and humanity's place within it.

The temporal dimension of sacrifice also acquired profound significance. The careful timing of ceremonies according to lunar phases, seasonal changes, and astronomical observations reflected an understanding of sacrifice as participation in cosmic rhythms. This temporal sensitivity contributed to the development of sophisticated calendrical systems and astronomical knowledge that would later influence various branches of Indian learning.

The increasing complexity of sacrificial ceremonies necessitated the development of a specialized priestly class with the knowledge, training, and authority to perform these elaborate rituals. This development fundamentally transformed Vedic society, creating new forms of social organization, economic relationships, and cultural authority that would profoundly influence Indian civilization.

The Emergence of Priestly Specialization

The earliest Vedic period appears to have been relatively egalitarian in religious practice, with family heads and tribal leaders performing basic sacrificial functions. However, as rituals became more complex and the stakes of proper performance increased, the need for specialized knowledge and training became apparent. This specialization initially emerged within existing social structures but gradually developed into a distinct occupational and social category.

The development of priestly specialization was accompanied by the creation of elaborate systems of religious education and knowledge transmission. Young men from priestly families underwent extensive training in hymn memorization, ritual procedure, and theological interpretation. This education system, characterized by strict oral transmission and master-disciple relationships, ensured both the preservation of religious traditions and the maintenance of priestly authority.

The specialization of priestly functions also led to internal hierarchies within the priestly class. Different types of priests assumed specific roles in sacrificial ceremonies: the hotar recited hymns, the adhvaryu performed ritual actions, the udgatr chanted melodies, and the brahman supervised the entire ceremony. This division of labor reflected not only practical considerations but also different types of religious knowledge and spiritual authority.

The consolidation of priestly authority contributed significantly to the development of the varna system, the fourfold division of society that became characteristic of Indian social organization. The Brahmanas, as the priestly class came to be known, claimed the highest position in this hierarchy, asserting their essential role in maintaining cosmic order and social stability.

The elevation of Brahmanas to the apex of social hierarchy involved both practical and ideological dimensions. Practically, their control over essential religious services made them indispensable to rulers and householders seeking divine favor and cosmic harmony. Ideologically, they developed elaborate theories about their inherent spiritual superiority and their unique capacity to mediate between human and divine realms.

The Brahmana texts themselves reflect this growing sense of priestly importance and authority. These ritual manuals not only provide detailed instructions for sacrificial performance but also elaborate theological justifications for priestly preeminence. The texts present Brahmanas as the earthly representatives of divine power, essential for the proper functioning of both cosmic and social order.

The development of Brahmanical authority was closely connected to economic changes in Vedic society. The performance of elaborate sacrifices required substantial resources, creating new forms of economic relationship between priests and their patrons. The system of dakshina (ritual fees) evolved from simple gifts to complex economic arrangements that could transfer significant wealth to priestly families.

The most elaborate sacrifices, particularly those sponsored by rulers, involved enormous expenditures that could affect entire kingdoms. The distribution of gifts during these ceremonies served multiple functions: demonstrating royal generosity, ensuring divine favor, and redistributing wealth in ways that strengthened social bonds. Priests often emerged from these ceremonies with substantial material rewards, including land grants, cattle, and precious objects.

The economic power of the priestly class also derived from their role as advisors to rulers and administrators of religious institutions. Their literacy skills, knowledge of legal traditions, and understanding of astronomical calculations made them valuable in various administrative capacities. This practical usefulness reinforced their social position and provided additional sources of income and influence.

Despite their growing power and social prominence, the Brahmanas faced various challenges to their authority. The increasing complexity and expense of sacrificial ceremonies created resentment among some social groups, particularly those excluded from full participation in ritual life. The development of alternative religious practices and philosophical speculations, which we will examine later, also posed challenges to traditional priestly authority.

The rise of powerful rulers who sought to legitimize their authority through means other than traditional sacrifice created tensions within the established religious order. Some rulers patronized non-Brahmana religious teachers or developed alternative sources of spiritual authority that bypassed traditional priestly mediation. These developments contributed to the religious ferment that characterized the later Vedic period.

Emergence of Philosophical Speculation

The ritualistic focus of early Vedic religion gradually gave way to more abstract and philosophical forms of religious inquiry. This transformation, which began during the later Vedic period, represents one of the most significant developments in world religious history. The emergence of philosophical speculation fundamentally altered the nature of religious discourse, introducing new questions, methods, and concerns that would dominate Indian intellectual life for centuries.

From Ritual to Philosophy

The transition from ritualistic to philosophical religion was neither sudden nor complete. Early Vedic hymns already contained speculative elements, questioning the nature of creation, the origin of the gods, and the fundamental principles governing the universe. The famous Nasadiya Sukta (Hymn of Creation) from the Rigveda exemplifies this early philosophical curiosity, presenting a sophisticated meditation on the origins of existence that acknowledges the limitations of human knowledge.

The development of the Brahmana texts marked an important intermediate phase in this evolution. While primarily concerned with ritual procedure, these texts also contain extensive theological speculation about the meaning and significance of sacrificial actions. The concept of ritual symbolism became increasingly sophisticated, with every aspect of ceremonial performance interpreted as representing deeper cosmic truths.

The Aranyakas, or "forest texts," represent a crucial transitional phase between ritual and philosophy. These texts, traditionally studied by hermits and forest dwellers, began to question the ultimate value of external sacrificial performance while developing more internalized and symbolic interpretations of religious practice. The emphasis shifted from physical ritual to mental contemplation, from external offerings to internal spiritual discipline.

The Nature of Early Philosophical Inquiry

The philosophical speculation that emerged during the later Vedic period was characterized by several distinctive features. First, it maintained a close connection to religious practice and spiritual experience, rarely developing into purely abstract intellectual exercise. Second, it emphasized direct experience and intuitive insight rather than logical argumentation as the primary means of gaining knowledge. Third, it focused on fundamental questions about the nature of reality, consciousness, and human existence rather than detailed analysis of specific problems.

The methodology of early Indian philosophy differed significantly from later Greek philosophical traditions. Rather than emphasizing logical demonstration and rational argumentation, Indian philosophical inquiry relied heavily on meditation, contemplation, and direct spiritual experience. This approach reflected the practical orientation of Indian religious thought, which sought not merely to understand reality but to transform human consciousness and achieve spiritual liberation.

The social context of philosophical development also influenced its character. The emergence of philosophical speculation coincided with the development of alternative religious movements and the questioning of traditional authority structures. This environment of religious experimentation and intellectual ferment provided fertile ground for innovative thinking and spiritual exploration.

Several fundamental concepts emerged during this period of philosophical development that would profoundly influence all subsequent Indian thought. The concept of Brahman, the ultimate reality underlying all existence, evolved from earlier notions of sacred power and cosmic order. This development represented a shift from polytheistic to more monistic forms of religious understanding, though the transition was gradual and often incorporated earlier religious concepts.

The relationship between the individual soul (atman) and ultimate reality (Brahman) became a central concern of philosophical speculation. Early philosophical texts explored various theories about the nature of consciousness, the relationship between mind and body, and the ultimate destiny of the human soul. These investigations laid the groundwork for later developments in Indian psychology and spiritual practice.

The concept of karma, the law of cause and effect governing moral actions, also emerged during this period. While earlier Vedic thought had recognized connections between human actions and their consequences, the philosophical elaboration of karma theory provided a comprehensive framework for understanding moral responsibility, social justice, and spiritual development. This concept would become fundamental to all later Indian religious and philosophical systems.

The Role of Meditation and Contemplative Practice

The development of philosophical speculation was closely connected to the evolution of contemplative practices and meditation techniques. The Aranyakas and early Upanishads describe various forms of mental discipline designed to transcend ordinary consciousness and achieve direct insight into ultimate reality. These practices included breath control, sensory withdrawal, concentration techniques, and various forms of contemplative meditation.

The emphasis on direct experience as the ultimate validation of philosophical insight distinguished Indian philosophical traditions from purely intellectual approaches to knowledge. This experiential orientation meant that philosophical speculation was always connected to practical spiritual discipline and personal transformation. The integration of theory and practice became a characteristic feature of Indian philosophical traditions.

The development of meditation practices also contributed to the emergence of alternative religious movements and the questioning of traditional ritual authority. Those who achieved direct spiritual experience through contemplative practice often felt less dependent on external religious institutions and priestly mediation. This development contributed to the democratization of spiritual authority and the proliferation of alternative religious paths.

Upanishadic Thought and Its Origins

The Upanishads represent the culmination of Vedic philosophical development and the foundation of later Indian philosophical traditions. These texts, composed between approximately 800 and 200 BCE, mark the transition from ritualistic to philosophical religion and introduce concepts that would dominate Indian intellectual life for centuries. The Upanishadic revolution in religious thought represents one of the most significant developments in world religious history.

The Historical Context of Upanishadic Development

The Upanishads emerged during a period of significant social, political, and intellectual change in ancient India. The expansion of Vedic civilization into the Gangetic plain, the development of urban centers, and the emergence of new forms of political organization created conditions conducive to religious and philosophical innovation. The growing complexity of society and the challenges posed by new social relationships stimulated fresh thinking about fundamental religious questions.

The economic prosperity of the period also contributed to the development of Upanishadic thought. The wealth generated by agricultural expansion and urban development provided the leisure necessary for contemplative practice and philosophical speculation. The emergence of a class of individuals who could dedicate themselves to spiritual pursuits without concern for immediate material needs created conditions favorable to intensive religious inquiry.

The political changes of the period, including the emergence of powerful kingdoms and the challenges to traditional tribal authority, also influenced religious development. The questioning of traditional political structures was accompanied by similar questioning of religious authority and conventional spiritual practices. This environment of intellectual ferment provided fertile ground for the revolutionary ideas that characterize Upanishadic thought.

The Literary and Textual Character of the Upanishads

The Upanishads differ significantly from earlier Vedic literature in their literary style, philosophical content, and religious orientation. While earlier Vedic texts were primarily concerned with ritual procedure and hymnic praise, the Upanishads focus on philosophical inquiry and spiritual instruction. The texts employ various literary forms, including dialogue, narrative, meditation, and symbolic exposition, to convey their philosophical insights.

The dialogical character of many Upanishadic texts reflects their origin in teacher-student relationships and contemplative communities. The conversations between spiritual masters and their disciples provide dramatic frameworks for exploring fundamental philosophical questions. These dialogues often employ paradox, metaphor, and indirect suggestion to convey insights that transcend ordinary conceptual understanding.

The symbolic and metaphorical language of the Upanishads represents a sophisticated development in religious expression. Abstract philosophical concepts are presented through concrete imagery and practical analogies that make complex ideas accessible to contemplative understanding. This literary approach reflects the experiential orientation of Upanishadic thought and its emphasis on direct spiritual realization rather than mere intellectual comprehension.

Fundamental Upanishadic Concepts

The Upanishads introduce several revolutionary concepts that fundamentally transformed Indian religious thought. The concept of Brahman as the ultimate reality underlying all existence represents a radical departure from earlier polytheistic understandings. This development involved not merely the elevation of one deity above others but a complete reconceptualization of the nature of divine reality and its relationship to the phenomenal world.

The identification of the individual soul (atman) with universal reality (Brahman) represents perhaps the most revolutionary insight of Upanishadic thought. This teaching, expressed in the famous mahavakya (great saying) "Tat tvam asi" (Thou art That), suggests that the ultimate goal of spiritual practice is the realization of one's fundamental identity with ultimate reality. This concept would become central to later Advaita Vedanta philosophy and influence all subsequent Indian spiritual traditions.

The Upanishadic understanding of the relationship between knowledge and liberation also represents a significant development in religious thought. The texts suggest that ignorance (avidya) is the fundamental cause of human suffering and that liberation (moksha) can be achieved through the attainment of true knowledge (jnana). This emphasis on knowledge as the path to salvation would profoundly influence later Indian philosophical and spiritual traditions.

The Upanishads provide the earliest systematic treatment of the doctrine of transmigration (samsara) and its relationship to moral action (karma). These concepts, which would become fundamental to all later Indian religious traditions, represent sophisticated attempts to address questions of moral responsibility, social justice, and ultimate spiritual destiny.

The doctrine of transmigration suggests that consciousness survives bodily death and takes on new forms according to the moral quality of past actions. This teaching provided a framework for understanding apparent inequalities in human circumstances while maintaining belief in ultimate moral justice. The concept also emphasized individual responsibility for spiritual development and the possibility of achieving liberation through proper understanding and ethical action.

The integration of transmigration doctrine with the concept of liberation (moksha) created a comprehensive worldview that could address both practical moral questions and ultimate spiritual aspirations. The possibility of transcending the cycle of rebirth through spiritual realization provided a goal that could orient and inspire lifelong spiritual practice.

Upanishadic Meditation and Spiritual Practice

The Upanishads describe various forms of contemplative practice designed to achieve direct realization of ultimate reality. These practices include meditation on sacred sounds (particularly the syllable OM), visualization techniques, breath control, and various forms of contemplative inquiry. The texts present these practices not merely as techniques for mental concentration but as means of transcending ordinary consciousness and achieving direct insight into the nature of reality.

The emphasis on direct experience as the ultimate validation of spiritual insight distinguishes Upanishadic spirituality from purely intellectual or ritualistic approaches to religion. The texts consistently emphasize that ultimate reality cannot be grasped through conceptual thought or external ritual but must be directly experienced through contemplative practice and spiritual realization.

The integration of philosophical insight with contemplative practice would become a characteristic feature of later Indian spiritual traditions. The Upanishadic model of the enlightened teacher who combines philosophical understanding with direct spiritual realization established patterns of spiritual authority that would influence Indian religious culture for centuries.

Popular Religion and Folk Practices

While the development of sophisticated philosophical and ritual traditions captured the attention of learned elites, the religious life of ordinary people continued to be shaped by folk practices, local traditions, and popular beliefs that often differed significantly from Brahmanical orthodoxy. These popular religious traditions, though less well-documented than elite practices, played crucial roles in shaping the overall character of Indian religious culture and providing alternative forms of spiritual expression and community identity.

The Persistence of Folk Traditions

Despite the growing influence of Brahmanical religion and the development of sophisticated philosophical systems, folk religious traditions maintained their vitality and continued to evolve throughout the Vedic period. These traditions, rooted in local customs, agricultural practices, and community life, provided forms of religious expression that were more accessible and immediately relevant to ordinary people than the complex rituals and abstract philosophies of the elite.

Folk religious practices often centered around local deities, natural phenomena, and seasonal celebrations that reflected the immediate concerns and experiences of rural communities. The worship of tree spirits, river goddesses, fertility deities, and protective spirits provided direct and personal forms of religious engagement that complemented or sometimes competed with more formal religious institutions.

The oral tradition of folk religion ensured the preservation and transmission of these practices across generations, often incorporating new elements while maintaining core symbolic and ritual patterns. This flexibility allowed folk traditions to adapt to changing circumstances while preserving essential cultural values and community identity.

The relationship between folk religious traditions and Brahmanical orthodoxy was complex and varied significantly across different regions and time periods. In some cases, local deities and practices were incorporated into the Brahmanical pantheon and ritual system, often through processes of identification with Vedic deities or transformation into subsidiary aspects of major gods.

This process of integration was not merely one-directional. Brahmanical religion was also influenced by folk traditions, incorporating popular practices, seasonal celebrations, and local customs into its own developing traditions. The evolution of later Hinduism reflects this ongoing process of mutual influence and adaptation between elite and popular religious traditions.

However, tensions also existed between folk practices and Brahmanical orthodoxy. The egalitarian character of many folk traditions conflicted with the hierarchical structure of Brahmanical society. The direct access to divine power claimed by folk practitioners challenged the mediating role of the priestly class. These tensions would continue to influence Indian religious development throughout subsequent periods.

Folk religious traditions often provided greater opportunities for women's religious participation than formal Brahmanical practices. Women played important roles as ritual specialists, healers, and spiritual teachers in many folk traditions, maintaining and transmitting religious knowledge and practices that were often excluded from or marginalized within Brahmanical orthodoxy.

The association of women with fertility cults, healing practices, and domestic religious observances reflected their central roles in community life and their responsibilities for maintaining household welfare and social continuity. These roles provided forms of religious authority and spiritual influence that existed alongside and sometimes competed with formal religious institutions.

The religious traditions associated with women often emphasized practical concerns such as family welfare, agricultural prosperity, and protection from disease and natural disasters. These concerns reflected the immediate realities of daily life and provided forms of religious expression that were more directly relevant to ordinary experience than abstract philosophical speculation.

The diversity of Indian geography and cultural traditions ensured that folk religious practices varied significantly across different regions. Local environmental conditions, cultural histories, and social structures influenced the development of distinctive regional traditions that reflected particular concerns and values while maintaining connections to broader cultural patterns.

Mountain regions developed traditions centered around local deities associated with peaks, forests, and natural phenomena. River valley civilizations emphasized the worship of water goddesses and fertility spirits. Desert regions focused on protective deities and practices designed to ensure survival in harsh environments. These regional variations contributed to the overall diversity of Indian religious culture and provided models for later religious development.

The integration of these diverse regional traditions into broader religious systems was facilitated by trade networks, political expansions, and cultural exchanges that brought different communities into contact with each other. This process of cultural interaction and synthesis would become a characteristic feature of Indian religious development.

Popular Festivals and Seasonal Celebrations

Folk religious traditions were particularly evident in the celebration of seasonal festivals and agricultural ceremonies that marked important transitions in the natural and social year. These celebrations often involved entire communities and provided opportunities for collective religious expression that transcended individual spiritual practice.

Harvest festivals, new moon celebrations, and seasonal transitions were marked by elaborate ceremonies that combined religious observance with social celebration. These events reinforced community bonds, provided opportunities for cultural transmission, and created shared experiences that strengthened collective identity and social cohesion.

The persistence of these celebratory traditions and their eventual incorporation into later Hindu religious calendars demonstrates the enduring influence of folk religious practices on Indian religious culture. Many of the major festivals and religious observances of later Hinduism can be traced back to these early folk traditions.

The Role of Sacred Geography

Folk religious traditions often emphasized the sacredness of particular places and natural features, creating networks of sacred geography that provided frameworks for religious pilgrimage and spiritual practice. Rivers, mountains, forests, and other natural phenomena were understood as manifestations of divine power and served as focal points for religious devotion and community gathering.

These sacred places often became centers for regional religious traditions and provided continuity across different historical periods. The identification of particular locations with divine presence created lasting connections between religious practice and geographic identity that would influence Indian religious culture for centuries.

The development of pilgrimage networks connecting various sacred sites facilitated cultural exchange and religious integration while maintaining respect for local traditions and regional variations. This balance between unity and diversity would become a characteristic feature of later Indian religious culture.

Conclusion

The religious evolution examined in this chapter represents one of the most significant transformations in human spiritual history. The journey from early Vedic sacrificial religion through the development of priestly hierarchy, philosophical speculation, and Upanishadic thought, combined with the persistent influence of folk traditions, created a rich and diverse religious culture that would profoundly influence not only Indian civilization but world religious consciousness.

The elaboration of sacrificial ceremonies demonstrated the human capacity for creating complex symbolic systems that connect individual action with cosmic significance. The development of priestly hierarchy revealed both the social power of religious authority and the tensions such authority creates within broader social structures. The emergence of philosophical speculation showed how religious consciousness could evolve from ritualistic to contemplative forms while maintaining essential spiritual concerns. The Upanishadic revolution in religious thought introduced concepts that would influence intellectual and spiritual development for millennia.

Perhaps most importantly, the persistent interaction between elite religious traditions and popular folk practices demonstrated the complex and dynamic nature of religious development. The ongoing process of mutual influence, adaptation, and creative synthesis between different forms of religious expression created a religious culture characterized by both remarkable diversity and underlying unity.

This religious evolution established patterns and precedents that would continue to influence Indian religious development throughout subsequent periods. The balance between ritual and philosophy, the tension between hierarchical and egalitarian forms of religious authority, the integration of diverse regional traditions, and the emphasis on direct spiritual experience would all remain characteristic features of Indian religious culture.

The period examined in this chapter thus represents not merely a historical phase but a foundational period that established the framework within which Indian religious consciousness would continue to evolve. The questions raised, the concepts developed, and the practices established during this time would provide the foundation for the rich tapestry of religious traditions that would emerge in subsequent centuries, making this period crucial for understanding not only ancient Indian religion but the broader development of human spiritual consciousness.

13
Agriculture and Trade

Settled Agriculture and Surplus Production

The shift to agriculture was not merely a change in food production methods; it was a comprehensive transformation that touched every aspect of human existence. As communities began to cultivate crops and domesticate animals, they experienced unprecedented population growth, developed complex social hierarchies, and created the first permanent settlements. These changes, in turn, facilitated the emergence of specialized crafts, the establishment of trade networks, and the development of increasingly sophisticated economic systems.

This chapter explores the multifaceted nature of early economic development, examining how settled agriculture created the conditions for surplus production, which became the catalyst for craft specialization, trade expansion, and urban growth. We will investigate how these interconnected developments led to the formation of guilds, the establishment of extensive trade networks, the evolution of currency systems, and the rise of urban centers that served as crucial marketplaces for economic exchange.

The Agricultural Transformation

The transition to settled agriculture, often referred to as the Neolithic Transformation, occurred independently in several regions around the world between 10,000 and 8,000 years ago. In the Fertile Crescent of the Middle East, communities began cultivating wheat, barley, and legumes while

domesticating sheep, goats, cattle, and pigs. Simultaneously, agricultural developments were taking place in other parts of the world: rice cultivation in East Asia, maize production in Mesoamerica, and the domestication of potatoes in the Andes.

The shift from foraging to farming was gradual rather than sudden, often taking centuries to complete. Early agricultural communities maintained hybrid economies, combining cultivation with continued hunting and gathering. This transitional period allowed societies to develop the knowledge and techniques necessary for successful agriculture while maintaining fallback options during times of crop failure or environmental stress.

The development of agriculture required significant innovations in technology and knowledge. Early farmers had to learn about seed selection, soil preparation, irrigation, and crop rotation. They developed new tools such as hoes, sickles, and eventually plows, which dramatically increased agricultural productivity. The domestication of animals provided not only meat and milk but also labor power for plowing fields and transportation.

Surplus Production and Its Implications

The most revolutionary aspect of settled agriculture was its capacity to generate surplus production beyond immediate subsistence needs. Unlike hunter-gatherer societies, which typically operated close to subsistence levels, agricultural communities could produce more food than they immediately consumed. This surplus became the foundation for all subsequent economic and social development.

Surplus production had several crucial implications. First, it allowed for population growth on an unprecedented scale. Agricultural communities could support much larger populations than huntergatherer groups, leading to the first significant increase in human population density. Villages of several hundred people became common, and some early agricultural settlements grew to accommodate thousands of inhabitants.

Second, surplus production enabled labor specialization. When not everyone needed to be directly involved in food production, some individuals could dedicate their time to other activities such as toolmaking, pottery, weaving, or religious ceremonies. This specialization led to increased efficiency and innovation in various crafts and technologies.

Third, agricultural surplus created the possibility of social stratification. Those who controlled surplus production—whether through land ownership, administrative roles, or religious authority—could accumulate wealth and power. This led to the emergence of social classes, with farmers, craftspeople, merchants, and elites occupying different positions in increasingly complex social hierarchies.

Storage and Preservation Technologies

The ability to generate surplus production was closely linked to advances in storage and preservation technologies. Early agricultural societies developed sophisticated methods for storing grain, including underground pits, ceramic vessels, and eventually large granaries. These storage facilities protected food from pests, moisture, and theft while allowing communities to maintain reserves for times of scarcity.

Preservation techniques such as drying, smoking, and fermentation extended the shelf life of various foods, enabling communities to maintain diverse diets throughout the year. The development of fermentation, in particular, led to the production of alcoholic beverages, which became important both for nutrition and social ceremonies.

The construction of storage facilities required significant labor investment and represented some of the earliest examples of public works projects. Large granaries became symbols of community wealth and security, often located in prominent positions within settlements and sometimes associated with religious or administrative buildings.

Environmental Management and Sustainability

Successful agricultural communities developed sophisticated understanding of environmental management and sustainability. They learned to manage soil fertility through crop rotation, fallowing, and the application of organic fertilizers. Irrigation systems were developed to control water resources, ranging from simple channel systems to complex networks of canals and reservoirs.

The relationship between agriculture and environment was not always harmonious. Some early agricultural societies experienced environmental degradation due to overfarming, deforestation, or salinization of irrigated land. These challenges forced communities to develop more sustainable practices or, in some cases, led to the abandonment of settlements.

The seasonal nature of agriculture also shaped social organization and cultural practices. Agricultural communities developed calendars based on seasonal cycles, celebrated harvest festivals, and organized their social activities around the agricultural year. This seasonal rhythm became deeply embedded in cultural traditions and religious practices.

Craft Specialization and Guilds

The Emergence of Specialized Crafts

As agricultural surplus freed individuals from direct food production, specialized crafts began to flourish. The earliest specialized crafts included pottery, weaving, metalworking, and toolmaking. These crafts required specialized knowledge, tools, and materials, making it more efficient for individuals to focus on particular skills rather than attempting to master all necessary technologies.

Pottery was among the first widespread specialized crafts. The production of ceramic vessels required knowledge of clay preparation, firing techniques, and decorative methods. Potters developed kilns capable of reaching high temperatures and experimented with different clay compositions and glazes. Pottery served both practical and ceremonial purposes, with specialized vessels for cooking, storage, serving, and religious rituals.

Textile production represented another crucial craft specialization. The processing of plant fibers and animal hair into thread, and the weaving of thread into cloth, required specialized tools such as spindles, looms, and various processing implements. Textile production often became associated with women's work, though this varied among different cultures.

Metalworking emerged as one of the most transformative craft specializations. Beginning with copper and later incorporating tin to create bronze, metalworkers developed techniques for mining, smelting, and shaping metals. The production of metal tools and weapons required extensive knowledge of ore sources, furnace construction, and metallurgical processes. Metalworking communities often developed around ore deposits, creating some of the earliest specialized economic settlements.

The Development of Expertise and Knowledge Transfer

Craft specialization led to the development of increasingly sophisticated expertise within specific fields. Master craftspeople accumulated knowledge through years of practice and experimentation, developing techniques that were often closely guarded secrets. This knowledge was typically passed down through family lines or apprenticeship systems, creating dynasties of skilled craftspeople.

The transfer of craft knowledge involved both practical training and theoretical understanding. Apprentices learned not only specific techniques but also the properties of materials, the principles underlying their craft, and the cultural significance of their products. This knowledge transfer system ensured continuity of traditions while also allowing for innovation and improvement.

Different crafts developed their own specialized vocabularies, tools, and techniques. Metalworkers, for example, developed complex understanding of alloy compositions, heat treatment, and forming techniques. Textile workers created sophisticated looms and developed intricate patterns and weaving methods. These specialized knowledge systems became increasingly complex and required dedicated learning periods.

The Formation of Guilds

As craft specialization became more established, craftspeople began organizing themselves into guilds or similar professional associations. These organizations served multiple functions: they protected the interests of their members, maintained quality standards, regulated training and apprenticeship, and often held significant political and economic power within their communities.

Guilds typically controlled entry into their trades through apprenticeship systems. Young people would serve as apprentices for several years, learning the basic skills of their craft while providing labor to established craftspeople. After completing their apprenticeship, they might become journeymen, working for wages while perfecting their skills. Eventually, they could achieve master status, allowing them to establish their own workshops and take on apprentices.

Quality control was another crucial function of guilds. They established standards for materials, workmanship, and finished products, often marking approved goods with special stamps or seals. This quality control system helped maintain consumer confidence and protected the reputation of guild members. Guilds also regulated pricing and working conditions, preventing unfair competition and ensuring reasonable profit margins for their members.

Many guilds developed strong social and religious dimensions. They often had patron deities or saints, held regular festivals and ceremonies, and provided mutual support for members and their families. Guild halls became important social centers, serving as meeting places, training facilities, and symbols of professional identity.

Technological Innovation and Competition

Craft specialization fostered technological innovation as craftspeople competed to improve their products and techniques. This competition drove developments in tool design, material processing, and production methods. Innovations in one craft often influenced others, creating networks of technological exchange and improvement.

The competitive environment also encouraged geographic specialization. Certain regions became known for particular crafts based on local resources, accumulated expertise, or favorable conditions. This geographic specialization contributed to the development of trade networks as communities sought to obtain goods they could not produce locally.

Technological secrets became valuable commodities. Master craftspeople often guarded their techniques carefully, and the theft of trade secrets could lead to serious conflicts. Some communities attempted to prevent the emigration of skilled craftspeople to protect their economic advantages, while others actively recruited skilled workers from other regions.

Trade Networks and Exchange

The Origins of Trade

Trade emerged naturally from the uneven distribution of resources and the development of craft specialization. No single community could produce everything its members needed or desired, creating opportunities for exchange between different groups. The earliest trade probably involved the exchange of raw materials such as obsidian, flint, or shells, which were valued for their utility in toolmaking or decoration.

As craft specialization developed, trade expanded to include finished goods. Communities with skilled potters, metalworkers, or textile producers could exchange their products for raw materials or goods they could not produce themselves. This trade in finished goods required more sophisticated systems of evaluation and exchange, as the value of crafted items was often difficult to determine.

The development of agriculture created new opportunities for trade. Different regions had varying agricultural products based on climate, soil conditions, and local expertise. Surplus grain from fertile regions could be traded for meat, dairy products, or specialized crops from other areas. Agricultural tools, seeds, and breeding animals also became important trade commodities.

Trade Routes and Networks

Early trade networks followed natural geographic features such as rivers, mountain passes, and coastal routes. Rivers provided convenient transportation for bulk goods, while mountain passes connected different regions despite challenging terrain. Coastal trade allowed for the exchange of goods across water bodies, though this required the development of suitable watercraft.

The establishment of regular trade routes led to the development of way stations and trading posts. These locations provided rest, supplies, and security for traveling merchants. Many of these trading posts eventually grew into permanent settlements, contributing to the spread of human habitation into new regions.

Long-distance trade networks created connections between distant communities, facilitating not only economic exchange but also cultural transmission. Ideas, technologies, and cultural practices spread along trade routes, contributing to the diffusion of innovations and the development of shared cultural elements across wide geographic areas.

The most famous ancient trade networks included the Silk Road connecting East and West Asia, the trans-Saharan trade routes linking North and sub-Saharan Africa, and the Mediterranean trade networks that connected Europe, Africa, and Asia. These networks facilitated the exchange of luxury goods, raw materials, and cultural innovations across vast distances.

Merchants and Trading Organizations

The expansion of trade led to the emergence of specialized merchants who dedicated themselves to commercial activities. These merchants developed expertise in evaluating goods, negotiating prices, and managing the risks associated with long-distance trade. They often accumulated significant wealth and became influential figures in their communities.

Merchant families often established trading dynasties, passing down commercial knowledge, connections, and resources through generations. These families developed extensive networks of contacts, including suppliers, customers, and other merchants, which gave them significant advantages in conducting business.

Trading organizations emerged to pool resources and share risks. Merchants might form partnerships for specific ventures, sharing costs and profits according to agreed-upon terms. These organizations could undertake larger and more complex trading expeditions than individual merchants could manage alone.

Some trading organizations developed sophisticated systems for managing long-distance commerce. They established standards for weights and measures, developed methods for extending credit, and created systems for settling disputes. These organizational innovations were crucial for the expansion of trade networks and the development of commercial law.

Trade Goods and Their Significance

The goods traded in early networks ranged from essential raw materials to luxury items. Basic materials such as metals, stone, and wood were crucial for toolmaking and construction. Salt, which was essential for food preservation and human health, became one of the most important trade commodities and was sometimes used as currency.

Luxury goods played a particularly important role in early trade networks. Items such as precious metals, gems, fine textiles, and exotic foods were highly valued by elites and often traveled great distances. The trade in luxury goods was often more profitable than bulk commodity trade, though it also involved greater risks.

Agricultural products formed another major category of trade goods. Surplus grain from fertile regions could be exchanged for animal products, vegetables, or specialized crops from other areas. The trade in agricultural products helped communities survive local crop failures and allowed for greater dietary diversity.

Technological products such as tools, weapons, and crafted items represented another important category of trade goods. Communities with skilled craftspeople could export their products in exchange for raw materials or other goods they needed. This trade in technological products helped spread innovations and improved living standards across different regions.

Currency and Economic Transactions

The Evolution from Barter to Currency

The earliest economic transactions were conducted through barter systems, where goods were directly exchanged for other goods without the use of a standardized medium of exchange. While barter systems could work effectively for simple transactions, they became increasingly cumbersome as trade networks grew more complex and diverse.

The limitations of barter systems became apparent as trade expanded. The "double coincidence of wants" problem arose when traders needed to find partners who not only had goods they wanted but also wanted the goods they offered. This problem was compounded by the difficulty of determining equivalent values between different types of goods.

To address these challenges, communities began adopting standardized items that could serve as media of exchange. These proto-currencies were typically goods that were widely valued, relatively durable, and easy to transport. Common examples included shells, beads, livestock, grain, and eventually metals.

The transition to currency systems was gradual and varied significantly between different regions and cultures. Some communities continued to use barter for local transactions while adopting currency for long-distance trade. Others developed complex systems that combined elements of both barter and currency exchange.

Types of Early Currency

Commodity currencies were among the earliest forms of standardized exchange media. These currencies were based on goods that had intrinsic value and practical uses beyond their monetary function. Cattle, for example, served as currency in many pastoral societies, providing a store of value that could also produce milk, meat, and labor.

Agricultural products such as grain or rice served as currency in many farming communities. These commodities had the advantage of being essential for survival, making them universally acceptable. However, their perishability and bulk made them less suitable for long-distance trade or long-term storage.

Precious metals gradually became the preferred medium of exchange in many societies. Gold, silver, and copper had several advantages as currency: they were durable, divisible, relatively rare, and had intrinsic value for decorative and practical purposes. The development of metalworking techniques allowed for the creation of standardized weights and measures, making metal currencies more practical.

The introduction of coined money represented a major advancement in currency systems. Coins provided standardized weights and purities of precious metals, backed by the authority of issuing governments or institutions. This standardization reduced transaction costs and facilitated trade by eliminating the need to weigh and test metals for each transaction.

Banking and Credit Systems

As economic transactions became more complex, communities developed systems for managing money and credit. Early banking functions included the storage of valuables, the exchange of different currencies, and the provision of credit for commercial ventures. These services were often provided by temples, wealthy merchants, or specialized banking houses.

Temple banking was common in many early civilizations, as religious institutions were often trusted with valuable goods and had the security needed to protect deposits. Temples sometimes issued loans for commercial ventures, using their religious authority to ensure repayment. They also served as neutral parties for settling commercial disputes.

Merchant banking emerged as trade networks expanded and commercial activities became more sophisticated. Wealthy merchants began offering financial services to other traders, including currency exchange, credit extension, and investment in commercial ventures. These merchant bankers often had extensive networks of contacts and knowledge of market conditions.

Credit systems allowed for more complex commercial transactions by enabling deferred payment arrangements. Merchants could obtain goods with promises to pay later, allowing them to conduct business even when they lacked immediate funds. These credit arrangements were often secured by collateral or backed by the reputation and relationships of the borrowers.

Record Keeping and Accounting

The development of currency systems required sophisticated record-keeping methods to track transactions, debts, and assets. Early accounting systems used various methods for recording economic information, including clay tablets, knotted strings, and marked sticks. These systems allowed businesses and governments to maintain detailed records of their financial activities.

Double-entry bookkeeping, which developed in medieval Europe, represented a major advancement in accounting methodology. This system required that every transaction be recorded in at least two accounts, ensuring that financial records remained balanced and providing better controls against errors and fraud.

The development of written contracts and legal documents supported the growth of complex economic transactions. These documents specified the terms of agreements, including prices, delivery schedules, and penalty clauses. Legal systems developed to enforce these contracts and resolve commercial disputes.

Standardized weights and measures were crucial for the functioning of currency and trade systems. Different communities developed their own measurement standards, but successful trade required either the adoption of common standards or the development of conversion systems. The standardization of weights and measures often became a function of central authorities or trade organizations.

Urban Centers and Marketplaces

The Rise of Urban Centers

The development of agriculture, craft specialization, and trade networks created the conditions for the emergence of urban centers. These early cities represented a fundamental shift in human settlement patterns, concentrating large populations in relatively small areas and creating new forms of social and economic organization.

Urban centers emerged in locations that offered advantages for trade and production. River valleys provided water for agriculture and transportation, while locations at the intersection of trade routes became natural gathering places for merchants and craftspeople. Coastal areas offered access to maritime trade, while regions with valuable natural resources attracted specialized industries.

The concentration of population in urban centers created new economic opportunities and challenges.

Cities required sophisticated systems for providing food, water, and other necessities to their inhabitants. They also needed systems for managing waste, maintaining security, and governing large, diverse populations.

Urban centers became focal points for innovation and cultural development. The concentration of skilled craftspeople, merchants, and scholars in cities created environments that fostered technological advancement and cultural exchange. Cities often became centers of learning, with schools, libraries, and other educational institutions.

Marketplaces and Commercial Districts

Marketplaces formed the economic heart of early urban centers. These spaces provided venues for the exchange of goods and services, bringing together producers, merchants, and consumers in organized settings. The design and organization of marketplaces reflected the economic needs and social structures of their communities.

Central marketplaces were often located in prominent positions within cities, sometimes adjacent to religious or governmental buildings. These locations reflected the importance of commerce in urban life and provided security and oversight for commercial activities. Market squares became important social spaces where people gathered not only for commerce but also for news, entertainment, and social interaction.

Specialized markets developed for different types of goods and services. Grain markets, livestock markets, and craft markets might be located in different areas of a city, each with facilities appropriate for their particular products. This specialization improved efficiency and allowed for better regulation of different types of trade.

The organization of marketplaces required sophisticated systems of governance and regulation. Market authorities established rules for trading, maintained standards for weights and measures, and resolved disputes between merchants and customers. They also collected taxes and fees that provided revenue for urban governments.

Urban Economic Organization

Urban centers developed complex economic systems that coordinated the activities of diverse populations. These systems included mechanisms for distributing food and raw materials, organizing production and services, and managing the flow of goods and money throughout the urban area.

Food distribution systems were crucial for urban survival. Cities required regular supplies of grain, meat, vegetables, and other foodstuffs from surrounding rural areas. These supplies were often organized through market systems, but some cities also developed public distribution systems for essential commodities.

Manufacturing districts emerged in many urban centers, concentrating particular crafts or industries in specific areas. These districts provided advantages through the sharing of resources, knowledge, and infrastructure. They also allowed for better regulation of industrial activities and management of environmental impacts.

Service sectors developed to meet the needs of urban populations. These included transportation services, construction, entertainment, and various personal services. The growth of service sectors reflected the increasing complexity of urban life and the specialization of economic activities.

Trade and Cultural Exchange

Urban centers became crucial nodes in trade networks, facilitating the exchange of goods between different regions and cultures. Cities often served as intermediaries, collecting goods from surrounding areas and redistributing them to distant markets. This intermediary function contributed to urban wealth and influence.

The concentration of merchants and traders in urban centers created opportunities for cultural exchange. Cities became melting pots where people from different backgrounds interacted, leading to the exchange of ideas, technologies, and cultural practices. This cultural mixing contributed to innovation and the development of new artistic and intellectual traditions.

Urban centers often developed distinctive cultural identities based on their economic activities and trade connections. Port cities might develop maritime cultures, while cities located on caravan routes might reflect the influences of diverse trading peoples. These cultural developments contributed to the richness and diversity of urban life.

The growth of urban centers also created new forms of social organization and governance. Cities required systems for managing large, diverse populations and coordinating complex economic activities. These requirements led to the development of new political institutions, legal systems, and administrative structures that would influence the development of civilization for centuries to come.

Conclusion

The economic developments explored in this chapter represent fundamental transformations in human society that continue to influence our world today. The transition from nomadic hunting and gathering to settled agriculture created the foundation for all subsequent economic development, while the emergence of craft specialization, trade networks, currency systems, and urban centers established the basic framework of economic organization that persists in modern societies.

The development of agricultural surplus production was perhaps the most crucial breakthrough, as it enabled population growth, social stratification, and the emergence of specialized roles within society. This surplus created the conditions for craft specialization, which in turn drove technological innovation and the development of complex skill-based hierarchies. The organization of craftspeople into guilds established important precedents for professional associations and quality control systems that remain relevant today.

Trade networks emerged as natural responses to resource distribution and specialization, creating connections between distant communities and facilitating the exchange of goods, ideas, and technologies. These networks required sophisticated organizational systems and gave rise to specialized merchant classes who played crucial roles in economic development. The evolution of currency systems from simple barter to complex monetary systems enabled increasingly sophisticated economic transactions and laid the groundwork for modern financial systems.

Urban centers represented the culmination of these economic developments, concentrating populations and economic activities in ways that fostered further innovation and growth. The marketplaces and commercial districts that emerged in these urban centers established patterns of economic organization that continue to influence how we think about commerce and trade.

These early economic developments also established important social and cultural patterns. The relationship between economic specialization and social stratification, the role of trade in cultural exchange, and the importance of urban centers as focal points for innovation and development all remain relevant to understanding contemporary economic systems.

The lessons learned from these early economic developments continue to inform our understanding of economic processes. The importance of surplus production for economic growth, the role of specialization in driving innovation, the value of trade networks for resource distribution, and the significance of urban centers for economic coordination all remain crucial concepts in modern economic theory and practice.

As we face contemporary economic challenges, the historical perspective provided by these early developments offers valuable insights into the fundamental processes that drive economic change and development. Understanding how our ancestors navigated the transition from simple subsistence economies to complex commercial systems can help us better understand the challenges and opportunities of our own economic evolution.

14
The Sacred Texts

The Eternal River of Knowledge

In the vast expanse of human civilization, few literary traditions can claim the antiquity, continuity, and profound influence of the Vedic corpus. Like an eternal river flowing through the landscape of human consciousness, the sacred texts of ancient India have carried forward the wisdom, rituals, and philosophical insights of countless generations across more than three millennia. The Vedic literature represents not merely a collection of ancient texts, but a living tradition that has shaped the spiritual, intellectual, and cultural fabric of one of the world's oldest continuous civilizations.

The story of Vedic literature is fundamentally the story of humanity's quest to understand the divine, the cosmos, and the human condition. From the earliest hymns composed by inspired seers (rishis) in the misty dawn of recorded Indian history to the sophisticated philosophical treatises that would later influence global thought, this literary tradition demonstrates remarkable continuity while simultaneously showing extraordinary capacity for growth and adaptation.

The four-fold structure of the Vedic corpus—the Samhitas (collections), Brahmanas (ritual explanations), Aranyakas (forest treatises), and Upanishads (philosophical texts)—represents not just a chronological development but a deepening of spiritual understanding. Each layer built upon the previous, creating a sophisticated theological and philosophical framework that would influence not only Indian thought but eventually, through various channels, contribute to the broader stream of human wisdom.

What makes the Vedic tradition particularly remarkable is its method of preservation and transmission. In an age when writing was either unknown or considered unsuitable for sacred knowledge, the ancient Indians developed sophisticated oral techniques that ensured the precise transmission of these texts across generations. This oral tradition, known as the Guru-Shishya Parampara (teacher-student tradition), created an unbroken chain of transmission that has preserved these texts with remarkable fidelity for over three thousand years.

The continuous thread that runs through this vast literary corpus is the search for truth—satya—and the understanding of dharma, the cosmic order that governs both the universe and human conduct. From the cosmic hymns of the Rig Veda to the profound philosophical insights of the Upanishads, we see the gradual evolution of human understanding of the relationship between the individual soul (atman) and the universal consciousness (Brahman).

The Foundation: Compilation of the Four Vedas

The four Vedas—Rig, Sama, Yajur, and Atharva—represent the foundational texts of not only Hinduism but of Indo-European religious thought. These collections, known as Samhitas, were compiled over several centuries, with the Rig

Veda being the earliest and most revered. The compilation process itself reflects the systematic approach of ancient Indian scholars to preserve and organize their sacred heritage.

The Rig Veda: The Ancient Hymnal

The Rig Veda, consisting of 1,028 hymns organized into ten mandalas (circles or books), stands as the oldest surviving text of the Indo-European language family. Composed between approximately 1500-1200 BCE, these hymns represent the religious and philosophical thoughts of the early Vedic people. The compilation was not a haphazard collection but a carefully structured anthology that reflects both chronological development and thematic organization.

The first and tenth mandalas contain some of the latest material and show signs of compilation, while mandalas two through seven, known as the family books, are attributed to specific priestly families and contain some of the oldest material. This structure reveals the sophisticated editorial process undertaken by the ancient compilers, who were not merely collecting verses but creating a coherent religious and literary work.

The hymns of the Rig Veda address various deities—Agni (fire), Indra (the warrior god), Varuna (the cosmic sovereign), Surya (the sun), and many others—but they also contain profound philosophical speculation. The famous Nasadiya Sukta (Creation Hymn) in the tenth mandala poses fundamental questions about the nature of existence and creation that continue to resonate with philosophical inquiry today. The hymn's uncertainty about the ultimate origin of the universe—"Who really knows? Who will here proclaim it?"—demonstrates the intellectual honesty and philosophical sophistication of the Vedic seers.

The continuous thread that emerges from the Rig Veda is the concept of Rita, the cosmic order that governs both natural phenomena and moral conduct. This concept would later evolve into the more familiar notion of dharma, but its seeds are clearly visible in the Rig Vedic hymns. The seers understood that the universe operated according to certain principles, and human society must align itself with these principles to achieve harmony and prosperity.

The Sama Veda: The Melodic Tradition

The Sama Veda, often called the "Veda of melodies," represents the musical dimension of Vedic worship. Consisting primarily of verses taken from the Rig Veda but arranged for chanting, the Sama Veda reveals the importance of sound and rhythm in Vedic religious practice. The compilation of the Sama Veda demonstrates the early recognition that spiritual truth could be conveyed not only through words but through the very vibrations of sound.

The Sama Veda is organized into two main parts: the Archika, containing the verses, and the Uttararchika, containing additional melodies. The text shows clear evidence of musical notation systems that were sophisticated for their time, indicating that the compilers understood the technical aspects of musical performance as well as the spiritual significance of sound.

The continuous thread from the Sama Veda is the understanding of sound as a spiritual force. The concept of Nada Brahman—the idea that the ultimate reality can be experienced through sound—finds its earliest expression in the Sama Veda. This understanding would later influence the development of Indian classical music, the practice of mantra recitation, and the philosophical concept of OM as the primordial sound.

The Yajur Veda: The Ritual Manual

The Yajur Veda exists in two main recensions: the Shukla (White) Yajur Veda and the Krishna (Black) Yajur Veda. This Veda consists of prose formulas and verses used in ritual worship, particularly in the performance of yajnas (fire sacrifices). The compilation of the Yajur Veda reflects the systematization of ritual practice and the recognition that proper performance of religious ceremonies required precise verbal formulations.

The Yajur Veda demonstrates the sophisticated understanding of ritual symbolism that characterized Vedic religion. Each ritual action was accompanied by specific mantras that were believed to activate the spiritual forces necessary for the ceremony's success. The compilation process shows evidence of careful attention to the practical needs of the adhvaryu priest, who was responsible for the physical aspects of the ritual.

The continuous thread from the Yajur Veda is the understanding of ritual as a means of maintaining cosmic order. The concept of yajna as a cosmic principle—the idea that sacrifice maintains the balance of the universe—emerges clearly from this text. This understanding would later be internalized in the Upanishads and the Bhagavad Gita, where external ritual becomes a metaphor for internal spiritual practice.

The Atharva Veda: The Practical Wisdom

The Atharva Veda, the latest of the four Vedas to be compiled, contains a different type of material from the other three. While the first three Vedas are primarily concerned with ritual and worship, the Atharva Veda contains practical spells, charms, and incantations for everyday life. It also contains some of the most profound philosophical material in the entire Vedic corpus.

The compilation of the Atharva Veda reflects the recognition that spiritual practice must address the practical needs of daily life. The text contains spells for healing, protection, prosperity, and success in various endeavors. But it also contains hymns that rival the philosophical depth of the Upanishads, such as the Prithvi Sukta (Earth Hymn), which expresses a profound ecological consciousness.

The continuous thread from the Atharva Veda is the integration of spiritual and practical wisdom. The text demonstrates that the Vedic seers understood that true spiritual practice must encompass all aspects of human existence. This holistic approach would become a defining characteristic of Indian philosophy and would influence the development of systems like Ayurveda, which integrate spiritual and physical healing.

The Brahmanas: Ritual Explanations and Theological Development

The Brahmanas represent the second layer of Vedic literature, composed roughly between 1000-800 BCE. These prose texts provide detailed explanations of the rituals outlined in the Samhitas, but they also contain significant theological and philosophical material. The Brahmanas mark a crucial stage in the development of Indian religious thought, as they show the transition from simple ritual performance to sophisticated theological speculation.

The Nature and Purpose of Brahmanas

Each Veda has associated Brahmanas, with the most important being the Aitareya and Kaushitaki Brahmanas of the Rig Veda, the Panchavimsha and Jaiminiya Brahmanas of the Sama Veda, the Shatapatha Brahmana of the Yajur Veda, and the Gopatha Brahmana of the Atharva Veda. These texts were composed by and for the Brahmin priests who performed the increasingly complex rituals of the Vedic religion.

The Brahmanas serve multiple purposes: they provide practical instructions for ritual performance, explain the symbolic meaning of ritual actions, and develop theological concepts that would later flower in the Upanishads. They represent the work of sophisticated theologians who were not content merely to perform rituals but sought to understand their deeper significance.

The continuous thread that emerges from the Brahmanas is the development of the concept of Brahman as the ultimate reality underlying all existence. While the Samhitas focus on various deities, the Brahmanas begin to explore the idea of a unified principle that transcends individual gods. This theological development would prove crucial for the later development of Indian philosophy.

The Shatapatha Brahmana: A Theological Masterpiece

The Shatapatha Brahmana, associated with the White Yajur Veda, is perhaps the most important of all Brahmanas. This massive text, consisting of 100 lessons (adhyayas), provides not only detailed ritual instructions but also sophisticated theological speculation. The text shows clear evidence of systematic theological thinking and demonstrates the intellectual sophistication of the Brahmana period.

One of the most significant contributions of the Shatapatha Brahmana is its development of the concept of Prajapati as the creator deity. The text presents Prajapati as the lord of creatures who creates the universe through sacrifice. This theological innovation represents a major step toward monotheistic thinking and provides a foundation for later philosophical developments.

The Shatapatha Brahmana also contains the famous story of Purusha, the cosmic person whose sacrifice creates the universe. This myth, which appears in various forms throughout Indian literature, establishes the principle that creation and sacrifice are intimately connected. The continuous thread here is the understanding that the universe itself is based on the principle of sacrifice and that human ritual activities participate in this cosmic process.

Ritual Symbolism and Cosmic Correspondence

The Brahmanas develop sophisticated theories of ritual symbolism that reveal the deep thinking of their authors. They establish correspondences between ritual actions and cosmic processes, between the sacrifice and the creation of the universe, and between the human person and the cosmic order. This system of correspondences, known as bandhu, would become a fundamental principle of Indian thought.

The principle of bandhu suggests that the macrocosm and microcosm are intimately connected and that human actions can influence cosmic processes. This understanding provides the theoretical foundation for ritual practice and establishes the importance of proper ritual performance for maintaining cosmic order.

The continuous thread from the Brahmanas is the development of a sophisticated understanding of the relationship between symbol and reality. The Brahmanas demonstrate that the Vedic thinkers understood that ritual actions were not merely external ceremonies but were effective precisely because they participated in the deeper structures of reality.

The Development of Theological Concepts

The Brahmanas mark a crucial stage in the development of several key theological concepts that would later become central to Indian philosophy. The concept of Brahman as the ultimate reality, the principle of dharma as cosmic order, and the understanding of sacrifice as a cosmic principle all receive systematic development in these texts.

The Brahmanas also develop the concept of tapas (austerity or spiritual heat) as a creative force. The idea that ascetic practices can generate spiritual power that influences both the practitioner and the cosmos becomes a central theme in later Indian religious thought. This concept provides a bridge between the ritual religion of the Vedic period and the ascetic traditions that would later develop.

The continuous thread here is the understanding that spiritual practice involves participation in cosmic processes. The Brahmanas establish the principle that human religious activity is not separate from the natural order but is an integral part of it. This understanding would later influence the development of yoga, tantra, and other spiritual practices that seek to align human consciousness with cosmic consciousness.

The Aranyakas: Forest Treatises and the Hermit Tradition

The Aranyakas, literally "forest texts," represent a transitional stage between the ritual-focused Brahmanas and the philosophical Upanishads. Composed roughly between 800-600 BCE, these texts reflect the concerns of Vanaprasthas (forest hermits) who had retired from active social life to pursue spiritual practice in the forest. The Aranyakas mark a crucial stage in the development of Indian spirituality, as they show the gradual shift from external ritual to internal meditation.

The Forest Tradition and Spiritual Practice

The Aranyakas emerge from the tradition of forest hermits who left their household lives to pursue spiritual practice in the wilderness. This tradition, which would later be formalized in the ashrama system, represents a significant development in Indian religious thought. The forest hermits were not rejecting society but were pursuing a different stage of spiritual development that required withdrawal from worldly concerns.

The Aranyakas reflect the spiritual concerns of these forest dwellers. They contain modifications of rituals that could be performed without the elaborate equipment and assistance required for the great public sacrifices. They also contain meditative practices that represent the internalization of ritual activity. The continuous thread here is the understanding that spiritual practice can take different forms depending on the practitioner's stage of life and spiritual development.

The Aitareya Aranyaka: Meditation and Symbolism

The Aitareya Aranyaka, associated with the Rig Veda, contains some of the earliest systematic presentations of meditative practices in Indian literature. The text describes various types of meditation, including meditation on the cosmic person (Purusha) and meditation on the syllable OM. These practices represent the beginning of the systematic development of meditation techniques that would later become central to Indian spirituality.

The Aitareya Aranyaka also develops sophisticated theories of symbolism that bridge the gap between ritual and philosophy. The text explains how ritual symbols can be used as objects of meditation and how meditation can achieve the same spiritual results as ritual performance. This understanding represents a crucial development in the evolution of Indian spiritual practice.

The continuous thread from the Aitareya Aranyaka is the understanding that external ritual and internal meditation are complementary aspects of spiritual practice. The text establishes the principle that the essential purpose of ritual is to achieve union with the divine, and that this union can be achieved through various means depending on the practitioner's circumstances and inclinations.

The Taittiriya Aranyaka: Cosmic Meditation

The Taittiriya Aranyaka, associated with the Black Yajur Veda, contains elaborate meditative practices focused on cosmic symbolism. The text describes meditation on the sun, the cosmic person, and various aspects of the sacrifice. These practices represent sophisticated techniques for achieving identification with cosmic principles.

The Taittiriya Aranyaka also contains important discussions of the nature of Brahman and the relationship between individual consciousness and cosmic consciousness. These discussions anticipate many of the themes that would later be developed in the Upanishads. The text demonstrates that the transition from ritual to philosophy was not abrupt but was a gradual process that involved the systematic exploration of the implications of Vedic symbolism.

The continuous thread here is the development of the understanding that individual consciousness and cosmic consciousness are ultimately identical. The Taittiriya Aranyaka establishes the principle that the goal of spiritual practice is not to achieve something external but to realize the true nature of one's own consciousness.

The Internalization of Ritual

The Aranyakas mark a crucial stage in the internalization of ritual practice. While the Brahmanas focus on external ritual performance, the Aranyakas begin to explore how ritual actions can be performed mentally. This development represents a major shift in Indian religious thought and provides the foundation for later developments in yoga and meditation.

The process of internalization involves understanding the symbolic meaning of ritual actions and then performing these actions mentally rather than physically. This practice, known as manasa yajna (mental sacrifice), represents a sophisticated understanding of the relationship between external action and internal consciousness.

The continuous thread from the Aranyakas is the understanding that the essential purpose of ritual is to achieve a particular state of consciousness. Once this understanding is achieved, the external aspects of ritual become less important, and the practitioner can focus on achieving the desired state of consciousness through direct means.

The Early Upanishads: Philosophical Breakthroughs

The Upanishads represent the culmination of Vedic thought and the beginning of systematic philosophy in India. Composed roughly between 800-400 BCE, the early Upanishads contain some of the most profound philosophical insights in human history. These texts mark a revolutionary development in human thinking about the nature of reality, consciousness, and the relationship between the individual and the universal.

The Revolutionary Nature of Upanishadic Thought

The Upanishads represent a philosophical revolution that transformed not only Indian thought but eventually influenced global philosophy. The central insight of the Upanishads is the identity of Atman (individual consciousness) and Brahman (universal consciousness), expressed in the famous formula "Tat tvam asi" (That thou art). This insight represents a radical departure from earlier religious thought and establishes the foundation for all later Indian philosophy.

The Upanishads also develop sophisticated theories of knowledge, reality, and ethical conduct. They establish the principle that true knowledge is not information about external objects but direct realization of the true nature of consciousness. This understanding represents a fundamental shift in the concept of knowledge and establishes the foundation for the later development of various schools of Indian philosophy.

The continuous thread from the Upanishads is the understanding that the ultimate goal of human existence is the realization of the true nature of consciousness. This understanding provides the foundation for all later Indian spiritual practice and establishes the principle that spiritual development is essentially a process of self-discovery.

The Chandogya Upanishad: The Science of Consciousness

The Chandogya Upanishad, one of the longest and most important early Upanishads, contains systematic teachings on the nature of consciousness and reality. The text presents these teachings through dialogues between teachers and students, a format that would become standard in Indian philosophical literature. The Chandogya Upanishad contains the famous teaching of Uddalaka Aruni to his son Shvetaketu, which establishes the fundamental principle of Advaita (non-dualism).

The Chandogya Upanishad also contains detailed discussions of meditation practices, including meditation on OM and various forms of symbolic meditation. These practices represent sophisticated techniques for achieving the realization of the identity of Atman and Brahman. The text demonstrates that the philosophical insights of the Upanishads were not merely intellectual but were based on direct experiential realization.

The continuous thread from the Chandogya Upanishad is the understanding that reality is essentially consciousness and that the apparent diversity of the world is ultimately illusory. This understanding, known as Advaita, would later be systematized by philosophers like Gaudapada and Shankara and would become one of the most influential philosophical systems in Indian thought.

The Brihad-Aranyaka Upanishad: The Great Forest Teaching

The Brihad-Aranyaka Upanishad, the longest of all Upanishads, contains some of the most profound philosophical teachings in the entire Vedic corpus. The text presents the teachings of great sages like Yajnavalkya, who is portrayed as the greatest philosopher of his time. The Brihad-Aranyaka Upanishad contains detailed discussions of the nature of the self, the process of death and rebirth, and the ultimate goal of human existence.

One of the most important teachings in the Brihad-Aranyaka Upanishad is the doctrine of the two selves —the empirical self that experiences the world and the transcendental self that is identical with Brahman. This teaching provides a sophisticated analysis of consciousness that anticipates many later developments in both Indian and Western philosophy.

The Brihad-Aranyaka Upanishad also contains detailed discussions of ethical conduct and the relationship between knowledge and action. The text establishes the principle that true knowledge naturally leads to ethical conduct and that spiritual realization involves the transformation of one's entire way of being.

The continuous thread from the Brihad-Aranyaka Upanishad is the understanding that the highest human achievement is the realization of the true nature of the self. This realization involves both intellectual understanding and experiential realization, and it results in the transformation of one's entire relationship with existence.

The Kena Upanishad: The Mystery of Consciousness

The Kena Upanishad, though brief, contains some of the most profound insights into the nature of consciousness in the entire Upanishadic corpus. The text begins with the famous question "By whom is the mind directed?" and proceeds to explore the mystery of consciousness itself. The Kena Upanishad establishes the principle that consciousness cannot be objectified or comprehended by the ordinary mind.

The Kena Upanishad also contains the famous story of the gods and Brahman, which illustrates the principle that ultimate reality transcends all conceptual categories. This story demonstrates the sophisticated understanding of the limitations of conceptual thinking that characterizes Upanishadic thought.

The continuous thread from the Kena Upanishad is the understanding that ultimate reality is beyond all mental categories and can only be realized through direct experience. This understanding establishes the foundation for the later development of various non-conceptual approaches to spiritual realization.

The Katha Upanishad: The Path to Immortality

The Katha Upanishad presents its teachings through the story of Nachiketa, a young boy who asks the god of death about the nature of life after death. This narrative framework allows the Upanishad to explore fundamental questions about the nature of existence, death, and immortality. The Katha Upanishad contains the famous teaching about the two paths—the path of pleasure and the path of spiritual realization.

The Katha Upanishad also contains one of the earliest systematic presentations of yoga philosophy, including discussions of the control of the senses and the mind. These teachings provide a bridge between the philosophical insights of the Upanishads and the practical techniques of yoga.

The continuous thread from the Katha Upanishad is the understanding that true immortality is not the continuation of individual existence but the realization of the eternal nature of consciousness. This understanding provides the foundation for the later development of various approaches to spiritual liberation.

Transmission and Preservation Methods: The Oral Tradition

The preservation and transmission of Vedic literature represents one of the most remarkable achievements in human history. For over three millennia, these texts have been transmitted orally with extraordinary fidelity, creating an unbroken chain of knowledge that connects the present with the distant past. The methods developed for this transmission are not only practically effective but also theoretically sophisticated, representing a profound understanding of the nature of language, memory, and consciousness.

The Guru-Shishya Parampara: The Sacred Chain

The foundation of Vedic transmission is the Guru-Shishya Parampara, the sacred teacher-student tradition that creates an unbroken chain of transmission from teacher to student across generations. This tradition is not merely a method of education but a spiritual practice that involves the complete transformation of the student through direct contact with the teacher's consciousness.

The Guru-Shishya relationship is understood to be a sacred bond that transcends the merely intellectual transmission of information. The teacher (Guru) is not simply someone who knows the texts but someone who has realized their inner meaning and can transmit not only the words but also the spiritual consciousness that the words represent. The student (Shishya) is not merely a recipient of information but a participant in a sacred process of transformation.

The continuous thread of the Guru-Shishya tradition is the understanding that true knowledge is not merely informational but transformational. The tradition establishes the principle that the highest forms of knowledge can only be transmitted through direct personal relationship and that the preservation of sacred texts requires the preservation of the consciousness that created them.

The Science of Recitation: patha methods and Vikritis

The Vedic tradition developed sophisticated techniques for ensuring the accurate transmission of texts through various methods of recitation known as patha methods . These methods involve different ways of combining and recombining the words of the text to ensure that any errors in transmission would be immediately apparent. The most important of these methods are the Samhita (continuous recitation), Pada (word-by-word recitation), and Krama (sequential recitation).

Beyond these basic methods, the tradition developed eleven vikritis (modifications) that involve complex patterns of recitation. These include the Jata (braid), Ghana (bell), and other intricate patterns that require the reciter to combine words in specific sequences. These methods serve not only as error-checking devices but also as spiritual practices that deepen the reciter's understanding of the text.

The continuous thread from the recitation tradition is the understanding that the sound of the text is as important as its meaning. The tradition establishes the principle that sacred texts are not merely collections of words but are living expressions of spiritual consciousness that must be preserved in their original form.

Memory Techniques and Cognitive Science

The Vedic tradition developed sophisticated memory techniques that represent an early form of cognitive science. These techniques involve the use of rhythm, melody, and physical movement to enhance memory and ensure accurate transmission. The tradition understood that effective memorization requires the engagement of multiple cognitive faculties and developed integrated approaches that involve the entire person.

The memory techniques also involve the use of elaborate mnemonic devices that help the student remember not only the words of the text but also their proper pronunciation, accent, and rhythm. These devices demonstrate a sophisticated understanding of the relationship between language, consciousness, and memory.

The continuous thread from the memory tradition is the understanding that consciousness and language are intimately connected and that the preservation of sacred texts requires the cultivation of particular states of consciousness. The tradition establishes the principle that memory is not merely a mechanical faculty but a spiritual practice that involves the entire person.

The Social Organization of Transmission

The transmission of Vedic literature required elaborate social organization that ensured the continuity of the tradition across generations. This organization involved the creation of specialized schools (charana or shakha) that were responsible for preserving particular texts or portions of texts. Each school developed its own methods of transmission and maintained its own lineage of teachers.

The social organization also involved the creation of complex systems of checks and balances that ensured the accuracy of transmission. These systems included regular assemblies where different schools would compare their versions of texts, competitive recitations that tested the accuracy of transmission, and elaborate ceremonies that celebrated the achievement of mastery.

The continuous thread from the social organization of transmission is the understanding that the preservation of sacred knowledge requires the commitment of entire communities and that this preservation is not merely an academic exercise but a sacred duty that involves the entire society.

The Relationship Between Oral and Written Tradition

Although the Vedic texts were eventually written down, the oral tradition remained primary and continues to this day. The tradition understood that written texts, while useful for certain purposes, could not capture the full meaning of the sacred texts, which required proper pronunciation, rhythm, and accent for their effective transmission.

The relationship between oral and written tradition in the Vedic context demonstrates a sophisticated understanding of the nature of language and consciousness. The tradition recognized that different modes of transmission serve different purposes and that the preservation of sacred texts requires the maintenance of multiple complementary approaches.

The continuous thread from the oral tradition is the understanding that the highest forms of knowledge require direct transmission from consciousness to consciousness and that no external medium can fully capture the essential meaning of sacred texts. This understanding continues to influence Indian approaches to education and spiritual practice.

The Continuous Threads: Connecting Millennia

The Vedic literary tradition represents one of the most remarkable examples of cultural continuity in human history. For over three thousand years, these texts have been preserved, studied, and practiced, creating an unbroken chain of wisdom that connects the present with the distant past. The continuous threads that run through this tradition represent not merely historical continuity but the preservation of essential insights into the nature of consciousness, reality, and human existence.

The Thread of Spiritual Inquiry

From the earliest hymns of the Rig Veda to the sophisticated philosophical treatises of the Upanishads, the Vedic tradition maintains a consistent focus on fundamental spiritual questions. The nature of ultimate reality, the relationship between individual consciousness and cosmic consciousness, and the means for achieving spiritual realization remain central concerns throughout the tradition.

This thread of spiritual inquiry demonstrates the remarkable consistency of the Vedic tradition while also showing its capacity for growth and development. The questions that concerned the earliest seers continue to be relevant, but the answers become increasingly sophisticated as the tradition develops more refined methods of inquiry and expression.

The continuous thread of spiritual inquiry establishes the principle that the highest human concern is the realization of truth and that this realization requires systematic inquiry conducted over many generations. The tradition demonstrates that spiritual development is not an individual achievement but a collective enterprise that requires the accumulated wisdom of countless seekers.

The Thread of Cosmic Consciousness

Throughout the Vedic tradition, there is a consistent understanding that individual consciousness and cosmic consciousness are ultimately identical. This understanding, which begins as an intuitive insight in the earliest hymns, gradually develops into sophisticated philosophical systems that explore the implications of this insight.

The thread of cosmic consciousness demonstrates the systematic nature of Vedic thought and its capacity to develop initial insights into comprehensive philosophical systems. The tradition shows how a fundamental insight can be explored from multiple perspectives and developed into practical methods for spiritual realization.

The continuous thread of cosmic consciousness establishes the principle that the ultimate goal of human existence is the realization of the universal nature of consciousness. This understanding provides the foundation for all later Indian philosophy and continues to influence contemporary approaches to consciousness studies.

The Thread of Ritual and Meditation

The Vedic tradition maintains a sophisticated understanding of the relationship between external ritual and internal meditation throughout its development. While the emphasis shifts from external ritual to internal meditation, the tradition maintains that both are valid approaches to spiritual realization and that they are ultimately complementary rather than contradictory.

This thread demonstrates the practical wisdom of the Vedic tradition and its understanding that spiritual practice must be adapted to different circumstances and different types of practitioners. The tradition shows how external practices can be internalized without losing their essential meaning and how internal practices can be expressed through external actions.

The continuous thread of ritual and meditation establishes the principle that spiritual practice involves the integration of all aspects of human existence and that true realization requires the harmonious development of thought, feeling, and action.

The Thread of Ethical Development

Throughout the Vedic tradition, there is a consistent emphasis on ethical conduct as both a means to spiritual realization and a natural expression of spiritual understanding. The concept of dharma, which begins as cosmic order in the earliest texts, gradually develops into a comprehensive ethical system that encompasses all aspects of human conduct.

The thread of ethical development demonstrates the practical nature of Vedic wisdom and its understanding that spiritual realization must be expressed through ethical conduct. The tradition shows that knowledge and conduct are inseparable and that true wisdom naturally leads to compassionate action.

The continuous thread of ethical development establishes the principle that spiritual development and ethical development are inseparable and that the ultimate test of spiritual realization is its expression through ethical conduct.

The Thread of Educational Method

The Vedic tradition developed sophisticated educational methods that ensure not only the transmission of information but also the development of the consciousness necessary to understand and apply that information. These methods, which are based on the Guru-Shishya relationship, represent a profound understanding of the nature of learning and consciousness.

The thread of educational method demonstrates the wisdom of the Vedic tradition in understanding that different types of knowledge require different methods of transmission and that the highest forms of knowledge can only be transmitted through direct personal relationship.

The continuous thread of educational method establishes the principle that true education involves the complete transformation of the student and that this transformation requires the guidance of someone who has achieved the realization that the education is designed to produce.

The Living Tradition: Contemporary Relevance

The Vedic literary tradition is not merely a historical phenomenon but a living tradition that continues to influence contemporary thought and practice. The texts continue to be studied, the practices continue to be followed, and the insights continue to be relevant to contemporary concerns. The living nature of the tradition demonstrates its essential timelessness and its capacity to address the fundamental concerns of human existence.

Modern Scholarship and Ancient Wisdom

Contemporary scholarship on the Vedic tradition has revealed both the historical development of the texts and their continuing relevance to modern concerns. Scholars have shown that the texts represent not merely ancient religious documents but sophisticated philosophical and spiritual treatises that address universal human concerns.

The encounter between modern scholarship and ancient wisdom has been mutually enriching. Modern methods of textual analysis have revealed the sophisticated literary and philosophical techniques used by the ancient authors, while the ancient texts have provided modern scholars with insights into the nature of consciousness, language, and reality that remain relevant to contemporary inquiry.

The continuous thread between ancient wisdom and modern scholarship demonstrates the essential timelessness of the Vedic insights and their capacity to enrich contemporary understanding of fundamental human concerns.

Spiritual Practice and Contemporary Life

The spiritual practices developed in the Vedic tradition continue to be followed by millions of people around the world. These practices, which include meditation, yoga, and various forms of devotional practice, have been adapted to contemporary circumstances while maintaining their essential character.

The continuing relevance of Vedic spiritual practices demonstrates their fundamental soundness and their capacity to address the spiritual needs of people in all times and circumstances. The practices provide effective methods for dealing with the stress and confusion of modern life while also offering pathways to deeper spiritual realization.

The continuous thread of spiritual practice demonstrates the practical wisdom of the Vedic tradition and its understanding that spiritual development requires systematic practice conducted over extended periods of time.

Philosophical Influence and Global Thought

The philosophical insights of the Vedic tradition have influenced not only Indian thought but also global philosophical development. The insights have been transmitted through various channels, including the work of philosophers like Schopenhauer and Heidegger, the teachings of spiritual teachers like Vivekananda and Krishnamurti, and the practices of yoga and meditation that have become widespread in the contemporary world.

The global influence of Vedic philosophy demonstrates the universal relevance of its insights and its capacity to enrich diverse cultural traditions. The philosophy provides frameworks for understanding consciousness, reality, and human existence that remain relevant to contemporary concerns.

The continuous thread of philosophical influence demonstrates the essential universality of the Vedic insights and their capacity to contribute to the development of global wisdom traditions.

The Eternal Wisdom

The Vedic literary tradition represents one of humanity's greatest achievements in the preservation and transmission of wisdom. For over three millennia, these texts have provided guidance for spiritual seekers, inspiration for philosophers, and practical methods for achieving spiritual realization. The tradition demonstrates the remarkable capacity of human consciousness to preserve and transmit the highest insights across vast spans of time and through countless generations.

The four-fold structure of the Vedic corpus—Samhitas, Brahmanas, Aranyakas, and Upanishads—reveals a sophisticated understanding of the different aspects of spiritual development and the need for different types of texts to address different levels of understanding. From the devotional hymns of the Samhitas to the philosophical treatises of the Upanishads, each layer of the tradition contributes essential elements to the complete picture of human spiritual development.

The methods of transmission developed by the Vedic tradition represent a profound understanding of the nature of consciousness, language, and learning. The oral tradition, with its emphasis on direct transmission from teacher to student, demonstrates the recognition that the highest forms of knowledge cannot be reduced to mere information but require the transmission of consciousness itself. The sophisticated techniques of recitation and memorization show the understanding that sacred texts are not merely collections of words but living expressions of spiritual realization.

The continuous threads that run through the Vedic tradition—the search for truth, the understanding of cosmic consciousness, the integration of ritual and meditation, the development of ethical conduct, and the sophisticated methods of education—demonstrate the essential coherence of the tradition despite its vast temporal span and diverse expressions. These threads show that the Vedic tradition is not merely a collection of ancient texts but a living wisdom that continues to address the fundamental concerns of human existence.

The Timeless Relevance of Vedic Wisdom

The continuing relevance of the Vedic tradition in the contemporary world demonstrates its essential timelessness. The questions that concerned the ancient seers—the nature of consciousness, the relationship between individual and universal, the means for achieving spiritual realization—remain as relevant today as they were three thousand years ago. The methods they developed for exploring these questions continue to be effective, and the insights they achieved continue to provide guidance for contemporary seekers.

The Vedic tradition's emphasis on direct experience rather than mere intellectual understanding provides a valuable corrective to the tendency in modern culture to reduce knowledge to information. The tradition demonstrates that the highest forms of knowledge require not only intellectual understanding but also the transformation of consciousness that comes through sustained spiritual practice.

The tradition's understanding of the relationship between individual consciousness and cosmic consciousness provides a framework for addressing the isolation and alienation that characterize much of modern life. The Vedic insight that individual consciousness and universal consciousness are ultimately identical offers a profound solution to the existential problems that continue to challenge human beings in all cultures and times.

The Integration of Ancient Wisdom and Modern Understanding

The encounter between Vedic wisdom and modern knowledge has been mutually enriching and continues to generate new insights and applications. The scientific study of consciousness, which has become increasingly important in contemporary research, has been greatly enriched by the sophisticated analysis of consciousness found in the Vedic texts. Similarly, modern methods of textual analysis and historical research have revealed the remarkable sophistication of the ancient authors and the systematic nature of their inquiry.

The integration of ancient wisdom and modern understanding demonstrates that the Vedic tradition is not opposed to scientific inquiry but can contribute to it in significant ways. The tradition's emphasis on systematic inquiry, careful observation, and rigorous analysis provides a foundation for scientific investigation that is often lacking in purely materialistic approaches to knowledge.

The practical applications of Vedic wisdom in fields such as medicine, psychology, and education demonstrate the continuing relevance of the tradition's insights. The holistic approach to human development found in the Vedic texts provides valuable guidance for addressing the fragmentation and specialization that characterize much of modern knowledge.

The Future of the Tradition

The Vedic literary tradition has survived for over three millennia because it addresses fundamental aspects of human existence that remain constant despite changes in external circumstances. The tradition's emphasis on the essential nature of consciousness, the importance of spiritual development, and the need for ethical conduct ensures its continuing relevance for future generations.

The challenge for contemporary practitioners and scholars is to maintain the essential character of the tradition while adapting it to contemporary circumstances. This requires a deep understanding of both the tradition itself and the contemporary context, as well as the wisdom to distinguish between essential elements that must be preserved and external forms that can be adapted.

The global spread of interest in Vedic wisdom demonstrates its universal relevance and its capacity to enrich diverse cultural traditions. The tradition's emphasis on the unity underlying diversity provides a foundation for the development of global wisdom traditions that can address the challenges facing humanity in the contemporary world.

The Eternal Message

The central message of the Vedic literary tradition is that consciousness is the fundamental reality and that the realization of this truth is the highest human achievement. This message, which appears in various forms throughout the tradition, remains as relevant today as it was when first expressed by the ancient seers. The tradition demonstrates that this realization is not merely an intellectual understanding but a transformation of consciousness that affects every aspect of human existence.

The Vedic tradition's understanding of the relationship between individual consciousness and universal consciousness provides a foundation for addressing the fundamental questions of human existence: Who am I? What is the nature of reality? How should I live? The tradition's answers to these questions are not dogmatic assertions but invitations to direct inquiry and experiential realization.

The tradition's emphasis on the importance of spiritual practice demonstrates that the realization of truth requires not only intellectual understanding but also the systematic cultivation of consciousness through sustained practice. The various practices developed within the tradition—meditation, yoga, ethical conduct, devotional practices—provide effective methods for achieving this realization.

The Vedic literary tradition represents humanity's most sustained and systematic inquiry into the nature of consciousness and reality. The insights achieved through this inquiry, the methods developed for pursuing it, and the techniques created for transmitting the results across generations represent one of humanity's greatest achievements. The tradition demonstrates that human consciousness has the capacity to transcend the limitations of time and space and to achieve realization of the eternal truths that govern existence.

As we stand at the threshold of a new millennium, the Vedic tradition offers both ancient wisdom and contemporary relevance. Its insights into the nature of consciousness provide guidance for addressing the challenges of modern life, while its methods of inquiry offer tools for continuing the search for truth. The tradition's emphasis on the unity underlying diversity provides a foundation for creating a more harmonious and integrated world.

The continuous threads that run through the Vedic tradition—stretching from the earliest hymns to contemporary practice—demonstrate the essential timelessness of its insights and the enduring relevance of its message. These threads connect us not only with the wisdom of the past but also with the possibilities of the future, showing that the search for truth is not a historical curiosity but a living reality that continues to shape human consciousness and human destiny.

In the end, the Vedic literary tradition stands as a testament to the highest aspirations of human consciousness and the deepest insights into the nature of existence. It reminds us that despite the apparent diversity and complexity of life, there is an underlying unity that can be realized through systematic inquiry and sustained practice. This realization, which the tradition calls the ultimate goal of human existence, remains as achievable today as it was for the ancient seers who first glimpsed its possibility and devoted their lives to its exploration and expression.

The tradition's message is ultimately one of hope and possibility: that human consciousness has the capacity to transcend its apparent limitations and realize its essential nature as consciousness itself. This realization, which the tradition presents not as a distant goal but as an immediate possibility, represents the ultimate fulfillment of human existence and the final answer to the questions that have driven human inquiry throughout history.

The Vedic literary tradition thus stands as both a historical achievement and a living invitation—an achievement that demonstrates what human consciousness can accomplish when directed toward the highest goals, and an invitation to continue the inquiry that began with the first seekers and continues with each individual who takes up the ancient quest for truth, understanding, and realization. In this way, the tradition bridges the gap between past and future, between individual and universal, between human and divine, showing that these apparent opposites are ultimately unified in the one consciousness that is the source, substance, and goal of all existence.

15
Science and Knowledge

The Cumulative Nature of Vedic Knowledge

The Vedic civilization inherited, preserved, and enhanced the intellectual achievements of countless generations, creating a foundation upon which Indian civilization would build for centuries to come.

The concept of knowledge accumulation in ancient India was fundamentally different from the modern notion of scientific revolution. Rather than sudden breakthroughs that overturned existing paradigms, Vedic knowledge evolved through a process of continuous refinement and expansion. Each generation of scholars, practitioners, and observers added to the collective understanding, creating a vast repository of practical and theoretical knowledge that was passed down through oral traditions and eventually codified in various texts.

This accumulated wisdom was not merely academic; it was deeply integrated into daily life, religious practice, and social organization. The Vedic people understood that knowledge was a living, breathing entity that required constant nurturing and application. They developed sophisticated systems for preserving and transmitting information across generations, ensuring that hard-won insights would not be lost to time.

Mathematics and Astronomy: The Eternal Dance of Numbers and Stars

The mathematical and astronomical knowledge of the Vedic period represents perhaps the most striking example of accumulated wisdom building upon itself across millennia. Long before the composition of the earliest Vedic texts, the inhabitants of the Indian subcontinent had been observing celestial patterns, developing counting systems, and creating mathematical concepts that would later be refined into sophisticated theoretical frameworks.

The Foundation of Mathematical Thought

The mathematical concepts that flowered during the Vedic Age had roots stretching back to the earliest agricultural communities of the Indus Valley and beyond. The need to measure land, calculate crop yields, and distribute resources had driven the development of basic arithmetic operations thousands of years before these concepts were formally articulated in Vedic literature. The decimal system, which would eventually become one of India's greatest contributions to world civilization, emerged from centuries of practical application in trade, construction, and administration.

The Vedic texts reveal a mathematical sophistication that could only have developed through generations of accumulated knowledge. The concept of zero, though not fully articulated until later periods, was implicit in Vedic mathematical thinking. The understanding of place value, essential for advanced calculations, demonstrates the inheritance of mathematical concepts that had been refined over countless generations of practical application.

Geometric principles, evident in the construction of altars and sacred spaces described in the Śulba Sūtras, represent the culmination of architectural and engineering knowledge passed down through generations of builders and craftsmen. The precise calculations required for altar construction, including the famous relationship between the sides of a right triangle (later known as the Pythagorean theorem), were not sudden discoveries but the result of millennia of practical experimentation and theoretical refinement.

Astronomical Observations and Celestial Mapping

The astronomical knowledge preserved in Vedic texts represents one of humanity's earliest systematic attempts to understand the cosmos. This understanding was built upon ten thousand years of careful observation, beginning with the earliest humans who noticed the correlation between celestial movements and seasonal changes. The Vedic astronomers inherited this vast database of observations and transformed it into a sophisticated system of celestial mechanics.

The lunar calendar system, fundamental to Vedic timekeeping, was the product of countless generations of moon-watchers who had gradually refined their understanding of lunar cycles. The recognition of the lunar month's length, the intercalation methods needed to align lunar and solar years, and the complex calculations required for accurate calendar keeping all represent accumulated knowledge that had been tested and refined over millennia.

The concept of the nakṣatras (lunar mansions) demonstrates how astronomical knowledge was preserved and transmitted across generations. These twenty-seven or twenty-eight stellar regions were not arbitrary divisions but represented a collective understanding of stellar positions that had been developed through centuries of observation. Each nakṣatra carried with it a wealth of information about seasonal changes, agricultural timing, and ceremonial requirements, representing the integration of astronomical knowledge with practical applications.

The Vedic understanding of planetary movements, while not as advanced as later developments, shows clear evidence of accumulated observations. The recognition of the five visible planets, their approximate orbital periods, and their relationship to the zodiacal system represents knowledge that could only have been developed through systematic observation over many generations. The mathematical models used to predict planetary positions were refined versions of computational methods that had been developed and tested over centuries.

The Integration of Mathematics and Astronomy

The sophisticated relationship between mathematical and astronomical knowledge in Vedic texts reveals the accumulated nature of this wisdom. The geometric principles used in altar construction were intimately connected to astronomical observations, creating a unified system of knowledge that integrated practical mathematics with celestial mechanics. This integration was not the work of a single genius but the result of generations of scholars who had gradually recognized the mathematical principles underlying astronomical phenomena.

The calculation of time periods, from the daily cycle to the cosmic ages (yugas), required mathematical concepts that had been refined through centuries of practical application. The understanding of large numbers, essential for astronomical calculations, was built upon counting systems that had been developed and refined through millennia of use in trade, administration, and religious practice.

Medicine and Healing Practices: The Wisdom of the Body

The medical knowledge that emerged during the Vedic period represents the culmination of ten thousand years of human experience with healing, representing perhaps the most vivid example of how practical knowledge accumulated across generations. The Vedic approach to medicine was fundamentally empirical, built upon countless observations of the human body, the effects of various substances, and the relationship between mind, body, and environment.

The Foundation of Herbal Medicine

The sophisticated understanding of medicinal plants evident in Vedic texts was the product of millennia of experimentation and observation. Early human communities had necessarily developed intimate knowledge of their plant environments, gradually learning through trial and error which plants could heal, which could harm, and which could alter consciousness. This knowledge was preserved and transmitted through oral traditions, creating a vast pharmacopeia that would later be systematized in medical texts.

The concept of plant energetics, fundamental to Vedic medicine, represents accumulated wisdom about the subtle effects of different substances on the human body. The classification of plants by taste, potency, and post-digestive effect was not theoretical speculation but the result of countless generations of careful observation and experimentation. The understanding that certain plants could balance specific constitutional types or treat particular conditions was built upon a foundation of empirical knowledge that had been tested and refined over thousands of years.

The seasonal and geographical variations in plant potency, well understood by Vedic physicians, represents knowledge that could only have been accumulated through generations of careful observation. The recognition that the same plant might have different effects depending on when and where it was harvested, how it was prepared, and in what combinations it was used, demonstrates the sophisticated understanding that emerged from centuries of practical experience.

Surgical Knowledge and Techniques

The surgical procedures described in later Vedic and post-Vedic medical texts were built upon a foundation of practical knowledge that had been accumulated over millennia. The understanding of human anatomy, while not as detailed as modern knowledge, was remarkably sophisticated for its time and represents the accumulated observations of countless healers who had treated injuries, performed procedures, and observed the effects of various interventions.

The development of surgical instruments, from simple cutting tools to specialized implements for specific procedures, represents the gradual refinement of technology over thousands of years. Each generation of healers had improved upon the tools and techniques inherited from their predecessors, creating an increasingly sophisticated arsenal of medical interventions.

The understanding of wound healing, infection prevention, and post-operative care evident in Vedic medical knowledge was built upon centuries of practical experience. The recognition that certain substances could prevent infection, that specific techniques could promote healing, and that particular dietary and lifestyle modifications could support recovery all represent accumulated wisdom that had been tested and refined through countless individual cases.

Diagnostic Methods and Constitutional Medicine

The sophisticated diagnostic methods described in Vedic medical texts were the product of millennia of careful observation of the human body and its variations. The understanding of constitutional types, fundamental to Vedic medicine, was built upon the recognition that different individuals responded differently to the same treatments, foods, and environmental conditions. This knowledge was accumulated through generations of healers who had observed and recorded the effects of various interventions on different types of people.

The pulse diagnosis, breath analysis, and other diagnostic techniques described in Vedic texts represent the culmination of centuries of empirical observation. The ability to detect subtle changes in physiological function and relate them to specific imbalances or conditions was not innate knowledge but the result of generations of careful observation and correlation.

The understanding of the relationship between mental and physical health, evident in Vedic medical approaches, was built upon millennia of observations about the effects of emotional states, stress, and psychological factors on physical well-being. The recognition that healing required attention to both body and mind was not theoretical insight but practical wisdom accumulated through countless cases and observations.

Metallurgy and Technology: The Mastery of Materials

The technological achievements of the Vedic period represent the culmination of thousands of years of human experimentation with materials and techniques. The sophisticated understanding of metallurgy, construction, and manufacturing evident in Vedic civilization was built upon a foundation of accumulated knowledge that had been refined through countless generations of craftsmen and innovators.

The Evolution of Metalworking

The metallurgical knowledge of the Vedic period was the product of millennia of experimentation with fire, ores, and alloying techniques. The transition from the use of native metals to the smelting of ores represents thousands of years of gradual technological development. The understanding of the properties of different metals, the techniques required for their extraction and purification, and the methods for creating alloys with specific characteristics all represent accumulated knowledge that had been refined through generations of practical experience.

The development of iron technology, which reached sophisticated levels during the Vedic period, was built upon centuries of experimentation with iron ores and smelting techniques. The recognition that iron could be made harder through specific heating and cooling processes, that different types of iron ore required different treatment methods, and that the addition of certain substances could improve the quality of the final product all represent accumulated wisdom that had been developed through trial and error over many generations.

The sophisticated understanding of bronze and copper alloys evident in Vedic artifacts was the result of centuries of experimentation with different combinations of metals. The knowledge of how to achieve specific properties through precise control of alloy composition, temperature, and processing techniques represents the culmination of accumulated technological knowledge that had been refined through countless iterations.

Construction and Engineering

The architectural and engineering achievements of the Vedic period were built upon millennia of accumulated knowledge about materials, structural principles, and construction techniques. The understanding of load-bearing principles, the selection of appropriate materials for different applications, and the techniques for creating durable structures all represent wisdom that had been developed and refined through generations of builders and engineers.

The sophisticated water management systems, including wells, channels, and reservoirs, represent the culmination of thousands of years of experimentation with hydraulic principles. The understanding of water flow, pressure, and storage was built upon practical experience that had been accumulated through generations of communities that had learned to harness and control water resources.

The development of tools and implements for various crafts and industries represents the gradual refinement of technology over millennia. Each generation of craftsmen had improved upon the tools inherited from their predecessors, creating increasingly sophisticated implements that enhanced productivity and quality. The understanding of the properties of different materials, the techniques for shaping and joining them, and the methods for creating durable and efficient tools all represent accumulated knowledge that had been refined through countless applications.

Agricultural Technology

The agricultural innovations of the Vedic period were built upon ten thousand years of accumulated knowledge about plant cultivation, soil management, and crop production. The understanding of seasonal cycles, soil fertility, and plant breeding was not theoretical knowledge but practical wisdom that had been developed through millennia of agricultural experimentation and observation.

The development of plowing techniques, irrigation methods, and crop rotation systems represents the gradual refinement of agricultural practices over thousands of years. Each generation of farmers had learned from the successes and failures of their predecessors, gradually developing more efficient and productive methods of food production.

The understanding of the relationship between different crops, the effects of various soil amendments, and the optimal timing for planting and harvesting all represent accumulated knowledge that had been tested and refined through countless growing seasons. The recognition that certain plants could improve soil fertility, that specific combinations of crops could maximize yields, and that particular techniques could prevent pest and disease problems all demonstrate the sophisticated understanding that emerged from millennia of practical experience.

Calendar Systems and Time-Keeping: The Rhythm of Existence

The sophisticated time-keeping systems of the Vedic period represent the culmination of thousands of years of accumulated observations about natural cycles and their relationship to human activities. The development of accurate calendars was essential for agricultural planning, religious observances, and social organization, and the systems that emerged during the Vedic period were built upon a foundation of accumulated knowledge that had been refined through countless generations of careful observation.

The Foundation of Temporal Measurement

The basic units of time recognized in Vedic texts were derived from natural phenomena that had been observed and correlated over millennia. The day-night cycle, the lunar month, and the solar year were not arbitrary divisions but represented the accumulation of observations that had been made and refined by countless generations of time-keepers. The understanding of the relationship between these different cycles and the methods for reconciling their differences were built upon practical experience that had been accumulated through thousands of years of calendar-keeping.

The recognition of seasonal variations in day length, the correlation between lunar phases and tidal patterns, and the relationship between stellar positions and seasonal changes all represent accumulated knowledge that had been developed through generations of careful observation. The ability to predict future celestial events based on past observations was not innate knowledge but the result of systematic record-keeping and correlation over many centuries.

The development of units for measuring smaller time intervals, from the day to the hour to more minute divisions, represents the gradual refinement of temporal measurement systems. Each generation of timekeepers had improved upon the methods inherited from their predecessors, creating increasingly precise and practical systems for dividing and measuring time.

The Integration of Natural and Human Cycles

The sophisticated understanding of the relationship between natural cycles and human activities evident in Vedic time-keeping systems was built upon millennia of accumulated observations. The recognition that certain agricultural activities were most successful when timed to coincide with specific lunar phases, that particular religious observances were most effective when aligned with astronomical events, and that human biological rhythms were influenced by celestial cycles all represent accumulated knowledge that had been developed through generations of practical experience.

The development of festival cycles and religious calendars was built upon the understanding of the relationship between celestial events and human psychological and spiritual states. The recognition that certain times of year were particularly suitable for specific types of activities, that particular combinations of astronomical factors created optimal conditions for different endeavors, and that the timing of religious observances could enhance their effectiveness all represent accumulated wisdom that had been refined through countless cycles of observation and practice.

The understanding of longer temporal cycles, including the concept of cosmic ages (yugas), was built upon the recognition of patterns that operated on scales beyond individual human lifetimes. The ability to conceive of and calculate such vast time periods was not theoretical speculation but the result of accumulated observations that had been passed down through generations of scholars and astronomers.

Practical Applications of Time-Keeping

The practical applications of Vedic time-keeping systems in agriculture, governance, and social organization represent the culmination of thousands of years of accumulated knowledge about the relationship between time and human activities. The understanding of optimal timing for planting, harvesting, and other agricultural activities was built upon generations of practical experience that had been codified into systematic guidelines.

The use of astronomical observations for navigation, both on land and water, was built upon accumulated knowledge that had been developed through centuries of travel and exploration. The recognition that certain stellar configurations could indicate direction, that particular celestial events could predict weather patterns, and that specific astronomical calculations could determine location all represent accumulated wisdom that had been refined through countless journeys and observations.

The integration of time-keeping with legal and administrative systems was built upon the understanding of the importance of accurate temporal measurement for social organization. The ability to coordinate activities across large populations, to maintain consistent legal and administrative procedures, and to preserve historical records all required sophisticated time-keeping systems that had been developed and refined through generations of practical application.

Agricultural Innovations: The Foundation of Civilization

The agricultural innovations of the Vedic period represent the culmination of ten thousand years of accumulated knowledge about plant cultivation, soil management, and food production. The sophisticated understanding of agricultural principles evident in Vedic texts was not theoretical knowledge but practical wisdom that had been developed through millennia of experimentation, observation, and refinement.

The Evolution of Crop Cultivation

The crop varieties and cultivation techniques described in Vedic texts were the product of thousands of years of plant breeding and agricultural experimentation. The understanding of the characteristics of different grain varieties, the techniques for improving crop yields, and the methods for developing new cultivars all represent accumulated knowledge that had been refined through countless generations of farmers and plant breeders.

The recognition of the relationship between soil conditions and crop performance was built upon millennia of observations about the effects of different soil types, drainage conditions, and fertility levels on plant growth. The understanding that certain crops thrived in specific soil conditions, that particular soil amendments could improve fertility, and that specific cultivation techniques could optimize growing conditions all represent accumulated wisdom that had been developed through generations of practical experience.

The development of irrigation systems and water management techniques was built upon thousands of years of experimentation with hydraulic principles and water control methods. The understanding of water flow, pressure, and distribution was accumulated through generations of communities that had learned to harness and control water resources for agricultural purposes.

Soil Management and Fertility

The sophisticated understanding of soil fertility and management evident in Vedic agricultural texts was the product of millennia of observations about the relationship between soil conditions and crop productivity. The recognition that soil fertility could be maintained and improved through specific practices, that different crops had different nutritional requirements, and that particular soil amendments could enhance growing conditions all represent accumulated knowledge that had been refined through countless growing seasons.

The understanding of the role of organic matter in soil fertility was built upon generations of observations about the effects of different types of organic materials on soil structure and plant growth. The recognition that certain plant residues could improve soil fertility, that particular composting techniques could enhance decomposition, and that specific applications of organic matter could optimize growing conditions all represent accumulated wisdom that had been developed through practical experience.

The development of crop rotation systems and intercropping techniques was built upon the understanding of the relationship between different plants and their effects on soil fertility and pest management. The recognition that certain crop combinations could maximize yields, that particular rotation sequences could maintain soil fertility, and that specific planting patterns could reduce pest and disease problems all represent accumulated knowledge that had been refined through generations of agricultural experimentation.

Integration with Natural Cycles

The sophisticated understanding of the relationship between agricultural activities and natural cycles evident in Vedic texts was built upon millennia of accumulated observations about the correlation between celestial events, seasonal changes, and optimal timing for various agricultural activities. The recognition that certain planting times produced better yields, that particular harvesting periods ensured optimal quality, and that specific processing techniques were most effective at certain times of year all represent accumulated wisdom that had been developed through generations of practical experience.

The understanding of the relationship between weather patterns and agricultural success was built upon thousands of years of observations about the effects of different climatic conditions on crop growth and yield. The ability to predict weather patterns based on astronomical observations, to prepare for seasonal variations, and to adapt agricultural practices to changing conditions all represent accumulated knowledge that had been refined through countless growing seasons.

The integration of agricultural activities with religious and social observances was built upon the understanding of the importance of community cooperation and spiritual practices in ensuring agricultural success. The recognition that certain religious observances could enhance agricultural productivity, that particular community activities could improve cooperation and coordination, and that specific spiritual practices could support the agricultural process all represent accumulated wisdom that had been developed through generations of practical experience.

The Preservation and Transmission of Knowledge

The remarkable preservation and transmission of accumulated knowledge through the Vedic period represents one of humanity's greatest achievements in information management. The sophisticated systems developed for maintaining and passing down complex technical, scientific, and cultural knowledge across generations were themselves the product of millennia of experimentation and refinement.

Oral Tradition and Memory Techniques

The elaborate systems of oral tradition that preserved Vedic knowledge were built upon thousands of years of accumulated experience in memorization and transmission techniques. The understanding of how to structure information for optimal retention, how to create mnemonic devices that would preserve complex data, and how to establish transmission protocols that would maintain accuracy across generations all represent accumulated wisdom that had been refined through countless iterations.

The recognition that different types of knowledge required different preservation methods was built upon practical experience with information transmission over many generations. The understanding that mathematical concepts could be preserved through rhythmic recitation, that technical procedures could be maintained through practical demonstration, and that complex theoretical knowledge could be transmitted through structured dialogue all represent accumulated insights that had been developed through generations of practical experience.

The development of quality control mechanisms for ensuring the accuracy of transmitted knowledge was built upon the understanding of the factors that could lead to information degradation over time. The recognition that certain types of errors were more likely to occur than others, that particular transmission methods were more reliable for different types of information, and that specific verification procedures could maintain accuracy all represent accumulated wisdom that had been refined through generations of practical experience.

The Integration of Knowledge Systems

The sophisticated integration of different types of knowledge evident in Vedic texts was built upon thousands of years of accumulated understanding about the relationships between different domains of knowledge. The recognition that mathematical principles could be applied to astronomical observations, that medical knowledge could be integrated with agricultural practices, and that technological innovations could be combined with spiritual insights all represent accumulated wisdom that had been developed through generations of practical experience.

The understanding of the practical applications of theoretical knowledge was built upon millennia of experimentation with the implementation of abstract concepts in real-world situations. The ability to translate theoretical understanding into practical techniques, to adapt general principles to specific circumstances, and to combine different types of knowledge to solve complex problems all represent accumulated skills that had been refined through countless applications.

The development of educational systems that could effectively transmit complex knowledge was built upon accumulated understanding of human learning processes and the factors that enhanced or impeded knowledge acquisition. The recognition that different individuals learned in different ways, that particular teaching methods were more effective for certain types of knowledge, and that specific educational structures could optimize learning outcomes all represent accumulated wisdom that had been developed through generations of practical experience.

The Eternal Accumulation of Wisdom

The scientific and technological achievements of the Vedic period represent not sudden breakthroughs but the crystallization of ten thousand years of accumulated human knowledge and experience. The sophisticated understanding of mathematics, astronomy, medicine, metallurgy, agriculture, and timekeeping that emerged during this period was built upon the patient observations, careful experimentation, and gradual refinement of countless generations of scholars, craftsmen, farmers, and healers.

This accumulated wisdom was not merely technical knowledge but represented a holistic understanding of the relationship between human beings and the natural world. The integration of scientific observation with practical application, the correlation of empirical data with theoretical understanding, and the synthesis of different domains of knowledge into coherent systems all represent the culmination of millennia of human intellectual development.

The preservation and transmission of this accumulated knowledge through sophisticated oral traditions and educational systems ensured that hard-won insights would not be lost to time. The recognition that knowledge was a living, evolving entity that required constant nurturing and application led to the development of systems that could maintain and enhance understanding across generations.

The Vedic period thus represents not the beginning of knowledge in Indian civilization but rather a crucial phase in the ongoing accumulation and systematization of human understanding. The foundations laid during this period, built upon ten thousand years of accumulated wisdom, would continue to support and inspire intellectual development for centuries to come. The understanding that knowledge is not invented but discovered, not created but accumulated, not individual but collective, represents perhaps the most profound insight of this remarkable period in human history.

The legacy of Vedic knowledge accumulation continues to influence how we understand the development of human civilization and the nature of knowledge itself. The recognition that wisdom is built upon the patient accumulation of observations, the careful testing of hypotheses, and the gradual refinement of understanding across generations provides a model for how human knowledge develops and evolves. The Vedic period thus stands as a testament to the power of accumulated wisdom and the importance of preserving and transmitting knowledge across the generations.

16
Art and Architecture

Evolution of Ceramic Traditions

The pottery of the Vedic period represents one of the most significant and well-documented aspects of material culture from this era. The transition from the earlier Harappan pottery traditions to distinctly Vedic ceramic styles marks a crucial phase in the development of Indian craftsmanship. Early Vedic pottery, characterized by its handmade construction and simple forms, gradually evolved into more sophisticated wheel-thrown vessels that demonstrated both technical mastery and artistic refinement.

The most distinctive ceramic tradition of the Vedic period is the Painted Grey Ware (PGW), which emerged around 1200 BCE and became widespread across the Gangetic plain. This pottery type is characterized by its fine grey fabric, thin walls, and distinctive painted decorations executed in black pigment. The PGW represents a significant technological advancement, requiring precise control of firing conditions to achieve the characteristic grey color and hard texture. The pottery was fired in a reducing atmosphere, which gave it its distinctive appearance and durability.

The decorative motifs on PGW vessels reveal sophisticated artistic sensibilities and symbolic content. Common patterns include geometric designs such as circles, dots, waves, and lattice work, often arranged in bands around the vessel's circumference. These motifs were not merely decorative but carried deeper meanings related to cosmic order, natural phenomena, and ritual significance. The circular patterns, for instance, may have represented the cyclical nature of time and the cosmic wheel, concepts that were central to Vedic cosmology.

Regional variations in pottery styles reflect the diverse cultural influences and local traditions that contributed to Vedic material culture. In the northwestern regions, pottery showed influences from Central Asian traditions, while in the eastern areas, indigenous techniques merged with Vedic innovations. This regional diversity demonstrates the adaptive nature of Vedic culture and its ability to incorporate local elements while maintaining distinctive characteristics.

Metalwork and Ornamental Arts

The Vedic period witnessed remarkable developments in metalworking, particularly in the production of bronze objects, iron tools, and precious metal ornaments. The transition from the Bronze Age to the Iron Age during the later Vedic period brought about significant changes in both technology and artistic expression. Iron technology, initially used for weapons and tools, gradually extended to decorative objects and architectural elements.

Bronze casting achieved new heights of sophistication during the Vedic period. Archaeological excavations have revealed bronze vessels, figurines, and ritual objects that demonstrate advanced casting techniques and artistic sensibilities. The lost-wax casting method, which allowed for the creation of complex forms and intricate details, was refined during this period. Bronze vessels often featured elaborate decorative elements, including animal motifs, geometric patterns, and religious symbols that reflected Vedic iconography.

Jewelry and personal ornaments from the Vedic period reveal the importance of decorative arts in expressing social status and religious identity. Gold, silver, and copper were worked into intricate designs that included necklaces, bracelets, rings, and hair ornaments. The craftsmanship of these pieces demonstrates sophisticated techniques in hammering, filigree work, and gem setting. Many ornaments incorporated symbolic elements derived from Vedic literature, such as solar discs, lotus motifs, and animal forms that held religious significance.

The production of textiles, while not preserved in the archaeological record due to their perishable nature, is extensively documented in Vedic literature. References to elaborate weaving techniques, dyed fabrics, and embroidered garments indicate a highly developed textile tradition. The Rigveda contains numerous references to different types of cloth, weaving processes, and the social importance of textile production. Archaeological evidence of spindle whorls, loom weights, and dyeing facilities suggests that textile production was a significant aspect of Vedic material culture.

The decorative arts of the Vedic period were deeply infused with symbolic meaning that reflected the religious and philosophical concepts of the time. The motifs used in pottery, metalwork, and other decorative objects were not merely ornamental but served as visual expressions of cosmic principles and divine concepts. Understanding these symbolic elements provides insight into the Vedic worldview and its material manifestations.

Solar symbolism was particularly prominent in Vedic decorative arts. The sun, revered as Surya in Vedic mythology, was represented through various motifs including radiating circles, wheel patterns, and stylized solar discs. These symbols appeared on pottery, metalwork, and architectural elements, reflecting the central importance of solar worship in Vedic religion. The wheel motif, which later became the chakra symbol, represented the cosmic order and the cyclical nature of time.

Water and fertility symbols were equally important in Vedic decorative traditions. Wave patterns, lotus motifs, and serpentine designs reflected the reverence for water as a life-giving force and the importance of fertility in agricultural society. The lotus, which would later become one of the most important symbols in Indian art, first appeared in Vedic decorative contexts as a representation of purity, creation, and cosmic manifestation.

Animal motifs played a significant role in Vedic decorative arts, with horses, bulls, and birds being particularly prominent. The horse, associated with the sun god and sacrificial rituals, appeared frequently in various artistic contexts. Bull imagery, connected to fertility and strength, was common in both religious and secular decorative schemes. Bird motifs, particularly those representing eagles and other solar birds, symbolized the connection between earthly and divine realms.

Early Architectural Forms

Foundations of Vedic Architecture

The architectural traditions of the Vedic period represent the earliest systematic development of building practices in the Indian subcontinent following the decline of the Harappan civilization. Unlike the sophisticated urban planning of the Harappan cities, early Vedic architecture was characterized by its adaptation to a semi-nomadic lifestyle and gradual transition to settled communities. The architectural forms that emerged during this period established fundamental principles that would influence Indian building traditions for millennia.

Early Vedic settlements were initially temporary or semi-permanent structures designed to accommodate the mobility of pastoral communities. Archaeological evidence suggests that the earliest Vedic dwellings were simple wooden structures with thatched roofs, designed for easy construction and dismantling. These buildings reflected the practical needs of communities that moved seasonally with their herds and followed agricultural cycles.

As Vedic society became more settled, particularly during the later Vedic period, architectural forms became more permanent and sophisticated. The development of village settlements led to the creation of more substantial buildings constructed from wood, mud brick, and stone. These structures demonstrated increasing architectural complexity, with evidence of planned layouts, specialized building types, and decorative elements.

The transition from temporary to permanent architecture was accompanied by the development of distinct building typologies. Residential structures evolved from simple huts to complex multi-room dwellings that reflected social hierarchies and family structures. Public buildings, including assembly halls and religious structures, emerged as communities developed more complex social and religious institutions.

Religious architecture during the Vedic period was fundamentally different from the monumental temple architecture that would later characterize Indian building traditions. Early Vedic religious practices were primarily conducted in temporary or semi-permanent structures that could be easily constructed for specific rituals and ceremonies. The most important of these was the sacrificial altar, which served as the focal point for Vedic religious practice.

The construction of fire altars (agni-chiti) represented one of the most sophisticated architectural achievements of the Vedic period. These structures were built according to precise geometric principles described in the Sulba Sutras, ancient mathematical texts that provided detailed instructions for altar construction. The altars were designed in various shapes, including squares, circles, and bird forms, each carrying specific symbolic meanings related to cosmic order and divine principles.

The bird-shaped altar (shyena-chiti) was particularly significant, representing the flight of the soul to the heavenly realm. These altars required sophisticated knowledge of geometry and construction techniques, demonstrating the advanced mathematical and architectural knowledge of Vedic builders. The precision required in altar construction led to the development of standardized measurement systems and construction techniques that would influence later architectural traditions.

Assembly halls (sabha and samiti) represented another important category of Vedic architecture. These structures served as venues for community gatherings, judicial proceedings, and religious ceremonies. Archaeological evidence suggests that these buildings were often circular or rectangular in plan, with wooden post-and-beam construction supporting thatched or wooden roofs. The design of these halls reflected principles of acoustics and spatial organization that facilitated communal activities.

Residential Architecture and Settlement Patterns

The evolution of residential architecture during the Vedic period reflects the gradual transformation of society from nomadic to settled agricultural communities. Early Vedic homes were simple structures designed for basic shelter and protection, but as society became more complex, residential architecture developed to accommodate changing social needs and technological capabilities.

The typical Vedic house was a rectangular structure constructed with a wooden frame and walls made from wattle and daub or mud brick. The roof was typically thatched with grass or reeds, providing effective protection from monsoon rains. Archaeological excavations have revealed evidence of hearths, storage areas, and drainage systems that indicate a sophisticated understanding of domestic architecture.

The internal organization of Vedic homes reflected social and religious principles. The hearth (agni) was the central focus of the dwelling, serving both practical and ritual functions. The positioning of the hearth and other internal elements followed principles described in Vedic texts, which prescribed specific orientations and spatial relationships based on cosmological concepts.

Larger residential complexes belonging to wealthy families or tribal leaders demonstrated more sophisticated architectural features. These buildings often included multiple rooms, courtyards, and specialized spaces for different activities. The use of decorative elements, such as carved wooden posts and painted walls, indicated the growing importance of aesthetic considerations in residential architecture.

Urban Planning and Settlement Organization

The development of urban centers during the later Vedic period marked a significant evolution in architectural planning and settlement organization. While early Vedic communities were primarily rural and dispersed, the growth of trade, craft specialization, and political centralization led to the emergence of more complex urban settlements.

Archaeological evidence from sites such as Hastinapura, Kaushambi, and Ujjain reveals sophisticated urban planning principles that may have drawn inspiration from earlier Harappan traditions while incorporating distinctly Vedic elements. These settlements demonstrated planned layouts with designated areas for different activities, including residential quarters, craft workshops, and religious precincts.

The organization of Vedic cities reflected social hierarchies and functional requirements. Elite residential areas were typically located in central or elevated portions of the settlement, while craft workshops and common residential areas were positioned in peripheral zones. This spatial organization reflected the social stratification that characterized later Vedic society.

Fortification systems became increasingly important as political competition intensified during the later Vedic period. Archaeological evidence reveals sophisticated defensive architecture, including walls, gates, and moats designed to protect urban centers from military threats. These fortifications demonstrated advanced engineering knowledge and the ability to organize large-scale construction projects.

Sculpture and Artistic Motifs

Early Sculptural Traditions

The sculptural traditions of the Vedic period represent the earliest systematic development of threedimensional artistic expression in the Indian subcontinent following the Harappan civilization. Unlike the sophisticated figurative sculpture of the Harappan period, early Vedic sculpture was primarily functional and symbolic, serving religious and ceremonial purposes rather than purely aesthetic ones.

The earliest Vedic sculptural works were primarily small-scale objects made from terracotta, bronze, and stone. These included figurines, ritual objects, and decorative elements that were integrated into architectural contexts. The style of these early sculptures was characterized by simplified forms, symbolic representation, and emphasis on spiritual rather than naturalistic expression.

Terracotta figurines from the Vedic period provide valuable insights into artistic traditions and religious practices. These small sculptures, often depicting human figures, animals, and mythological beings, served various functions including religious worship, magical protection, and decorative purposes. The style of these figurines shows a gradual evolution from simple, geometric forms to more naturalistic representations.

Animal sculpture held particular significance in Vedic artistic traditions. Horses, bulls, and birds were commonly depicted in various media, reflecting their importance in Vedic religious and social contexts. The horse, associated with solar worship and sacrificial rituals, was frequently represented in bronze and terracotta sculptures. These animal figures often served as votive offerings or religious symbols rather than purely decorative objects.

Iconographic Development

The development of iconographic traditions during the Vedic period established fundamental principles that would influence Indian artistic expression for centuries to come. The symbolic language that emerged during this period combined indigenous traditions with Vedic religious concepts, creating a unique artistic vocabulary that expressed complex philosophical and spiritual ideas.

The representation of divine figures in Vedic art was initially aniconic, reflecting the abstract nature of early Vedic religious concepts. Fire, water, and celestial bodies were represented through symbolic forms rather than anthropomorphic images. This aniconic tradition influenced the development of symbolic representation in later Indian art, where abstract forms carried profound spiritual meanings.

The gradual development of anthropomorphic representation marked a significant evolution in Vedic artistic traditions. As religious concepts became more personalized and complex, artists began to create human-like images of divine beings. These early anthropomorphic representations were often simplified and stylized, emphasizing symbolic attributes rather than naturalistic details.

The integration of multiple symbolic elements in single sculptural works demonstrated the sophisticated conceptual framework that guided Vedic artistic expression. Composite figures combining human and animal elements, geometric patterns with organic forms, and terrestrial imagery with celestial symbols created complex visual narratives that conveyed multiple layers of meaning.

Decorative Relief Work

Relief sculpture during the Vedic period developed primarily in architectural contexts, where decorative elements were integrated into building structures to enhance both aesthetic appeal and symbolic meaning. These relief works represented some of the most sophisticated artistic achievements of the period, demonstrating advanced technical skills and artistic sensibilities.

Wooden architectural elements provided the primary medium for relief sculpture during the Vedic period. Door frames, pillars, and roof supports were often decorated with carved motifs that included geometric patterns, floral designs, and narrative scenes. The relatively soft nature of wood allowed for intricate carving techniques that produced detailed and expressive relief works.

The subject matter of Vedic relief sculpture reflected the religious and cultural preoccupations of the period. Solar symbols, fertility motifs, and protective deities were commonly represented in architectural relief work. These decorative elements served both aesthetic and apotropaic functions, beautifying buildings while providing spiritual protection for inhabitants.

The stylistic characteristics of Vedic relief sculpture emphasized clarity of form and symbolic content over naturalistic representation. Figures were often depicted in profile or frontal positions with simplified features that emphasized their symbolic significance. The use of repeated motifs and geometric frameworks created rhythmic patterns that enhanced the visual impact of relief compositions.

Artistic Techniques and Materials

The technical aspects of Vedic sculpture reveal sophisticated knowledge of materials and manufacturing processes that enabled artists to create works of remarkable quality and durability. The choice of materials and techniques was influenced by both practical considerations and symbolic meanings associated with different substances.

Bronze casting represented one of the most advanced technical achievements in Vedic sculpture. The lost-wax casting process allowed for the creation of complex forms with intricate details that would have been impossible to achieve through other methods. Vedic bronze workers developed sophisticated techniques for creating hollow castings, composite sculptures, and decorative inlays that demonstrated remarkable technical skill.

Stone carving during the Vedic period was relatively limited compared to later periods, but the works that survive demonstrate sophisticated understanding of stone properties and carving techniques. The selection of appropriate stone types, the use of iron tools, and the development of finishing techniques all contributed to the creation of durable and aesthetically pleasing sculptural works.

The integration of color in Vedic sculpture added another dimension to artistic expression. Evidence suggests that many sculptural works were originally painted with mineral pigments and organic dyes. The use of color enhanced the symbolic meaning of sculptures and created more visually striking artistic effects. The combination of sculptural form with color decoration established precedents for later Indian artistic traditions.

Music and Dance Traditions

Foundations of Musical Expression

The musical traditions of the Vedic period represent the earliest systematic development of musical theory and practice in the Indian subcontinent. The Sama Veda, one of the four principal Vedic texts, is essentially a collection of musical compositions that were chanted during religious ceremonies. This text provides invaluable insights into the musical practices, theoretical concepts, and aesthetic principles that governed Vedic musical expression.

The chanting of Vedic hymns required sophisticated knowledge of musical intervals, rhythmic patterns, and vocal techniques. The Sama Veda prescribes specific melodic patterns (saman) for different verses, indicating a developed system of musical notation and theory. The seven-note scale (sapta svara) that forms the basis of Indian classical music has its origins in Vedic musical theory, demonstrating the fundamental importance of this period in the development of musical traditions.

The performance of Vedic music was closely integrated with religious ritual and ceremonial practice. Different types of chanting were prescribed for various ritual contexts, including simple recitation (patha), melodic chanting (gana), and elaborate musical performances (stotra). The complexity of these musical forms required extensive training and specialized knowledge, leading to the development of hereditary musical traditions and professional musician classes.

Instrumental music during the Vedic period complemented vocal traditions and provided rhythmic accompaniment for religious ceremonies. Archaeological evidence and textual references indicate the use of various musical instruments, including drums, flutes, and stringed instruments. The development of these instruments required sophisticated knowledge of acoustics and craftsmanship, contributing to the broader artistic achievements of the period.

Rhythmic Systems and Meter

The development of rhythmic systems during the Vedic period established fundamental principles that would influence Indian musical traditions for millennia. The Vedic concept of meter (chhandas) was based on the systematic organization of syllables, beats, and rhythmic patterns that created structured musical compositions. This rhythmic framework provided the foundation for both musical and poetic expression.

The Rigveda contains numerous references to different metrical patterns that were used in musical compositions. The most common meters included the gayatri (24 syllables), tristubh (44 syllables), and jagati (48 syllables), each with specific rhythmic characteristics and ceremonial applications. The precise organization of these meters required sophisticated mathematical knowledge and contributed to the development of both musical theory and mathematical concepts.

The integration of rhythm with melodic and textual elements created complex musical compositions that served multiple functions. The rhythmic patterns were not merely temporal frameworks but carried symbolic meanings related to cosmic order, natural cycles, and spiritual concepts. The correlation between musical rhythm and cosmic rhythm reflected the Vedic understanding of music as a manifestation of universal principles.

Percussion instruments played a crucial role in establishing and maintaining rhythmic patterns during Vedic musical performances. The dundubhi (large drum) and other percussion instruments provided rhythmic foundation for chanting and ceremonial music. The construction and tuning of these instruments required advanced knowledge of acoustics and materials, contributing to the technical sophistication of Vedic musical traditions.

Dance as Sacred Expression

Dance traditions during the Vedic period were primarily religious and ceremonial in nature, serving as a means of expressing devotion, enacting mythological narratives, and facilitating spiritual transformation. The integration of dance with music and ritual created comprehensive artistic performances that engaged multiple senses and levels of meaning.

The Rigveda contains numerous references to dance performances that were conducted during religious festivals and ceremonies. These dances often involved the enactment of mythological stories, the celebration of natural phenomena, and the invocation of divine beings. The performers, known as nartakas, were skilled artists who combined physical movement with vocal expression and dramatic interpretation.

The choreographic principles of Vedic dance emphasized symbolic gesture, rhythmic movement, and spiritual expression rather than purely aesthetic display. The movements were designed to convey specific meanings and emotions, creating a sophisticated system of non-verbal communication that complemented the verbal content of religious texts. This symbolic approach to dance established precedents for the highly codified classical dance traditions that would later emerge in India.

Different types of dance were prescribed for various ritual contexts and seasonal celebrations. Fertility dances, victory celebrations, and seasonal festivals each had distinctive choreographic characteristics and performance requirements. The diversity of dance forms reflected the complex social and religious life of Vedic communities and the importance of artistic expression in maintaining cultural identity.

Musical Instruments and Technology

The development of musical instruments during the Vedic period represents a significant achievement in both artistic and technological terms. The creation of instruments required sophisticated knowledge of materials, acoustics, and manufacturing techniques that contributed to the broader technological advancement of Vedic civilization.

String instruments (tata vadya) mentioned in Vedic texts include the vina and other plucked string instruments that provided melodic accompaniment for vocal music. The construction of these instruments required precise knowledge of string tension, resonance, and tonal relationships. The development of frets and tuning systems enabled musicians to produce accurate pitches and complex melodic patterns.

Wind instruments (sushira vadya) played important roles in Vedic musical traditions, with the flute (vamsa) being particularly significant. The construction of flutes required precise calculations of hole placement and bore dimensions to produce accurate pitches and pleasant tonal qualities. The development of multiple sizes and types of flutes created a family of instruments capable of producing different tonal ranges and timbres.

Percussion instruments (avanaddha vadya) were essential components of Vedic musical ensembles, providing rhythmic foundation and ceremonial emphasis. The construction of drums required sophisticated knowledge of skin preparation, frame construction, and tuning techniques. Different types of drums were used for various ceremonial contexts, each with specific acoustic properties and symbolic associations.

The integration of instrumental music with vocal traditions created rich and complex musical textures that enhanced the effectiveness of religious ceremonies and cultural celebrations. The combination of different instrument types produced layered musical compositions that engaged listeners on multiple levels and created immersive artistic experiences.

Archaeological Evidence of Material Culture

Excavation Sites and Findings

Archaeological investigations of Vedic period sites have provided crucial evidence for understanding the material culture and artistic achievements of this formative period in Indian civilization. Major excavation sites across the Indo-Gangetic plain have yielded extensive collections of artifacts that illuminate various aspects of Vedic life, including artistic practices, technological capabilities, and cultural traditions.

The site of Hastinapura, identified as one of the most important Vedic settlements, has produced significant archaeological evidence of material culture spanning several centuries. Excavations have revealed multiple occupation levels that document the evolution of Vedic society from early settlement to complex urban development. The artifact assemblages from Hastinapura include sophisticated pottery, metalwork, and architectural remains that demonstrate the artistic achievements of Vedic craftsmen.

Kaushambi, another major Vedic site, has yielded extensive evidence of urban planning and architectural development. The excavations have revealed sophisticated fortification systems, residential complexes, and craft workshops that indicate advanced organizational and technical capabilities. The artistic remains from Kaushambi include terracotta sculptures, decorated pottery, and bronze objects that represent some of the finest examples of Vedic material culture.

The site of Atranjikhera has provided valuable insights into the transition from early to later Vedic periods through its well-stratified archaeological deposits. The material culture from this site demonstrates the gradual evolution of artistic traditions and technological capabilities over several centuries. The pottery sequences, tool assemblages, and architectural remains from Atranjikhera have been crucial for understanding the chronological development of Vedic civilization.

Stratigraphy and Chronological Development

The stratigraphic analysis of Vedic period sites has revealed important information about the chronological development of material culture and artistic traditions. The careful excavation and recording of archaeological layers has enabled researchers to trace the evolution of various artistic forms and technological practices over time.

The earliest Vedic levels at major sites are characterized by relatively simple material culture, including handmade pottery, basic metal tools, and simple architectural remains. These early deposits reflect the semi-nomadic lifestyle of early Vedic communities and their limited technological capabilities. The artistic expressions from these early levels are primarily functional in nature, with minimal decorative elaboration.

The middle Vedic period levels show significant developments in material culture, including the introduction of wheel-made pottery, more sophisticated metalwork, and more complex architectural forms. The artistic achievements of this period demonstrate increasing technical skill and aesthetic sophistication. The development of distinctive decorative styles and the standardization of production techniques indicate the emergence of specialized craft traditions.

The later Vedic period levels reveal the full flowering of material culture and artistic achievement. The archaeological deposits from this period contain sophisticated pottery, elaborate metalwork, and complex architectural remains that represent the culmination of Vedic artistic traditions. The diversity and quality of artistic remains from later Vedic contexts demonstrate the advanced state of cultural development achieved by the end of the period.

Artifact Analysis and Interpretation

The detailed analysis of artifacts from Vedic period sites has provided crucial insights into the

technological, artistic, and cultural achievements of this formative period. The systematic study of pottery, metalwork, stone tools, and other material remains has enabled researchers to reconstruct various aspects of Vedic life and cultural practices.

Pottery analysis has been particularly important for understanding chronological development and regional variations in Vedic material culture. The study of vessel forms, decorative techniques, and production methods has revealed information about technological capabilities, artistic preferences, and cultural influences. The analysis of pottery assemblages has also provided insights into functional aspects of Vedic life, including food preparation, storage, and ritual practices.

Metalwork analysis has revealed sophisticated knowledge of metallurgy and advanced technical skills in the production of tools, weapons, and decorative objects. The study of bronze casting techniques, iron working methods, and precious metal craftsmanship has demonstrated the high level of technological achievement attained by Vedic craftsmen. The analysis of metal objects has also provided insights into trade networks, resource procurement, and technological transmission.

The analysis of architectural remains has revealed important information about building techniques, spatial organization, and aesthetic principles. The study of construction methods, material selection, and decorative elements has provided insights into the technological capabilities and cultural preferences of Vedic builders. The analysis of settlement patterns and urban organization has also contributed to understanding of social structure and cultural development.

Technological Innovations and Craft Specialization

Archaeological evidence from Vedic period sites demonstrates significant technological innovations and the development of specialized craft traditions. The analysis of production techniques, tool assemblages, and workshop remains has revealed the advanced state of technological development achieved during this period.

The introduction of iron technology during the later Vedic period represents one of the most significant technological innovations of the era. Archaeological evidence shows the gradual adoption of iron tools and weapons, which provided superior performance compared to bronze implements. The development of iron working techniques required sophisticated knowledge of metallurgy and contributed to significant improvements in agricultural productivity and military capabilities.

The development of specialized craft workshops indicates the emergence of professional artisan classes and the standardization of production techniques. Archaeological excavations have revealed evidence of pottery workshops, metalworking facilities, and textile production centers that operated on a scale suggesting commercial production. The specialization of craft activities contributed to improvements in quality and efficiency while enabling the development of distinctive artistic styles.

The evidence for long-distance trade networks demonstrates the sophisticated economic and cultural connections that linked Vedic communities with distant regions. The presence of non-local materials and imported objects at Vedic sites indicates extensive trade relationships that facilitated the exchange of both goods and ideas. These trade connections contributed to technological innovation and cultural development through the introduction of new materials, techniques, and artistic influences.

Regional Variations and Cultural Synthesis

Geographic Distribution of Artistic Traditions

The Vedic period witnessed the development of distinct regional traditions that reflected local cultural influences, environmental conditions, and historical circumstances. The geographic distribution of artistic styles and material culture patterns reveals the complex processes of cultural interaction and adaptation that characterized Vedic civilization.

The northwestern regions of the Indian subcontinent, where the earliest Vedic settlements were established, developed artistic traditions that showed influences from Central Asian and Iranian cultures. The pottery styles, metalwork techniques, and architectural forms from these regions demonstrate the synthesis of indigenous and foreign elements that characterized early Vedic culture. The horse-related imagery and solar symbolism that became prominent in Vedic art may have originated in these northwestern regions.

The Gangetic plain region developed distinctive artistic traditions that reflected the transition from nomadic to agricultural lifestyles. The sophisticated pottery traditions, including the Painted Grey Ware culture, emerged in this region and spread throughout northern India. The artistic expressions from Gangetic sites demonstrate the successful adaptation of Vedic culture to new environmental and social conditions.

The peninsular regions of India developed unique syntheses of Vedic and indigenous traditions that created distinctive regional styles. The interaction between Vedic settlers and local populations produced hybrid artistic forms that combined Vedic symbolic elements with indigenous techniques and aesthetic preferences. These regional variations demonstrate the adaptive nature of Vedic culture and its ability to incorporate diverse influences.

Cultural Exchange and Synthesis

The artistic traditions of the Vedic period were shaped by extensive cultural exchange and synthesis that occurred through trade, migration, and cultural contact. The analysis of artistic styles, technological innovations, and symbolic systems reveals the complex processes of cultural interaction that contributed to the development of Vedic material culture.

The influence of earlier Harappan traditions can be detected in various aspects of Vedic material culture, including pottery techniques, urban planning principles, and artistic motifs. The continuity of certain technological and aesthetic elements suggests that aspects of Harappan culture were preserved and transmitted to Vedic communities through indigenous populations. This cultural synthesis contributed to the distinctive character of Vedic artistic traditions.

The interaction with Central Asian and Iranian cultures introduced new artistic elements, including specific decorative motifs, metallurgical techniques, and architectural forms. The horse and solar symbolism that became prominent in Vedic art may have originated through these cultural contacts. The synthesis of these foreign influences with indigenous traditions created the unique artistic vocabulary that characterized Vedic culture.

The gradual expansion of Vedic culture throughout the Indian subcontinent facilitated extensive cultural exchange with diverse indigenous populations. The interaction between Vedic settlers and local communities produced regional variations in artistic traditions that reflected local preferences and conditions. This process of cultural synthesis contributed to the rich diversity of Indian artistic traditions.

Legacy and Influence on Later Traditions

The artistic achievements of the Vedic period established fundamental principles and traditions that profoundly influenced subsequent developments in Indian art and architecture. The symbolic systems, technical innovations, and aesthetic principles developed during this period provided the foundation for the classical traditions that would emerge in later centuries.

The iconographic traditions established during the Vedic period continued to influence Indian artistic expression throughout history. The symbolic motifs, including solar imagery, lotus patterns, and animal symbolism, became integral elements of later Indian art. The aniconic traditions of early Vedic art also influenced the development of abstract and symbolic representation in later periods.

The architectural principles developed during the Vedic period, including the use of geometric proportions, cosmic symbolism, and ritual significance, became fundamental aspects of Indian building traditions. The temple architecture of later periods incorporated many elements that originated in Vedic architectural practices, including the emphasis on cardinal directions, cosmic symbolism, and ritual function.

The musical and dance traditions of the Vedic period provided the foundation for the sophisticated classical traditions that would emerge in later centuries. The theoretical principles, rhythmic systems, and performance practices developed during this period continued to influence Indian musical and dance traditions throughout their historical development.

Conclusion

The material expressions of the Vedic period represent a remarkable achievement in human creativity and cultural development. The artistic traditions that emerged during this formative period established fundamental principles that would influence Indian civilization for millennia. The integration of functional utility with symbolic meaning, the synthesis of indigenous and foreign influences, and the development of sophisticated technical capabilities all contributed to the distinctive character of Vedic material culture.

The pottery traditions of the Vedic period, exemplified by the Painted Grey Ware culture, demonstrated advanced technical skills and aesthetic sensibilities that reflected the sophisticated cultural development of the period. The decorative motifs and symbolic systems developed in ceramic arts provided visual expressions of cosmic principles and religious concepts that were central to Vedic worldview.

The architectural achievements of the Vedic period, from simple residential structures to complex urban settlements, established building traditions that would influence Indian architecture throughout history. The integration of functional requirements with symbolic meaning and the development of sophisticated construction techniques demonstrated the advanced state of architectural knowledge achieved during this period.

The sculptural traditions of the Vedic period, though limited in scope compared to later periods, established fundamental principles of iconography and symbolic representation that would profoundly influence subsequent artistic developments. The emphasis on symbolic content over naturalistic representation and the integration of multiple meaning systems created a distinctive artistic vocabulary that became characteristic of Indian artistic traditions.

The music and dance traditions of the Vedic period provided the theoretical and practical foundation for the sophisticated classical traditions that would emerge in later centuries. The development of musical theory, rhythmic systems, and performance practices demonstrated the advanced state of cultural achievement attained during this formative period.

The archaeological evidence of Vedic material culture provides crucial insights into the daily life, technological capabilities, and cultural achievements of this foundational period in Indian civilization. The systematic analysis of artifacts, architectural remains, and settlement patterns has enabled researchers to reconstruct various aspects of Vedic life and cultural practices.

The regional variations in Vedic artistic traditions demonstrate the adaptive nature of the culture and its ability to incorporate diverse influences while maintaining distinctive characteristics. The synthesis of indigenous and foreign elements created rich and varied artistic traditions that reflected the complex cultural interactions that characterized the Vedic period.

The legacy of Vedic artistic achievements extends far beyond the historical period itself, providing the foundation for the sophisticated classical traditions that would emerge in later centuries. The principles of symbolism, technical innovation, and aesthetic expression developed during the Vedic period continued to influence Indian artistic traditions throughout their historical development, demonstrating the enduring significance of this formative period in Indian civilization.

The study of Vedic art and architecture reveals the profound creativity and cultural sophistication of early Indian civilization. The material expressions of this period serve as testament to the remarkable achievements of human creativity and the enduring power of artistic expression to convey complex ideas and cultural values. The artistic legacy of the Vedic period continues to inspire and influence contemporary artistic traditions, demonstrating the timeless relevance of these ancient cultural achievements.

17
The Lasting Influence

Impact on Later Hindu Traditions

The relationship between Vedic religion and later Hindu traditions represents one of the most complex and fascinating examples of religious evolution in human history. While Hinduism as we know it today differs significantly from the religion practiced by the early Vedic peoples, the fundamental structures, concepts, and practices that emerged from the Vedic period form the bedrock upon which later Hindu traditions were built.

The pantheon of Vedic deities underwent remarkable transformation as they were incorporated into later Hindu worship. Indra, the mighty storm god and king of the devas in Vedic literature, gradually diminished in importance while other deities like Vishnu and Shiva, who had relatively minor roles in the earliest Vedic texts, evolved into the supreme deities of major Hindu traditions. Vishnu, mentioned briefly in the Rig Veda as a solar deity known for his three strides across the universe, eventually became the supreme deity of

Vaishnavism, with elaborate mythologies surrounding his various avatars. Similarly, Rudra, a fierce deity associated with storms and healing in the Vedic texts, transformed into Shiva, one of the principal deities of Hinduism.

The concept of Brahman, which appears in the later Vedic texts, particularly the Upanishads, as the ultimate reality underlying all existence, became central to Hindu philosophical thought. This abstract, impersonal principle of ultimate reality provided the theological foundation for later Hindu concepts of the divine that transcends personal deities while simultaneously manifesting through them. The Upanishadic teaching that Atman (the individual soul) and Brahman are ultimately identical became a cornerstone of Advaita Vedanta and influenced virtually all subsequent Hindu philosophical schools.

Ritual practices established in the Vedic period continued to evolve and adapt within Hindu traditions. The elaborate fire sacrifices (yajnas) of the Vedic period, while maintaining their theoretical importance, were gradually supplemented and often replaced by temple worship, devotional practices (bhakti), and personal meditation. However, the underlying structure of Vedic ritual, with its emphasis on precise performance, sacred syllables, and the transformative power of correctly executed ceremonies, remained influential. The concept of mantra, derived from Vedic chanting traditions, became fundamental to Hindu practice, whether in temple worship, personal devotion, or meditative practices.

The Vedic concept of dharma, initially referring to the cosmic order maintained through proper ritual performance, expanded to encompass ethical conduct, social duty, and natural law. This evolution of dharma from a primarily ritual concept to a comprehensive moral and social framework demonstrates how Vedic ideas provided the conceptual foundation for later Hindu ethical systems. The Dharmasutras and Dharmashastra literature, which codified Hindu law and social organization, explicitly traced their authority back to

Vedic sources, even as they addressed concerns far beyond the scope of early Vedic society.

The caste system, while not explicitly outlined in the earliest Vedic texts, found its theological justification in the Purusha Sukta of the Rig Veda, which describes the cosmic man being divided into four parts corresponding to the four varnas. Later Hindu texts elaborated this into a comprehensive social system that governed marriage, occupation, and social interaction. Despite significant criticism and reform movements, the influence of this Vedic-derived social organization continues to shape Indian society.

The tradition of guru-disciple relationship, fundamental to Hindu spiritual practice, has its roots in the Vedic system of transmitting sacred knowledge. The concept of the guru as not merely a teacher but as a living embodiment of divine wisdom, worthy of reverence equal to the gods themselves, stems from Vedic traditions of preserving and transmitting sacred texts through oral tradition. The relationship between teacher and student in the Vedic tradition was seen as sacred, and this understanding profoundly influenced later Hindu approaches to spiritual instruction.

Hindu concepts of time and cosmology also reflect Vedic influence. The cyclical understanding of time, with its vast epochs (yugas) and recurring cosmic cycles, while elaborated in later texts like the Puranas, has its conceptual origins in Vedic hymns that describe the recurring cycles of creation and destruction. The idea that the universe undergoes periodic dissolution and recreation, governed by cosmic principles rather than historical contingency, became fundamental to Hindu cosmological thinking.

The integration of Vedic elements with non-Vedic traditions created the syncretic character that defines Hinduism. Local deities, tribal practices, and regional customs were incorporated into the broader Hindu framework by establishing connections with Vedic precedents or by reinterpreting Vedic texts to accommodate new elements. This process of integration and reinterpretation, guided by the authority of Vedic texts, allowed Hinduism to maintain both continuity with ancient traditions and adaptability to changing circumstances.

Influence on Law and Social Organization

The Vedic tradition's impact on Indian legal and social systems extends far beyond religious practice into the fundamental structures that have governed Indian society for millennia. The concept of dharma, as it evolved from Vedic literature, became the organizing principle for an entire civilization's understanding of law, duty, and social order.

The earliest legal literature in India, the Dharmasutras composed between approximately 800-200 BCE, explicitly claimed Vedic authority for their prescriptions. These texts, including works attributed to Apastamba, Gautama, and Baudhayana, presented themselves as explanations and applications of Vedic principles to practical social situations. While they addressed many issues not directly covered in Vedic literature, they maintained that their authority derived from Vedic sources, either through direct citation or through claimed continuation of Vedic tradition.

The more elaborate Dharmashastra literature, including the influential Manusmriti (Laws of Manu), further developed this legal tradition while maintaining its Vedic foundations. These texts created comprehensive legal systems covering criminal law, civil disputes, royal duties, and social organization, all justified by reference to Vedic principles. The concept that law must conform to dharma, and that dharma finds its ultimate source in Vedic revelation, established a theoretical framework that influenced Indian legal thinking for centuries.

The varna system, while not fully developed in early Vedic texts, found its theological justification in Vedic literature and became the organizing principle for Indian social structure. The Purusha Sukta's description of the cosmic being divided into brahmins (priests), kshatriyas (warriors), vaishyas (merchants), and shudras (laborers) provided religious sanction for social hierarchy. Later legal texts elaborated this into detailed prescriptions for social behavior, occupational duties, and inter-group relationships.

This system created a complex web of mutual obligations and restrictions that governed marriage, dining, occupation, and social interaction. The concept of ritual purity and pollution, while having some basis in Vedic ritual requirements, was expanded into a comprehensive system that regulated social contact and created elaborate hierarchies within and between social groups. The influence of these Vedic-derived social categories persisted even as Indian society encountered other legal traditions, including Islamic law during the medieval period and British colonial law.

The idea of royal dharma (rajadharma), developed in later texts but rooted in Vedic concepts of cosmic order, established principles for governance that influenced Indian political thought. The king was seen not as an absolute ruler but as a maintainer of dharma, obligated to protect the social order and ensure that all groups fulfilled their dharmic duties. This concept created a theoretical framework for limited government, where royal power was constrained by religious and moral principles derived from Vedic tradition.

The legal concept of evidence and testimony also drew from Vedic precedents. The importance of truthfulness, established in Vedic literature as both a cosmic principle and a practical necessity for ritual effectiveness, became fundamental to legal procedures. The idea that false testimony corrupts both the individual and society reflected Vedic understanding of the interconnectedness of cosmic and social order.

Property law in classical Indian legal texts reflected Vedic principles about the relationship between individuals, community, and the cosmic order. While private property was recognized, it was understood within a framework of dharmic obligations that limited absolute ownership rights. The concept that wealth should be used in accordance with dharmic principles, including obligations to support religious activities and help those in need, showed clear Vedic influence.

The institution of joint family property, which became characteristic of Hindu law, reflected Vedic emphasis on family and lineage. The idea that property belonged not just to individuals but to family lines, with complex rules governing inheritance and management, drew from Vedic concepts of ancestral obligations and the continuity of family traditions.

Marriage law showed particularly strong Vedic influence, with the concept of marriage as a sacrament (samskara) rather than merely a civil contract. The various forms of marriage described in later legal texts, from the highly recommended brahma marriage to the conditionally acceptable forms, were justified by reference to Vedic practices. The emphasis on marriage within appropriate varna boundaries, the importance of family consent, and the religious ceremonies required for valid marriage all reflected Vedic origins.

The legal status of women in classical Hindu law, while varying significantly across different periods and regions, was profoundly influenced by interpretations of Vedic texts. Some Vedic hymns suggest relatively high status for women in ritual contexts, while others reflect patriarchal assumptions. Later legal texts, claiming Vedic authority, generally restricted women's legal rights while acknowledging their importance in religious and family contexts.

Criminal law in classical Indian texts also showed Vedic influence, particularly in the concept that crimes disrupted both social and cosmic order. The idea that punishment should restore balance rather than merely deter future crimes reflected Vedic understanding of the interconnectedness of moral and natural law. The principle of proportionality in punishment, and the consideration of factors like intent, social status, and circumstances, showed sophisticated legal thinking rooted in Vedic concepts of justice.

Literary and Linguistic Legacy

The linguistic and literary influence of the Vedic tradition on Indian civilization cannot be overstated. Sanskrit, the language of most Vedic texts, became not only the sacred language of Hindu tradition but also the medium for philosophy, science, law, and literature across the Indian subcontinent for over two millennia. The preservation and transmission of Vedic texts created sophisticated techniques for linguistic analysis and grammatical study that influenced educational and intellectual traditions throughout Indian history.

The oral tradition that preserved Vedic texts developed remarkable techniques for ensuring accurate transmission across generations. The Vedic schools (shakhas) developed different methods of chanting that included various combinations and repetitions designed to prevent errors in transmission. This tradition of precise verbal transmission created a culture of linguistic precision that influenced all subsequent Sanskrit literature.

The grammatical tradition initiated by Panini in his Ashtadhyayi, while not exclusively focused on Vedic language, was fundamentally concerned with systematizing Sanskrit grammar in a way that would preserve the linguistic precision necessary for Vedic study. Panini's work, which represents one of the most sophisticated grammatical analyses in human history, established standards for linguistic description that influenced not only Indian traditions but eventually comparative linguistics worldwide.

The Vedic tradition established Sanskrit as a trans-regional language of learning that transcended local linguistic boundaries. While various Indian regions developed their own languages, Sanskrit remained the medium for scholarly discourse, religious texts, and literary creation. This created a shared intellectual culture across diverse linguistic communities, with Sanskrit serving as the Latin of Indian civilization.

The poetic techniques developed in Vedic literature profoundly influenced later Sanskrit poetry. The complex meters of Vedic hymns, the sophisticated use of imagery and metaphor, and the development of particular literary devices can be traced through classical Sanskrit literature. The concept of rasa (aesthetic flavor) in later poetic theory, while not explicitly formulated in Vedic texts, drew from Vedic understanding of how properly constructed language could evoke specific emotional and spiritual responses.

The philosophical vocabulary developed in Vedic literature, particularly in the Upanishads, provided the technical terminology for virtually all subsequent Indian philosophical schools. Terms like dharma, karma, moksha, samsara, and countless others originated in or were given their technical meanings by Vedic texts. This shared vocabulary enabled sophisticated philosophical discourse across different schools and traditions, even when they disagreed fundamentally about the meaning and implications of these terms.

The influence of Vedic literary forms extended beyond Sanskrit literature into regional languages. The hymnal structure of Vedic texts influenced devotional poetry in languages like Tamil, Telugu, Marathi, and Hindi. The concept of sacred poetry as a means of approaching the divine, established in Vedic tradition, became fundamental to bhakti literature across India.

The Vedic tradition of commentary (bhashya) and sub-commentary established methods of textual interpretation that influenced Indian literary and philosophical discourse. The technique of explaining difficult passages through reference to other texts, the careful analysis of grammatical forms, and the systematic examination of different possible interpretations became standard approaches to textual study throughout Indian intellectual traditions.

Epic literature, including the Mahabharata and Ramayana, while post-Vedic in composition, drew heavily from Vedic linguistic traditions and incorporated Vedic hymns and concepts throughout their narratives. These epics served as vehicles for transmitting Vedic ideas to broader audiences who might not have direct access to Vedic texts themselves.

The tradition of oral performance that characterized Vedic transmission influenced Indian approaches to literature more generally. The concept that texts were meant to be heard rather than read silently, that proper pronunciation and rhythm were essential to meaning, and that the performance context was crucial to understanding remained important throughout Indian literary history.

Dramatic literature also showed Vedic influence, particularly in the understanding that properly performed words could create transformative experiences. The theory of drama developed by Bharata and others drew from Vedic concepts about the power of correctly executed ritual performance, adapting these ideas to secular entertainment and instruction.

The Vedic emphasis on precision in language use influenced Indian approaches to translation and interpretation. The concept that slight changes in wording could completely alter meaning, essential to Vedic ritual practice, created sophisticated approaches to textual analysis that influenced legal interpretation, philosophical argument, and literary criticism.

Regional languages throughout India borrowed extensively from Sanskrit vocabulary rooted in Vedic texts. Modern Indian languages contain thousands of words derived from Sanskrit sources, many of which originated in or were defined by Vedic literature. This linguistic inheritance created shared conceptual frameworks across diverse linguistic communities throughout the subcontinent.

Philosophical Contributions to Indian Thought

The philosophical revolution initiated in the later Vedic period, particularly in the Upanishads, established foundational concepts and methods of inquiry that shaped virtually all subsequent Indian philosophical development. The transition from the ritualistic religion of the early Vedic period to the philosophical sophistication of the Upanishads represents one of the most remarkable intellectual developments in human history, creating conceptual frameworks that continue to influence philosophical discourse today.

The concept of Brahman as ultimate reality represents perhaps the most significant philosophical contribution of the Vedic tradition. The Upanishadic teaching that behind the apparent diversity of the phenomenal world lies a single, unchanging reality provided a metaphysical foundation that influenced every subsequent school of Indian philosophy, even those that rejected this particular formulation. The systematic exploration of the relationship between appearance and reality, between the many and the one, established fundamental questions that drove philosophical inquiry for millennia.

The identity between Atman (individual self) and Brahman, proclaimed in the Upanishadic statement "Tat tvam asi" (That thou art), created a unique approach to the problem of individual identity and cosmic reality. This teaching suggested that the deepest truth about individual existence was not separateness but fundamental unity with ultimate reality. This concept influenced not only explicitly Vedantic philosophies but also Buddhist and Jain approaches to understanding the nature of individual existence.

The method of philosophical inquiry developed in the Upanishads, characterized by dialogue between teacher and student, systematic questioning of apparent certainties, and the use of analogies and thought experiments to illuminate abstract concepts, became the standard approach for Indian philosophical discourse. The Upanishadic technique of using familiar examples to explain unfamiliar concepts, such as comparing the relationship between individual and universal consciousness to that between rivers and the ocean, influenced pedagogical methods throughout Indian intellectual history.

The concept of maya (illusion or creative power), while not fully developed in the earliest Upanishads, emerged from Vedic speculation about the relationship between appearance and reality. This concept became central to Advaita Vedanta and influenced other philosophical schools' approaches to understanding perception, knowledge, and the nature of phenomenal existence.

The doctrine of karma, while having roots in Vedic ritual theory, was philosophically developed in the Upanishads into a comprehensive theory of moral causation that extended beyond individual lifetimes. The idea that actions create consequences that may manifest in future existences provided a framework for understanding moral responsibility and cosmic justice that influenced virtually all subsequent Indian religious and philosophical traditions.

The concept of moksha (liberation) as the ultimate human goal emerged from Vedic traditions but was philosophically elaborated in the Upanishads. The teaching that human existence involves bondage to ignorance and that liberation requires correct understanding of reality established soteriological goals that influenced all Indian religions, even those that rejected specific Vedic formulations.

The Upanishadic development of meditation techniques and contemplative practices provided practical methods for achieving the philosophical insights described in these texts. The emphasis on direct experience (anubhava) as the ultimate validation of philosophical truth, rather than mere logical argument or scriptural authority, created an empirical dimension to philosophical inquiry that distinguished Indian traditions from purely rational approaches to metaphysics.

The philosophy of language developed in Vedic traditions, particularly the understanding that properly used words could reveal or even create reality, influenced Indian approaches to logic, epistemology, and hermeneutics. The concept that sacred sounds (mantras) possessed inherent power independent of their semantic meaning provided a framework for understanding language that influenced not only religious practice but also philosophical theories about the relationship between words and reality.

The Vedic understanding of time as cyclical rather than linear created distinctive approaches to questions about causation, progress, and ultimate meaning. The concept that cosmic and individual existence moved through recurring cycles of manifestation and dissolution influenced Indian philosophical approaches to questions about the nature of change, permanence, and ultimate reality.

The epistemological frameworks developed in Vedic traditions, particularly the recognition of different sources of valid knowledge (pramanas) including perception, inference, and revelation, provided methodological foundations for later philosophical schools. While different schools developed different theories about the number and nature of valid knowledge sources, the basic framework for epistemological inquiry was established in Vedic traditions.

The ethics that emerged from Vedic philosophical development emphasized the connection between understanding reality correctly and acting appropriately. The concept that moral action flowed naturally from correct knowledge, rather than being imposed by external authority, created approaches to ethics that integrated metaphysical understanding with practical conduct.

The influence of Vedic philosophical methods extended beyond explicitly Hindu traditions to influence

Buddhist and Jain philosophical development. While these traditions rejected Vedic authority and specific Vedic doctrines, they adopted many of the methods of philosophical inquiry, technical vocabulary, and conceptual frameworks developed in Vedic traditions.

Global Influence: Impact on East, West, and the World

The influence of Vedic traditions extends far beyond the boundaries of the Indian subcontinent, creating ripple effects that have touched civilizations across Asia and, in modern times, throughout the entire world. This global dissemination of Vedic concepts, practices, and philosophical insights demonstrates the universal appeal and applicability of ideas that emerged from the ancient Indian synthesis of spiritual inquiry and intellectual sophistication. The global dissemination of Vedic knowledge reveals a fundamental aspect of human civilization: we are fundamentally an information-sharing species. The mechanisms by which Vedic philosophy, religion, and science spread across continents in ancient times demonstrate sophisticated networks of knowledge transmission that parallel, in many ways, our modern digital information systems. Understanding these ancient pathways of intellectual exchange provides insight into both the enduring human drive to share knowledge and the revolutionary impact that new information technologies can have on civilizations.

Ancient Networks of Knowledge Transmission

The spread of Vedic knowledge occurred through remarkably sophisticated networks that functioned as the ancient equivalent of modern information systems. Unlike today's instantaneous digital communication, ancient knowledge transfer required physical movement of people, creating dense networks of intellectual and spiritual exchange that connected distant civilizations.

The most significant pathway was through traveling scholars, monks, and teachers who carried oral traditions, manuscripts, and practical knowledge across vast distances. Buddhist monks, in particular, created what might be considered the world's first international educational network. Monasteries from Nalanda in India to Dunhuang in China served as nodes in this network, preserving texts, training scholars, and facilitating the exchange of ideas across cultural and linguistic boundaries. These institutions functioned much like modern universities, research centers, and digital platforms combined - they were simultaneously repositories of knowledge, centers for creating new understanding, and hubs for distributing information to wider networks.

Trade routes served as crucial information highways, with merchants carrying not only goods but also ideas, practices, and texts. The Silk Road functioned as an ancient internet, connecting India with Central Asia, China, the Middle East, and eventually Europe. Caravanserais along these routes became informal centers of intellectual exchange, where travelers shared stories, philosophies, and practical knowledge. Archaeological evidence shows that Indian mathematical texts, medical treatises, and philosophical works traveled these same routes that carried spices and silk.

Royal courts and political networks also facilitated knowledge transmission. When Southeast Asian rulers adopted Indian political and religious concepts, they created formal channels for importing Indian scholars, architects, artists, and religious practitioners. The construction of Angkor Wat required not only Vedic cosmological knowledge but also sophisticated engineering and mathematical understanding that had to be transmitted from India to Cambodia through networks of skilled practitioners.

The guru-disciple tradition created uniquely effective systems for preserving and transmitting complex knowledge. Unlike written texts, which could be copied incorrectly or misinterpreted, the oral tradition ensured that knowledge was transmitted with deep understanding. Students would spend years with teachers, absorbing not only information but also the subtle aspects of practice and interpretation that couldn't be captured in written form. This system created networks of authenticated knowledge that maintained remarkable consistency across vast distances and long time periods.

Marriage and kinship networks also served as conduits for knowledge transmission. When Indian princesses married into Southeast Asian royal families, they brought with them not only cultural practices but also the scholars, priests, and artists who maintained these traditions. These human networks created lasting channels for ongoing cultural and intellectual exchange.

Eastern Influence: The Buddhist and Southeast Asian Connection

The most immediate and profound international impact of Vedic traditions came through Buddhism, which, despite rejecting Vedic authority, carried many Vedic concepts and practices throughout Asia. The Buddhist understanding of karma, samsara, dharma, and moksha (nirvana in Buddhist terminology) directly derived from Vedic and Upanishadic sources, even as Buddhism reinterpreted these concepts within its own framework. As Buddhism spread throughout Central Asia, China, Southeast Asia, Korea, and Japan, it carried these Vedic-derived concepts to cultures that had no direct contact with Indian civilization.

The philosophical methodology developed in Vedic traditions, particularly the dialectical approach of the Upanishads and the systematic analysis of consciousness and reality, profoundly influenced Buddhist philosophical schools. The Madhyamika school's analysis of emptiness (sunyata) and the Yogacara school's investigation of consciousness showed clear methodological continuities with Upanishadic inquiry, even while reaching different conclusions. This philosophical sophistication, rooted in Vedic intellectual traditions, became fundamental to Buddhist thought throughout Asia.

In Southeast Asia, the direct influence of Vedic traditions was even more apparent. Hindu kingdoms in Cambodia, Java, Bali, and other regions adopted not only Vedic deities and practices but also Sanskrit as a language of learning and administration. The magnificent temple complexes of Angkor Wat,

Borobudur, and Prambanan demonstrate how Vedic cosmology, mythology, and architectural principles were transplanted to Southeast Asian contexts while adapting to local conditions and aesthetic preferences.

The concept of the divine king (devaraja), which became central to Southeast Asian political theory, drew directly from Vedic and post-Vedic Indian concepts of royal dharma and the connection between earthly and cosmic order. This political theology influenced governmental structures throughout the region for centuries and continues to influence contemporary Southeast Asian political thought.

Traditional medicine systems throughout Asia show clear Vedic influence through Ayurveda, which was based on principles derived from Vedic understanding of cosmic elements, human constitution, and the relationship between microcosm and macrocosm. Chinese traditional medicine, Tibetan medicine, and traditional medical systems throughout Southeast Asia incorporated Ayurvedic principles, creating syncretic systems that combined local knowledge with Indian medical theory.

The practice of yoga and meditation, rooted in Vedic traditions and systematized in later Indian texts, spread throughout Buddhist Asia and influenced local contemplative traditions. Zen meditation in China and Japan, while developed within Buddhist contexts, showed clear influences from Indian meditative techniques that ultimately traced back to Vedic practices.

Western Encounter: Colonial Period to Contemporary Spirituality

The Western encounter with Vedic traditions began seriously during the colonial period, when European scholars first gained access to Sanskrit texts and began translating Vedic literature. The work of scholars like Max Müller, who edited and translated the Rig Veda, and Paul Deussen, who translated the

Upanishads, introduced Vedic thought to European intellectual circles and sparked significant interest in comparative religion and philosophy.

The German Romantic movement found in Vedic literature, particularly the Upanishads, confirmation of their own philosophical intuitions about the unity underlying apparent diversity. Philosophers like Arthur Schopenhauer explicitly acknowledged their debt to Upanishadic thought, with Schopenhauer calling the Upanishads "the consolation of my life and will be of my death." This philosophical influence contributed to broader European movements away from purely materialistic worldviews toward more holistic understandings of reality.

The Transcendentalist movement in America, led by figures like Ralph Waldo Emerson and Henry David Thoreau, drew heavily from Vedic and Upanishadic sources. Emerson's concept of the "Over-Soul" showed clear influence from Upanishadic teachings about Brahman, while Thoreau's approach to simple living and contemplative practice reflected his reading of Indian philosophical texts. This influence contributed to distinctly American philosophical traditions that combined European rationalism with Indian spiritual insight.

The late nineteenth and early twentieth centuries saw more direct transmission of Vedic-influenced teachings through figures like Swami Vivekananda, who presented Vedanta philosophy to Western audiences in ways that emphasized its universal applicability rather than its specifically Hindu cultural context. This presentation of Vedic wisdom as universal truth rather than ethnic religion enabled its adoption by Western practitioners without requiring conversion to Hinduism as a cultural system.

The counterculture movements of the 1960s marked a significant expansion of Western interest in Vedic traditions. The Beatles' study with Indian teachers, the popularity of Transcendental Meditation, and the establishment of numerous yoga centers throughout the West brought Vedic practices to mainstream Western culture. This period saw the beginning of serious Western engagement with Vedic texts, practices, and worldviews outside purely academic contexts.

Contemporary Western psychology and neuroscience have increasingly engaged with concepts and practices derived from Vedic traditions. The scientific study of meditation, much of which involves techniques ultimately rooted in Vedic traditions, has demonstrated measurable benefits for mental and physical health. Concepts like mindfulness, while often presented in secular contexts, reflect understanding of consciousness and attention that can be traced back to Vedic sources.

The global yoga phenomenon represents perhaps the most visible contemporary manifestation of Vedic influence in the West. While modern yoga often emphasizes physical postures (asanas) more than the comprehensive philosophical system from which they emerged, the underlying concepts of union between individual and universal consciousness, the systematic approach to spiritual development, and the understanding of the body-mind connection all derive from Vedic traditions.

Comparing Ancient and Modern Information Systems

The parallels between ancient and modern information networks are striking and reveal consistent patterns in how humans create, preserve, and share knowledge. Like modern social media influencers, ancient gurus and teachers built followings based on their expertise and ability to communicate complex ideas effectively. The most successful teachers were those who could adapt their message to different audiences while maintaining essential content - much like contemporary content creators who tailor their presentations for different platforms and demographics.

Ancient manuscript libraries functioned remarkably like modern databases and search engines. Scholars at institutions like Nalanda developed sophisticated cataloging systems, cross-referencing methods, and preservation techniques that allowed them to store and retrieve vast amounts of information efficiently. The difference was one of scale and speed rather than fundamental approach to information management.

The role of translation in ancient knowledge networks parallels the function of modern communication technologies in breaking down language barriers. Just as Google Translate and other digital tools enable instant communication across linguistic boundaries, ancient translator-scholars created bridges between different cultural and linguistic communities. The translation of Sanskrit texts into Chinese, Arabic, Greek, and other languages required not only linguistic skill but also deep cultural understanding - creating a class of intellectual intermediaries who functioned like modern cross-cultural communication specialists.

The verification and authentication of knowledge in ancient systems shows sophisticated understanding of information quality control that parallels modern concerns about fake news and misinformation. The guru-disciple tradition included elaborate methods for ensuring that students had truly understood teachings before being authorized to transmit them further. Monastic institutions developed rigorous scholarly standards for copying and preserving texts. These quality control mechanisms were actually more effective in some ways than modern digital systems, since they required demonstrated competence rather than mere access to information.

The speed of information transfer, while obviously much slower in ancient times, followed similar patterns of exponential spread that we see in viral content today. When a new philosophical insight or practical technique proved valuable, it could spread throughout entire regions within a few generations through the same network effects that drive modern information dissemination.

Human Nature and Information Sharing

The success of both ancient and modern information systems reveals fundamental aspects of human nature that transcend technological capabilities. Humans appear to be inherently driven to share significant discoveries, insights, and innovations with others. This drive operates independently of material incentives and seems to reflect a deep understanding that knowledge increases in value when it is shared rather than hoarded.

The ancient spread of Vedic knowledge demonstrates that humans naturally create redundant, interconnected networks for preserving and transmitting important information. Just as modern internet protocols route around damage to maintain connectivity, ancient knowledge networks developed multiple pathways for preserving essential insights. The survival of Vedic texts through different manuscript traditions, oral lineages, and cultural adaptations shows the same resilience that characterizes robust modern information systems.

The human tendency to adapt and localize information while preserving core insights also remains constant. Ancient practitioners modified Vedic concepts to fit local cultural contexts while maintaining essential philosophical and practical content, just as modern users adapt digital technologies and online content to their specific needs and circumstances.

The role of authority and credibility in information networks has remained remarkably consistent. In ancient times, the reputation of teachers, the prestige of institutions, and the demonstrated effectiveness of practices determined which information gained widespread acceptance. Modern information systems show the same patterns, with content from credible sources, prestigious institutions, and demonstrably effective practices achieving broader dissemination.

Implications for Understanding Cultural Evolution

Examining ancient knowledge transmission systems alongside modern digital networks reveals that technological change accelerates and amplifies existing human tendencies rather than creating entirely new behaviors. The fundamental human drive to seek, create, preserve, and share knowledge remains constant, but the tools available for these activities continue to evolve and improve.

The ancient spread of Vedic knowledge suggests that truly valuable ideas possess intrinsic qualities that enable them to transcend cultural, linguistic, and geographical boundaries. The philosophical insights, practical techniques, and organizational principles that spread most successfully were those that addressed universal human needs and concerns. This pattern continues in the modern digital age, where content that addresses fundamental human experiences achieves global reach regardless of its cultural origins.

The comparison also reveals the importance of human relationships in knowledge transmission, even in highly technological environments. Ancient knowledge networks depended on personal trust, demonstrated competence, and ongoing relationships between teachers and students. Modern successful information systems, despite their technological sophistication, still depend on similar human factors - credibility, relationship-building, and demonstrated value.

Understanding these patterns helps explain why certain ancient traditions like those derived from Vedic sources continue to find receptive audiences in contemporary global culture. The knowledge transmission systems that successfully carried Vedic insights across ancient Asia have evolved into modern networks that continue to disseminate these same fundamental insights about consciousness, reality, and human potential to global audiences seeking timeless wisdom for contemporary challenges.

Continuities and Transformations

Understanding the Vedic heritage requires careful analysis of both the elements that remained constant across millennia and the profound transformations that adapted ancient insights to changing circumstances. The relationship between continuity and change in the Vedic tradition illustrates how living traditions maintain identity while responding to new challenges and opportunities.

The most obvious continuity lies in the preservation of Vedic texts themselves. The remarkable accuracy with which Vedic texts have been transmitted across more than two and a half millennia, verified by comparison of manuscripts from different regions and traditions, demonstrates the effectiveness of traditional preservation methods. However, this textual continuity coexisted with significant evolution in the interpretation and application of these texts.

The authority of Vedic texts remained constant throughout Indian history, but the methods of establishing and interpreting this authority changed dramatically. Early Vedic religion emphasized the literal performance of prescribed rituals, while later traditions developed sophisticated hermeneutical techniques that found philosophical, devotional, or practical meanings in the same texts. The concept of shruti (revealed scripture) maintained Vedic authority while allowing for creative reinterpretation through smriti (remembered tradition) texts.

The pantheon of deities worshipped in Indian traditions shows both continuity and transformation. Gods like Agni, Surya, and Indra remained objects of worship, but their relative importance, mythological associations, and ritual requirements changed significantly. Meanwhile, deities like Vishnu and Shiva, who had relatively minor roles in early Vedic texts, became supreme deities of major traditions while maintaining connections to their Vedic origins.

Ritual practice demonstrates perhaps the most complex relationship between continuity and transformation. The basic structure of Vedic ritual, with its emphasis on fire sacrifice, precise performance, and sacred formulas, remained theoretically authoritative throughout Hindu history. However, actual ritual practice evolved to emphasize temple worship, devotional practices, and meditation, while maintaining that these newer forms ultimately derived from Vedic precedents.

The caste system illustrates how Vedic concepts could be transformed into institutions that would have been unrecognizable to early Vedic practitioners. The four-fold varna system mentioned in the Purusha Sukta evolved into a complex hierarchy of thousands of castes with elaborate rules governing social interaction. Yet this transformation was legitimized by reference to Vedic authority, showing how ancient texts could provide foundations for entirely new social arrangements.

Philosophical development shows both the deepest continuities and most creative transformations within the Vedic tradition. The Upanishadic insight that ultimate reality transcends phenomenal appearances remained fundamental to most Indian philosophical schools, but the methods of understanding and achieving this insight varied dramatically. Schools like Advaita Vedanta claimed to represent the pure Vedic teaching, while others like Dvaita Vedanta argued for different interpretations of the same foundational texts.

The concept of dharma underwent perhaps the most significant transformation while maintaining claims to Vedic authority. Originally referring primarily to cosmic order maintained through ritual performance, dharma evolved to encompass personal ethics, social duty, natural law, and ultimate reality. This conceptual expansion allowed dharma to remain relevant across changing social conditions while maintaining connection to Vedic origins.

Language represents another area of both continuity and transformation. Sanskrit remained the sacred language of Hindu tradition and the medium for learned discourse, maintaining direct connection to Vedic linguistic traditions. However, the meaning and usage of Sanskrit terms evolved significantly, and regional languages developed their own religious and philosophical vocabularies while borrowing extensively from Sanskrit sources.

The relationship between Vedic traditions and non-Vedic elements shows the creative power of traditional frameworks to incorporate new materials. Local deities, tribal practices, regional customs, and foreign influences were integrated into Hindu traditions through creative interpretation that established connections with Vedic precedents. This process of integration maintained the authority of Vedic tradition while creating space for cultural diversity and innovation.

Women's roles within Vedic traditions illustrate the complex interplay between textual authority and social transformation. Some Vedic texts suggest relatively high status for women in ritual contexts, while others reflect patriarchal assumptions. Later traditions selectively emphasized different aspects of this complex inheritance, sometimes restricting women's religious roles while acknowledging their spiritual potential, sometimes finding in Vedic texts justification for women's religious authority.

The geographic expansion of Vedic traditions required constant adaptation to new environments, peoples, and cultural contexts. The transformation of Vedic traditions as they spread throughout the Indian subcontinent and beyond created regional variations that maintained connection to common sources while developing distinctive characteristics suited to local conditions.

The encounter with other religious traditions, including Buddhism, Jainism, Islam, and Christianity, prompted both defensive reactions that emphasized traditional Vedic authority and creative adaptations that found new ways to express Vedic insights. These encounters often resulted in mutual influence that enriched all traditions involved while maintaining distinct identities.

Modern developments, including colonialism, nationalism, and globalization, created new challenges and opportunities for Vedic traditions. Reform movements emphasized different aspects of the Vedic heritage, sometimes claiming to return to original Vedic teachings while actually creating innovative interpretations suited to contemporary concerns. The global spread of yoga, meditation, and Indian philosophy represents a new phase in the transformation of Vedic traditions for modern audiences.

The continuing vitality of Vedic traditions depends precisely on this capacity for creative transformation while maintaining essential continuities. The challenge for contemporary practitioners and scholars involves distinguishing between elements that represent the essential genius of Vedic traditions and those that reflect particular historical adaptations. This ongoing process of interpretation and reinterpretation ensures that the Vedic heritage remains a living tradition capable of addressing contemporary questions while maintaining connection to ancient wisdom.

The study of continuities and transformations within Vedic traditions provides insight into how human cultures maintain identity across time while adapting to changing circumstances. The Vedic heritage demonstrates that tradition and innovation need not be opposed but can work together to create intellectual and spiritual resources adequate to the challenges of each new generation. Understanding this dynamic relationship between continuity and change remains essential for appreciating both the historical significance and contemporary relevance of the Vedic tradition.

In conclusion, the Vedic heritage represents one of humanity's most remarkable achievements in creating intellectual and spiritual frameworks capable of maintaining relevance across millennia while providing foundations for continuous cultural creativity. The lasting influence of Vedic traditions on Hindu practice, legal systems, literature, philosophy, and social organization demonstrates the power of foundational insights to generate ongoing cultural development. The capacity of Vedic traditions to maintain essential continuities while adapting to changing circumstances provides a model for how human cultures can preserve wisdom from the past while remaining creative and responsive to contemporary needs. The continuing study and practice of Vedic traditions ensures that this ancient heritage will continue to contribute to human understanding and spiritual development for generations to come.

18
Understanding India

What appears as disorder to the untrained eye is actually the world's most sophisticated example of civilizational specialization—a 15,000-year in human adaptation that has produced regional excellence unmatched anywhere on Earth.

Modern India is not a collection of disparate parts struggling to hold together it is the living embodiment of the world's oldest continuous civilization, where each region has evolved into a specialized center of excellence perfectly adapted to its unique environmental, climatic, and geographical demands. This diversity is the feature that has made Indian civilization not just survive, but thrive through millennia of change, conquest, and transformation.

To understand India's true nature, we must abandon the Western notion that uniformity equals strength and diversity equals weakness. Instead, we must recognize that India's regional specialization represents humanity's most successful experiment in sustainable civilizational development, where each region has become world-class in precisely those skills, knowledge systems, and cultural practices that their specific environment demanded.

The Foundation Environmental Determinism and Cultural Evolution

India's extraordinary diversity begins with its unparalleled environmental variety. Spanning from the world's highest mountains to tropical coastlines, from the world's largest desert to some of its most fertile river valleys, from monsoon-soaked forests to arid plateaus, India contains virtually every climate and ecosystem found on Earth. This environmental diversity created the foundational condition for what would become the world's most sophisticated system of regional specialization.

Over 15,000 years, human communities across the subcontinent faced vastly different survival challenges.The fishing communities of Kerala developed entirely different skill sets from the pastoralists of Rajasthan. The rice cultivators of Bengal evolved different social systems from the spice traders of the Western Ghats. The mountain peoples of Himachal Pradesh created different architectural solutions from the delta dwellers of Sundarbans. Each group was forced by their environment to become world-class specialists in their particular domain.

This process was not random or chaotic—it was the natural result of human intelligence adapting to maximize survival and prosperity in specific environmental niches. What makes India unique is that this specialization occurred within a shared civilizational framework that allowed for exchange, learning, and mutual support while maintaining regional distinctiveness.

The Kerala Model Maritime Excellence and Spice Mastery

Consider Kerala, often called "God's Own Country," which exemplifies how environmental demands created world-class regional specialization. The state's unique position—with the Western Ghats creating a rain shadow effect, abundant monsoons, and extensive coastline—demanded expertise in maritime navigation, spice cultivation, and sophisticated water management.

Over millennia, Keralites became the world's premier spice traders and navigators. They developed the sophisticated system of Ayurveda, which was perfectly adapted to their humid, tropical environment. Their martial art, Kalaripayattu, evolved as a fighting system suited to their terrain and lifestyle. Their architecture, with its distinctive sloping roofs and wooden construction, represents perfect adaptation to heavy monsoon conditions.

The Keralite model of boat building—exemplified by the famous Uru boats—became legendary across the Indian Ocean. These boats, constructed without nails using a complex system of ropes and wooden joints, could flex with ocean swells while remaining watertight. This technology was so advanced that Arab and European traders relied on Keralite shipbuilders for centuries.

Kerala's spice expertise went far beyond simple cultivation. Keralites developed sophisticated knowledge of spice processing, preservation, quality grading, and international trading practices. They created complex trading networks that stretched from Southeast Asia to Europe, becoming the intermediaries in global spice commerce centuries before European colonial powers arrived.

This wasn't accidental—it was the result of 15,000 years of communities perfecting their responses to environmental demands. Kerala's excellence in these areas didn't emerge from nowhere; it represents the accumulated wisdom of countless generations who refined their practices to achieve world-class mastery.

Rajasthan Desert Innovation and Architectural Mastery

At the opposite environmental extreme, Rajasthan demonstrates how scarcity breeds innovation. The harsh desert environment of western Rajasthan demanded entirely different specializations: water conservation, desert navigation, fortification building, and trade across arid landscapes.

Rajasthani communities developed the world's most sophisticated desert water management systems. The stepwells (baolis) of Rajasthan are engineering marvels that allowed communities to access groundwater in areas where surface water was scarce. These structures were not just functional—they were architectural masterpieces that combined engineering excellence with aesthetic beauty.

The famous havelis of Rajasthan represent perfect adaptation to desert conditions. Their thick walls, small windows, courtyards designed to create cooling air currents, and intricate jali work (stone lattice screens) all served specific functions in managing extreme heat while creating beautiful living spaces. This architectural tradition produced buildings so well-adapted to their environment that they remained comfortable without any mechanical cooling systems.

Rajasthani communities also became master traders, developing the business networks and commercial practices that made them India's premier merchant class. The Marwari trading community's practices— including sophisticated credit systems, long-distance trade management, and risk assessment—became so advanced that they dominated Indian commerce for centuries.

The military traditions of Rajasthan, exemplified by the Rajputs, evolved specifically to deal with desert warfare and the defense of trade routes. Their cavalry techniques, fortification strategies, and warrior codes were perfectly adapted to their environment and strategic position.

Bengal Agricultural Innovation and Intellectual Excellence

Bengal's position in the Ganges-Brahmaputra delta created different environmental demands that led to different specializations. The region's fertile alluvial soil, abundant water, and complex river systems demanded expertise in intensive agriculture, river management, and intellectual pursuits that could flourish in an environment of relative abundance.

Bengali communities developed the world's most sophisticated rice cultivation techniques, creating hundreds of varieties adapted to different microclimates and growing conditions. Their methods of managing river floods, creating fish ponds, and integrating agriculture with aquaculture became models of sustainable farming that produced some of the highest yields in the ancient world.

The intellectual traditions that emerged in Bengal—from the ancient universities of Nalanda and Vikramashila to the Bengali Renaissance of the modern era—were not accidents. They emerged from a society that agricultural prosperity allowed to dedicate significant resources to learning, philosophy, and cultural development.

Bengali contributions to literature, philosophy, science, and arts reached world-class levels because the region's environmental advantages created conditions where intellectual pursuits could flourish. The tradition of debate, analysis, and cultural refinement that characterizes Bengali society developed over millennia as communities that had solved their basic survival challenges turned their attention to higher pursuits.

Punjab Agricultural Powerhouse and Military Tradition

Punjab's position in the fertile Indus Valley system created different environmental pressures that produced different specializations. The region's five rivers, fertile alluvium, and strategic position as the gateway to the Indian subcontinent demanded excellence in intensive agriculture and military organization.

Punjabi communities became the subcontinent's agricultural specialists, developing farming techniques so advanced that the region became known as India's breadbasket. Their expertise in wheat cultivation, irrigation management, and agricultural organization allowed them to feed not just their own population but much of northern India.

The military traditions of Punjab emerged from the region's strategic position as the entry point for invasions from the northwest. Punjabi communities developed martial traditions—exemplified by the Sikh military organization—that made them some of the most formidable fighters in Indian history. Their ability to organize, equip, and deploy agricultural communities for military purposes became legendary.

The entrepreneurial spirit of Punjabi communities, their work ethic, and their ability to migrate and establish successful communities worldwide all stem from millennia of adaptation to an environment that rewarded hard work, organization, and the ability to maximize agricultural potential.

Tamil Nadu Temple Technology and Classical Excellence

Tamil Nadu's unique position in southern India, with its distinct Dravidian cultural heritage and specific climatic conditions, produced specializations in temple architecture, classical arts, and sophisticated governance systems.

The temple complexes of Tamil Nadu represent some of the world's most sophisticated architectural achievements. These structures were not just religious buildings—they were complex institutions that served as centers of learning, economic activity, cultural preservation, and community organization. The engineering techniques used to build temples like those at Thanjavur, with their massive stone domes constructed without mortar, represent technological achievements that modern engineers still study.

Tamil classical traditions in music, dance, and literature reached levels of sophistication that made them the foundational systems for much of South Indian classical culture. The Sangam literature of ancient Tamil Nadu represents one of the world's oldest and most sophisticated literary traditions, while

Bharatanatyam and Carnatic music achieved levels of technical and aesthetic complexity that made them global art forms.

The governance systems developed in Tamil Nadu, including sophisticated methods of village selfgovernment, water management, and community organization, became models that influenced administrative practices across South India.

The Himalayan Regions High-Altitude Mastery

The communities of India's Himalayan regions—from Kashmir to Arunachal Pradesh—developed specializations demanded by high-altitude environments. These communities became world experts in mountain agriculture, high-altitude animal husbandry, alpine medicine, and spiritual practices adapted to extreme environments.

Kashmiri communities developed saffron cultivation techniques, carpet weaving traditions, and architectural styles (exemplified by houseboats and wooden architecture) perfectly adapted to their unique alpine valley environment. Their

Pashmina goat herding and wool processing created some of the world's finest textiles.

Communities in Himachal Pradesh and Uttarakhand developed sophisticated systems of terraced agriculture, forest management, and seasonal migration that allowed them to thrive in vertical ecosystems. Their traditional knowledge of medicinal plants and high-altitude agriculture became invaluable resources for modern sustainable development.

The spiritual traditions that emerged in these regions—from Kashmir Shaivism to Tibetan Buddhist practices—were specifically adapted to the contemplative possibilities and challenges of high-altitude living.

The Deccan Plateau Mineral Wealth and Strategic Mastery

The Deccan Plateau's unique geology and strategic position created different environmental demands that produced specializations in mining, metallurgy, and strategic governance. Communities in this region became experts in working with the plateau's mineral wealth while developing political and military systems adapted to the region's strategic importance.

The Vijayanagara Empire exemplified how Deccan communities combined expertise in hydraulic engineering, urban planning, and strategic governance to create one of the world's most prosperous medieval cities. Their techniques for managing water resources in a semi-arid environment, their architectural innovations, and their systems for integrating diverse communities became models for successful governance in challenging environments.

The metallurgical traditions of the Deccan, exemplified by the famous Wootz steel that became legendary as Damascus steel in international markets, represented technical knowledge accumulated over millennia of working with the region's iron ore deposits.

The Coastal Regions Maritime Networks and Cultural Exchange

India's extensive coastline created multiple maritime civilizations, each adapted to specific coastal conditions. The Gujarati coast developed different specializations from the Coromandel coast, which differed from the Malabar coast, which differed from the Bengal coast.

Gujarati maritime communities became masters of monsoon navigation, developing trading networks that stretched from Southeast Asia to East Africa. Their ship-building techniques, navigation methods, and commercial practices made them dominant players in Indian Ocean trade for over a millennium.

The coastal communities of Andhra Pradesh and Tamil Nadu developed different maritime specializations, becoming experts in textile production and export, temple-based urban planning, and the integration of inland and coastal economies.

Each coastal region developed unique solutions to the challenges of maritime trade, monsoon management, and the integration of land and sea-based economic activities.

The Integration Principle Unity Through Specialization

What makes India's regional specialization extraordinary is not just the depth of expertise achieved in each region, but the sophisticated systems that emerged to integrate these diverse specializations into a functioning civilizational whole. This integration occurred through multiple mechanisms that allowed regions to benefit from each other's expertise while maintaining their distinctive specializations.

The pilgrimage system created networks that connected every region of India, allowing for the exchange of ideas, techniques, and cultural practices. A merchant from Gujarat on pilgrimage to Kanyakumari would encounter and learn from the specialized knowledge of every region along the way.

Trade networks created economic incentives for regions to maintain their specializations while trading their products and expertise with other regions. The famous trade routes that crisscrossed India carried not just goods but knowledge, techniques, and cultural practices.

Marriage networks, particularly among trading and artisan communities, created kinship connections that spanned regions and facilitated the sharing of specialized knowledge across vast distances.

The guru-shishya tradition created educational networks that allowed specialized knowledge to be transmitted and refined across regions. A student might learn foundational skills in one region and advanced techniques in another, creating individuals who could bridge different specializations.

The Colonial Disruption and Modern Recovery

The arrival of European colonial powers in the 18th and 19th centuries disrupted many of these traditional systems of regional specialization. Colonial policies deliberately broke down traditional networks, imposed uniform administrative systems, and redirected regional specializations toward colonial economic needs rather than indigenous development.

The textile expertise of Bengal and Gujarat was deliberately destroyed to create markets for British manufactured goods. Traditional educational networks were disrupted to create a colonial administrative class. Regional specializations in metallurgy, shipbuilding, and other technical fields were abandoned as colonial policies discouraged indigenous manufacturing.

However, the underlying foundation of regional specialization proved remarkably resilient. Even under colonial rule, regional communities maintained much of their distinctive knowledge and cultural practices. The independence movement itself drew strength from the diversity of regional traditions and the sophisticated networks that connected them.

Since independence, India has been engaged in a process of recovering and modernizing its traditional systems of regional specialization. The Green Revolution built on Punjab's agricultural expertise. India's software industry emerged partly from regions with strong mathematical and educational traditions. The country's pharmaceutical industry drew on regions with traditional knowledge of medicinal plants and chemical processes.

Specialization in the Global Economy

Understanding India's traditional system of regional specialization provides crucial insights for navigating the modern global economy. Rather than viewing India's diversity as a challenge to be overcome, we can recognize it as a strategic advantage that allows the country to compete simultaneously in multiple global sectors.

Kerala's expertise in spices and maritime trade has evolved into leadership in international commerce and tourism. Karnataka's historical position as a center of learning has made it a natural hub for information technology. Gujarat's trading traditions have made it a center for modern industrial development. Punjab's agricultural expertise continues to feed not just India but contributes to global food security.

Each region's historical specializations provide a foundation for modern economic development that is more sustainable and authentic than imposed uniformity would be. Rather than trying to make every region identical, India's development strategy can build on each region's distinctive strengths while creating modern networks for integration and exchange.

The Civilizational Achievement

What India has achieved over 15,000 years represents humanity's most successful experiment in sustainable civilizational development. By allowing regions to specialize deeply in response to their specific environmental conditions while maintaining sophisticated systems for integration and exchange, Indian civilization created a model that maximized both local expertise and collective prosperity.

This system proved remarkably resilient, surviving invasions, colonial rule, and the challenges of modern development. It created a civilization that was simultaneously deeply rooted in local conditions and globally connected through networks of trade, pilgrimage, and cultural exchange.

The regional specializations that developed in India were not just economic or technical—they encompassed entire ways of life that integrated practical skills with cultural practices, spiritual traditions, and social organizations. This holistic approach to specialization created communities that were not just economically successful but culturally rich and spiritually fulfilling.

Greatest Gift to Humanity

India's greatest gift to humanity is not any single invention or philosophy, but rather the demonstration that civilization can achieve unprecedented depth and sophistication by embracing rather than suppressing diversity. Over 15,000 years, India proved that unity doesn't require uniformity—that a civilization can become stronger, more resilient, and more innovative by allowing different regions to specialize deeply in response to their unique conditions while maintaining sophisticated networks for integration and exchange. This model created the world's most sustainable form of human organization, one that simultaneously maximized local expertise and collective prosperity, survived countless invasions and transformations, and produced contributions to mathematics, science, philosophy, arts, and spirituality that continue to enrich human knowledge. At a time when the modern world struggles with the tension between global integration and local identity, between economic development and cultural preservation, between technological advancement and spiritual fulfillment, India's 15,000-year experiment offers a proven template for how human societies can thrive by celebrating rather than erasing their internal complexity. This is civilization's most valuable lesson: that diversity is not chaos to be controlled, but wisdom to be cultivated, and that humanity's greatest achievements emerge not from forced uniformity but from the symphonic harmony of specialized excellence working in conscious unity.

India's greatest contributions to humanity include the revolutionary concept of zero and the decimal system that made modern mathematics and science possible, transforming how the entire world calculates and thinks about numbers. Ayurveda provided the world's first comprehensive system of holistic medicine, understanding the human body as an integrated whole and pioneering concepts like preventive healthcare, personalized treatment, and the mind-body connection that modern medicine is only now rediscovering. Yoga offered humanity a complete science of physical, mental, and spiritual well-being, giving the world practical techniques for managing stress, achieving mental clarity, and exploring consciousness that have become essential tools for millions globally. Beyond these, India gifted humanity the philosophical frameworks of Vedanta and Buddhism that revolutionized human understanding of consciousness and ethics, the surgical techniques of Sushruta that laid foundations for modern surgery, the astronomical calculations that accurately predicted eclipses and planetary movements, the metallurgical knowledge that produced the world's finest steel, the architectural principles that created earthquake-resistant structures, the linguistic analysis of Sanskrit grammar that influenced modern linguistics, and the democratic village governance systems that demonstrated self-rule millennia before modern democracy. These weren't isolated achievements but emerged from a civilization that perfected the art of deep inquiry—whether into the nature of reality, the workings of the human body, the movements of celestial bodies, or the possibilities of human consciousness—creating knowledge systems so profound that they continue to offer solutions to humanity's most pressing challenges in health, sustainability, governance, and spiritual fulfillment.

India's contributions to humanity extend far beyond the famous examples to encompass virtually every domain of human knowledge and achievement. In mathematics, beyond zero and decimals, India developed algebra, trigonometry, calculus concepts (centuries before Newton and Leibniz), infinite series, and the binary number system that underlies all modern computing. In medicine, beyond Ayurveda, Indian physicians pioneered cataract surgery, plastic surgery, cesarean sections, and created the world's first hospitals and medical universities. In philosophy, India didn't just give Buddhism and Vedanta but developed logical systems like Nyaya, epistemological frameworks like Samkhya, and ethical philosophies like Dharma that influenced moral thinking worldwide. In science, Indian astronomers calculated the Earth's circumference, discovered that the Earth rotates on its axis, identified that the Moon causes tides, and created astronomical models more accurate than those used in Europe for centuries. In technology, India invented the spinning wheel, developed the world's finest textiles (inspiring the Industrial Revolution), created the most advanced metallurgy (producing rust-resistant iron pillars that still stand today), and built hydraulic engineering marvels like stepwells and sophisticated irrigation systems. In governance, India pioneered concepts of religious tolerance, federal systems, local self-rule, and created administrative structures so effective that they governed populations larger than entire continents. In linguistics, Sanskrit grammar provided the foundation for all modern linguistic analysis, while India's preservation of oral traditions demonstrated sophisticated memory techniques and knowledge transmission systems. In arts, India created classical music systems with mathematical precision, dance forms that became complete languages of expression, architectural principles that produced earthquake-resistant temples, and literary traditions that influenced storytelling worldwide. In agriculture, India developed crop rotation, selective breeding, and sustainable farming techniques that fed the world's largest populations while maintaining soil fertility for millennia. In psychology, India mapped states of consciousness, developed meditation techniques for mental training, and created therapeutic systems for emotional and spiritual healing that modern psychology is only beginning to understand. Even in commerce, India pioneered banking systems, insurance concepts, international trade networks, and business ethics that shaped global economic practices. These achievements weren't isolated discoveries but emerged from a civilization that approached every aspect of human existence with systematic inquiry, producing integrated knowledge systems that addressed not just practical needs but the deepest questions of human purpose and potential.

The Symphony Continues

Modern India's diversity is the continuation of a 15,000-year symphony of specialization that represents humanity's longest and most successful civilizational development. Each region's distinctive traditions, skills, and cultural practices are movements in this larger symphony, contributing their unique voice to a civilizational composition of unprecedented complexity and beauty.

Understanding this perspective transforms how we view everything about India—from its politics to its economics, from its social systems to its cultural expressions. Rather than seeing diversity as a problem to be solved, we can recognize it as India's greatest strength and the source of its unique contributions to human civilization.

The challenge for modern India is not to overcome its diversity but to update and modernize the systems that allow this diversity to function as a integrated whole. This means creating modern networks for exchange and integration while preserving and developing each region's distinctive specializations.

India's future lies not in becoming more uniform but in becoming better at being diverse—in perfecting the art of unity through specialization that has been its civilizational signature for 15,000 years. In a global economy that increasingly values specialized knowledge and cultural authenticity, India's model of deep regional specialization within civilizational unity offers insights that extend far beyond the subcontinent itself.

The modern world's challenges—from climate change to cultural preservation, from economic development to social integration—all require the kind of sophisticated balance between specialization and unity that India has been perfecting for millennia. Rather than chaos, India's diversity represents one of humanity's most valuable experiments in how civilizations can thrive by embracing rather than suppressing their internal complexity.

This is the true story of Indian diversity—not fragmentation overcome by artificial unity, but specialization so deep and integration so sophisticated that they created a civilization unlike any other in human history. The symphony continues, and its music has never been more relevant to the challenges facing humanity in the 21st century.

Glossary of Key Terms

A

- **Arya** – A term in the Rigveda used to describe noble or free members of society, often contrasted with *Dasa* or *Dasyu*.
- **Atman** – The inner self or soul; a central concept in the Upanishads representing the individual essence connected to *Brahman*.

B

- **Bhimbetka** – A site in central India known for prehistoric cave paintings dating back over 15,000 years; considered one of the earliest examples of cultural continuity.
- **Brahman** – The ultimate, unchanging reality in Vedic and Upanishadic philosophy, often identified with the cosmic principle.

C

- **Caste System** – A social stratification that began forming in the Vedic period, with divisions like Brahmins (priests), Kshatriyas (warriors), Vaishyas (traders), and Shudras (servants).

D

- **Dasa/Dasyu** – Non-Aryan people in the Rigvedic texts, often portrayed as enemies or outsiders.
- **Dholavira** – A major urban center of the Indus Valley Civilization noted for its advanced water management and city planning.

G

- **Gurukul** – The traditional Vedic education system where students lived with their teacher (*guru*) to receive holistic education.

H

- **Harappan Civilization** – Another name for the Indus Valley Civilization; known for urban planning, standardized weights, and script.
- **Hymns (Rigveda)** – Poetic compositions devoted to deities like Agni, Indra, and Varuna, forming the core of Vedic religious texts.

I

- **Indus-Sarasvati Civilization** – A term emphasizing the geographical and cultural expanse of the Harappan civilization along the Indus and now-dry Sarasvati rivers.
- **Iron Age** – The later Vedic period marked by the use of iron tools and the rise of more complex political and social systems.

K

- **Kalibangan** – An archaeological site in Rajasthan with evidence of early fire altars and ritual practices.

- **Kula** – A clan or extended family unit, fundamental to Vedic social organization.

L

- **Lothal** – A port city of the Harappan Civilization known for its dockyard and maritime trade.

M

- **Mehrgarh** – One of the earliest known Neolithic settlements in South Asia, significant for early agricultural and craft development.
- **Mantra** – A sacred utterance, sound, or phrase believed to have spiritual power; central to Vedic rituals.

R

- **Raja** – Tribal chief or king in the Vedic period; not an absolute monarch but a leader with both secular and spiritual responsibilities.
- **Rigveda** – The oldest of the four Vedas, composed of 1,028 hymns and central to understanding early Vedic society.

S

- **Sabha and Samiti** – Tribal assemblies in the Vedic age; the *sabha* was more elite, while the *samiti* was a general council of the people.
- **Sanskrit** – The classical language of ancient India used in Vedic and other scholarly texts.
- **Swastika** – An ancient symbol found in early Indian cave art representing auspiciousness, cosmic order, and the sun.

U

- **Upanishads** – Philosophical texts that explore the nature of reality, the self, and the universe; part of the later Vedic literature.

V

- **Vedas** – The foundational texts of Hinduism composed in early Sanskrit, including Rigveda, Samaveda, Yajurveda, and Atharvaveda.
- **Vedic Period** – The era in ancient Indian history (approx. 1500–500 BCE) when the Vedas were composed and Vedic culture flourished.
- **Vis** – Term for the common people or clans in the Rigvedic society; part of the early social order.

Appendix A: Chronological Timeline

Prehistoric and Early Settlements (100,000–3300 BCE)

Period	Key Events / Developments
~100,000–60,000 BCE	Early human migration to India from Africa via coastal routes (genetic and archaeological evidence).
~15,000 BCE	Cave paintings begin at Bhimbetka; marks the world's longest continuous artistic tradition.
9000–7000 BCE	Agriculture begins at Mehrgarh; domestication of wheat, barley, and animals.
7000–3300 BCE	Formation of early villages; beginnings of craft specialization, pottery, and trade networks.

Urban Bronze Age – Indus-Sarasvati Civilization (3300–1300 BCE)

Phase	Key Events / Sites
3300–2600 BCE	Early Harappan phase: sites like Rehman Dheri, Kot Diji emerge.
2600–1900 BCE	Mature Harappan phase: flourishing urban centers like Harappa, Mohenjo-daro, Dholavira, Lothal, Rakhigarhi.
1900–1300 BCE	Late Harappan phase: gradual decline, eastward migration, transition to rural settlements.

Vedic Age (1500–500 BCE)

Sub-Period	Key Events / Literary Milestones
1500–1200 BCE	Composition of early Rigvedic hymns; semi-nomadic, pastoral society.
1200–1000 BCE	Development of iron tools; Painted Grey Ware Culture begins.
1000–800 BCE	Later Vedic period; agriculture expands in Ganges plain; rise of political assemblies (sabha, samiti).
800–500 BCE	Upanishads composed; philosophical shift toward metaphysical concepts.

Literary Composition Periods

Text / Corpus	Approximate Date
Rigveda	1500–1200 BCE
Samaveda, Yajurveda, Atharvaveda	1200–1000 BCE
Brahmanas (ritual texts)	1000–800 BCE
Upanishads	800–500 BCE

Appendix B: Glossary of Terms

Sanskrit Terms and Concepts

- **Atman** – The inner self or soul; the individual essence that is ultimately identical with *Brahman* in Upanishadic philosophy.
- **Brahman** – The unchanging, infinite, immanent, and transcendent reality that is the divine ground of all matter, energy, time, space, and being.
- **Dharma** – Moral order, law, and duty; a central concept in Indian religion and philosophy.
- **Karma** – The principle of cause and effect where intent and actions influence the future of the individual.
- **Mantra** – A sacred utterance, sound, or syllable believed to have spiritual power.
- **Raja** – A chieftain or king during the Vedic period, selected by tribal assemblies and supported by priestly rituals.
- **Sabha / Samiti** – Early Vedic tribal assemblies; *Sabha* was more elite and judicial, *Samiti* more democratic and political.
- **Yajna** – Vedic ritual of fire sacrifice performed to honor deities and ensure cosmic harmony.

Technical Vocabulary

- **Megalithic** – Refers to large stone structures or burials used in prehistoric times across India.
- **Painted Grey Ware (PGW)** – A type of pottery associated with the later Vedic period, found in archaeological sites along the Ganges.
- **Urban Planning** – A hallmark of Indus-Sarasvati cities such as Mohenjo-daro and Dholavira, including grid layouts and drainage systems.
- **Iron Age** – Refers to the period (c. 1200–600 BCE) marked by the use of iron tools and the expansion of agriculture and polity in the Vedic region.
- **Oral Tradition** – The method by which Vedic texts were preserved and transmitted with high precision before the invention of writing.

Names and Places

- **Bhimbetka** – Site of prehistoric rock shelters and cave paintings in Madhya Pradesh, representing over 15,000 years of artistic tradition.
- **Dholavira** – A major Harappan urban site in Gujarat known for its water conservation systems and monumental architecture.
- **Mehrgarh** – One of the earliest agricultural settlements in South Asia, dating back to 7000 BCE.
- **Rigveda** – The oldest of the four Vedas, composed of hymns dedicated to Vedic deities and forming the core of early Indian spiritual thought.
- **Indus-Sarasvati Civilization** – A vast urban civilization centered on the Indus and Ghaggar-Hakra (Sarasvati) rivers, characterized by standardized city planning and long-distance trade.

- **Kalibangan** – Harappan site in Rajasthan known for its early fire altars and evidence of agricultural field patterns.
- **Rakhigarhi** – The largest Indus-Sarasvati site discovered in India, located in present-day Haryana.
- **Lothal** – An ancient port city in Gujarat, known for its dockyard and maritime trade.

Appendix C: Maps and Illustrations

Refer to the visual maps showing:

Archaeological Sites Like Indus Valley in India

The Indus Valley Civilization (IVC), known for its advanced urban planning and architecture, has numerous archaeological sites across India that share similar historical significance. Below is a detailed comparison of some notable sites.

Site Name	Location	Period	Key Features
Harappa	Punjab, Pakistan	3300–1300 BCE	Urban planning, drainage systems, granaries

Site Name	Location	Period	Key Features
Mohenjo-daro	Sindh, Pakistan	3300–1300 BCE	Citadel, Great Bath, advanced drainage
Dholavira	Gujarat, India	3000–1500 BCE	Water conservation systems, large reservoirs
Rakhigarhi	Haryana, India	3300–1300 BCE	Largest IVC site in India, urban layout
Kalibangan	Rajasthan, India	3000–1500 BCE	Fire altars, evidence of plowed fields
Lothal	Gujarat, India	2400–1900 BCE	Dockyard, bead-making industry, trade links
Kunal	Haryana, India	3000–1500 BCE	Evidence of early agriculture, pottery
Farmana	Haryana, India	3000–1500 BCE	Urban layout, pottery, and seals
Bhagwanpura	Haryana, India	3000–1500 BCE	Urban planning, drainage systems

Site Name	Location	Period	Key Features
Sutkagen Dor	Balochistan, Pakistan	3000–1500 BCE	Fortified settlement, trade links with Mesopotamia

Site Name	Location	Period	Key Features
Chandraketugarh	West Bengal, India	400 BCE–200 CE	Urban settlement, trade links with the IVC
Bhirrana	Haryana, India	6500–3000 BCE	Evidence of early agriculture, pottery, and urban life
Kot Diji	Sindh, Pakistan	3000–2500 BCE	Pre-Harappan culture, fortified settlement

Site Name	Location	Period	Key Features
Nageshwar	Gujarat, India	3000–1500 BCE	Evidence of a coastal settlement, trade activities
Sutkagen Dor	Balochistan, Pakistan	3000–1500 BCE	Fortified settlement, trade links with Mesopotamia
Manda	Jammu and Kashmir, India	3000–1500 BCE	Urban planning, pottery, and seals
Kutch	Gujarat, India	3000–1500 BCE	Evidence of trade and maritime activities
Dharamraj	Madhya Pradesh, India	3000–1500 BCE	Urban layout, pottery, and seals

Site Name	Location	Period	Key Features
Brahmapuri	Maharashtra, India	3000–1500 BCE	Evidence of urban planning and trade
Paharpur	West Bengal, India	3000–1500 BCE	Monastic complex, trade links with the IVC

MAP OF KEY SITES

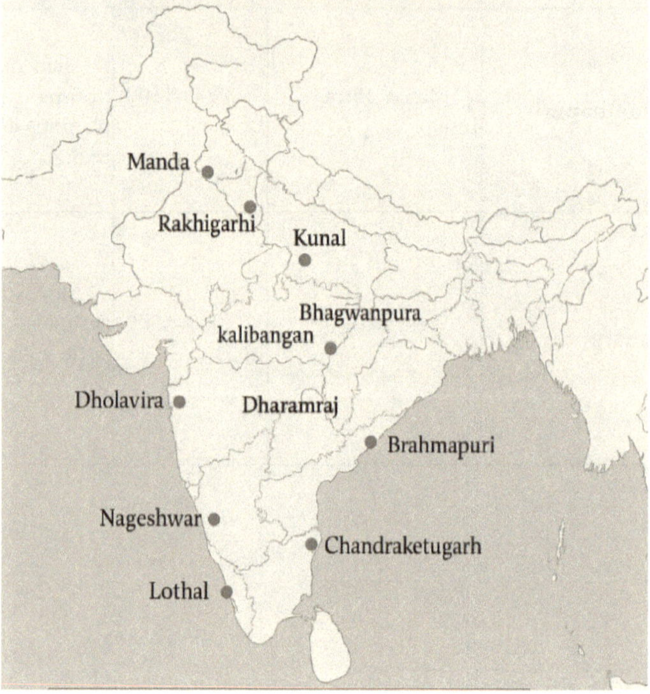

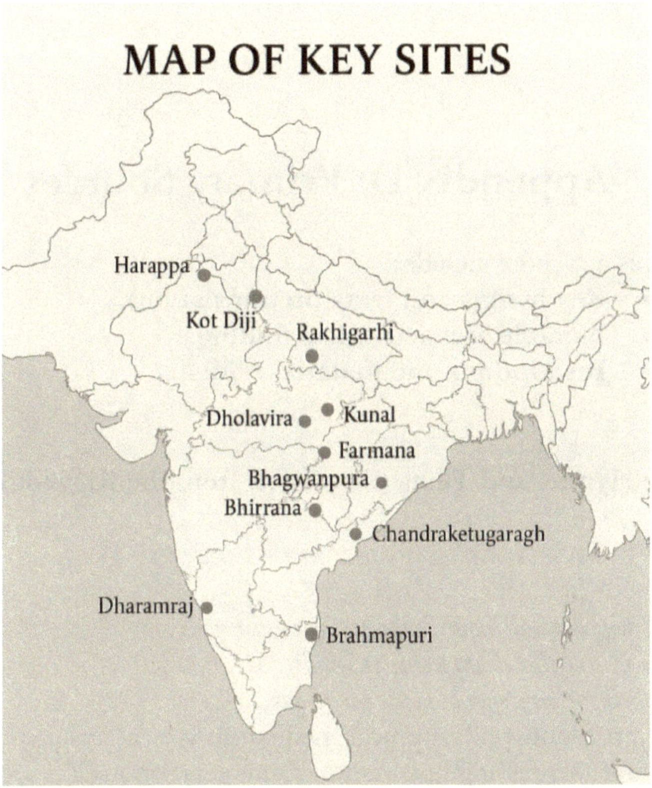
MAP OF KEY SITES
Harappa
Kot Diji
Rakhigarhi
Dholavira
Kunal
Farmana
Bhagwanpura
Bhirrana
Chandraketugaragh
Dharamraj
Brahmapuri

Appendix D: Primary Sources

This appendix includes:

- **Key hymns and texts (in translation)**
- **Notable archaeological findings**
- **Inscriptions and material evidence**

Key Hymns and Texts (Selections from the Rigveda)

1. Nasadiya Sukta (Creation Hymn – Rigveda 10.129)

"Then even nothingness was not, nor existence…
There was neither death nor immortality then,
No distinguishing sign of night nor of day…"
– A profound philosophical meditation on the origins of the universe, expressing uncertainty about creation itself.

2. Purusha Sukta (Cosmic Man – Rigveda 10.90)

"The Purusha is all that yet hath been and all that is to be;
He is the Lord of immortality which waxes greater still by food."
– Describes the cosmic being whose body was sacrificed to create the world and the social orders.

3. Gayatri Mantra (Rigveda 3.62.10)

"Om Bhur Bhuvah Swaha
Tat Savitur Varenyam
Bhargo Devasya Dhimahi
Dhiyo Yo Nah Prachodayat"
– A revered mantra invoking the sun and spiritual illumination.

Archaeological Findings

Site	Finding	Significance
Mehrgarh	Evidence of earliest farming in South Asia (7000 BCE)	Transition from foraging to settled life
Dholavira	Massive water reservoirs and urban layout	Advanced engineering in arid environments
Kalibangan	Fire altars and ploughed fields	Ritual activity and early agriculture
Rakhigarhi	India's largest Harappan city, with metallurgy workshops	Center of trade and craftsmanship
Lothal	Dockyard and port infrastructure	Evidence of maritime trade with Mesopotamia

Inscriptions and Material Evidence

- **Seals (Harappan)**
  Depict animals, script, and possibly proto-religious symbols (e.g. "proto-Shiva", bull, pipal tree). Still undeciphered but suggest a complex symbolic system.
- **Iron tools (Painted Grey Ware sites)**
  Found in Vedic period sites like Hastinapur and Ahichchhatra; mark transition into the Iron Age.
- **Weights & Measures**
  Uniform across sites like Harappa and Lothal; evidence of standardized trade systems.
- **Terracotta Figurines**
  Represent fertility goddesses, animals, and dancers; reflect beliefs and daily life.

Appendix E: Further Reading

This section includes **scholarly sources, popular works,** and **digital resources** for deeper exploration of Indian civilization and the Vedic era.

Academic Sources

Title	Author / Institution	Notes
The Vedic Age	R.C. Majumdar (Bharatiya Vidya Bhavan Series)	Authoritative work on early Vedic society
The Rigveda: A Historical Analysis	Shrikant G. Talageri	Argues for an indigenous origin of the Vedic people
Ancient India: From the Earliest Times to the First Century A.D.	Romila Thapar	Concise and critical overview of early Indian history
India: A Sacred Geography	Diana L. Eck	Explores how geography and pilgrimage shape Indian cultural identity
The Early Aryans of India	B.G. Tilak	A classic but dated attempt to localize Aryan origins in India

Popular Works

Title	Author	Notes
Lost River: On the Trail of the Sarasvati	Michel Danino	Investigates the mythical river Sarasvati with archaeological support
In Search of the Cradle of Civilization	Georg Feuerstein, Subhash Kak, David Frawley	Introduces readers to Vedic roots of Indian civilization
The Wonder That Was India	A.L. Basham	Accessible, classic introduction to India's ancient past
Sapiens: A Brief History of Humankind	Yuval Noah Harari	Includes broader context of prehistoric migration into India
The Discovery of India	Jawaharlal Nehru	Philosophical and political reflections with historical insights

Digital Resources

Website	Description
Digital South Asia Library (DSAL)	Maps, texts, and historical archives hosted by University of Chicago
Sanskrit Documents Archive	Vedic texts with translations and recitations
Indus Script Database	Ongoing efforts to document and decipher the Harappan script
Internet Sacred Text Archive	Public domain translations of the Vedas and other scriptures
Archaeological Survey of India (ASI)	Official reports and findings from Indian heritage sites

Acknowledgement

This book is the result of the collective efforts, insights, and support of many individuals and institutions whose contributions I gratefully acknowledge.

First and foremost, I express deep gratitude to the archaeologists, historians, and scholars whose decades of rigorous research laid the foundation for this work. Their dedication to uncovering the layers of India's ancient past—through excavations, textual analysis, and comparative study—has made this journey of exploration both possible and meaningful.

I am particularly thankful to the libraries, archives, and digital platforms, including the Digital South Asia Library, Sanskrit Documents Archive, and the Archaeological Survey of India, whose open access to invaluable resources enriched this project.

A special note of appreciation goes to the editors, peer reviewers, and academic mentors who offered their time and expertise in shaping and refining the manuscript. Their critical feedback helped sharpen both the clarity and depth of the content.

To my family and friends, thank you for your patience, encouragement, and unwavering belief in this endeavor. Your support carried me through the long hours of writing, research, and revision.

Finally, this book is dedicated to the students, readers, and lifelong learners who continue to seek a deeper understanding of India's civilizational heritage. May this work inspire further inquiry, dialogue, and appreciation for the richness of the past.

With sincere thanks,

Umang Kartikey

www.ingramcontent.com/pod-product-compliance
Lightning Source LLC
Chambersburg PA
CBHW050010170726
48282CB00025B/341
* 9 7 8 9 3 3 4 3 7 4 7 2 8 *